MW00917664

CRAZIFORNIA

How California Is Destroying Itself
- And Why It Matters to America

LAER PEARCE

CRAZIFORNIA

Published by
Intercontinental Words and Pictures, Inc.
22892 Mill Creek Drive
Laguna Hills, CA 92653, USA

Copyright © 2012 Laer Pearce

All rights reserved, including the right to reproduce,
store, or transmit this book or portions thereof in any
form whatsoever without prior written permission of
the copyright owner and publisher of this book.

Library of Congress Cataloging-in-Publication Data is
available upon request.

Jacket design by Dan Dankberg

Print and Electronic Editions Type and Format Design
by Shawn Bell

v2.07

ISBN: 1478357339
ISBN-13: 978-1478357339

The heart of the wise inclines to the right,
but the heart of the fool to the left.
- Ecclesiastes 10:2

This book is dedicated to my clients, who have always held tenaciously to a vision for a better California, and were kind enough to give me the privilege of helping them fight to realize it.

It is also dedicated to my incredible wife Beth. She has been an encourager, wise counselor and unwavering supporter - not just with Crazifornia, but with everything.

"Anyone who is concerned about California's future or who fears that California's maladies will spread to their state should read Crazifornia. Laer Pearce, whom I've known as a public affairs pro for as long as I've lived in California, has written the most insightful and entertaining book I've ever read on the genesis, depth and - surprisingly - deep funniness of California's perilous condition. Thankfully, this isn't a boring tome touting the next ultimately futile formula for supposedly fixing all that ails California. Rather, it's a story book, full of one astonishing tale after another about what really goes on in California, and why, and what it means to you. In the end, you'll learn a great deal and enjoy it a great deal."

- Hugh Hewitt, national radio talk show host

'Crazifornia' made me laugh, it made me cry. No, really - one rarely reads such a funny account of such a sad subject. California, my beloved home, has gone from the destination spot in the nation to a pathetic basket case run into the ground by lunatics. Pearce pins the blame where it belongs. You won't find any solutions in this book, but solutions are pointless because the crazies who still run the state, and the crazies who vote those people, would never accept any solutions. This is a great book to read, tearfully, as you pack the house in Orange County and wait for the moving van to take you to Nevada.

- Steven Greenhut, California-based author and columnist

"If California history is one of your passions, then Crazifornia will provide the road map of where this state is and where it is going. With so much potential, California is being driven into a ditch. It's crazy. With an adroit morning-commentary writing style, Laer Pearce provides a dose of reality. But it may drive you crazy."

- John Moorlach, Orange County Supervisor

"Want to know what's happening in America's nuttiest state? Read Crazifornia. It's the most incisive, and funniest, dissection of what happened to the formerly Golden State. It's all there: punishing taxes, environmental extremism, cultural rot, Gov. Moonbeam and the Schwarzenegger meltdown. And even if you don't live there, given California's immense influence, what Laer Pearce details is coming soon to your state."

- John Seiler, Managing Editor, CalWatchDog.com

"Before we can hope to return California to good governance and fiscal health, we need to understand just how dysfunctional the state has become and who is responsible for its deterioration. Crazifornia tells us that story, relaying an entertaining history of progressive ideology, failed liberal experiments and regulatory excesses. Pearce's exposition helps us understand why California is teetering on the precipice. And more important, it helps us see a path forward."

Sally Pipes, President and CEO
Pacific Research Institute,
Author, The Pipes Plan: The Top Ten Ways to
Dismantle and Replace Obamacare

TABLE OF CONTENTS

Author's note: Each chapter of Crazifornia stands alone, so you can read it in whatever order interests you most. The chapters in Part One provide history and perspective; those in Part Two look at the current state of affairs in the Tarnished State.

INTRODUCTION

As catastrophes loom like so many high-speed train wrecks, California still excels at clinging defiantly to its Progressive ideals.

NEAR SAN FRANCISCO, there's a California neighborhood in a California town that's named after an 11th Century monk who was known for the clarity of his teaching. That's fitting, because we can learn a lot about how the once-golden state of California became a perma-nent state of dysfunction called Crazifornia if we look at what happened in that town, San Bruno, on September 9, 2010.

Roughly equidistant between the Pacific Ocean to the west and San Francisco International Airport to the east, San Bruno is modest. In one modest San Bruno neighborhood - the one that became tragically famous on that pleasant fall day in 2010 - Honda Accords and Dodge minivans fill the driveways of homes that have a simple, no-nonsense architectural style dominated by pastel wood siding and inexpensive asphalt shingles. This is a place not at all like the wealthier enclaves of

Nob Hill to the north or Palo Alto to the south, where the Bay Area's blue bloods and high-tech billionaires live. It is instead a neighborhood called home primarily by the working stiffs of the Bay Area.

Just west of the neighborhood is a jagged depression that's so pronounced it's visible to airline passengers flying in and out of San Francisco International. It's the San Andreas Fault, but it wasn't this unstable and dangerous neighbor that made the neighborhood famous. It was the ineptitude of California's government.

It was late afternoon, and the big Orange California sun was dropping toward Sweeney Ridge. Families were preparing dinner and catching up on the day's activities when, at 6:11 p.m., a section of pipe in a 30-inch-diameter intrastate natural gas pipeline owned by Pacific Gas & Electric ruptured near the corner of Glenview Drive and Earl Avenue, at the entry to the neighborhood. A half-million cubic feet of natural gas gushed out of the pipeline in the first minute after the rupture, and for every one of the 94 additional minutes that passed before PG&E finally was able to shut down the flow of natural gas. Almost instantly after the first molecules of the highly explosive gas escaped the pipeline's confines, something ignited it - quite possibly a gas stove heating up dinner in one of the nearby homes. The resulting explosion and inferno obliterated that home and 37 others and killed eight people. It created a crater, now filled in, that was big enough to swallow any of the houses destroyed in the explosion. The twisted remains of the ruptured section of pipe, weighing 3,000 pounds and about as long as three elephants lined up nose-to-tail, lay smoking where the explosion hurled it, 100 feet away.

Tammy Zapata was cooking dinner in her house on Earl Drive and her husband, Mike, and daughter Amanda were watching television when the natural gas exploded into a roaring, roiling Hell. On the first anniversary of the explosion, Tammy told the San Francisco public television station KQED what it was like:[1]

> *No matter how high up you looked, all you could see was fire. You couldn't see anything. My daughter was so freaked out that she couldn't move. And Mike kept trying to get her out of the house; he actually picked her up and like tossed her. It wasn't so much what you could see at that point, it was the noise. The noise was so loud, it was deafening. You couldn't hear yourself, let alone anyone else. It sounded just like a plane crashed in our backyard.*

> *We were trapped. When you're in a dream and you're trying to run as fast as you can, but you feel like you're getting nowhere like you're in quicksand? That's how it felt. No matter how fast or how hard you tried to move, the house just kept sucking you back in.*

Just then, their neighbor Joe Ruigomez, a 19-year-old college student, ran up from his house next door to the Zapatas. It had just been destroyed, killing his girlfriend, who had been watching the season's first football game with him, less than two hours after Ruigomez had posted on his Facebook page, "Finally the NFL season has arrived, gonna be a good year." [2] Zapata continued her story:

> *He had no skin. It looked like he had a shredded t-shirt, but it was the skin all melted off him. His face was all white. You could hardly see features. In fact, he still had smoke coming off his entire body. When he tried to open the door to get in, he couldn't. Because his hands were so badly burned.*

Just 300 yards from the explosion site, firefighters at the San Bruno Fire Station felt the explosion shake their station before they heard it, and as they rushed to the scene, they could see ugly gushing flames and black smoke just ahead of them. It would be two days until they could roll up their hoses after the last flames were finally extinguished.

WRONG-HEADED REGULATION

The pipeline accident report of the National Transportation Safety Board (NTSB),[3] which regulates pipelines and investigates their explosions, found 28 contributing factors to the explosion, but two stand out. The first is that the section of pipe that ruptured had defects so pronounced they should have been visible to the PG&E work crews and state inspectors when the pipe was installed in 1954. The second is that the California Public Utilities Commission (PUC) decided against all logic in 1961 that its newly adopted pipeline inspection standards would not be applied to pipelines that were in place prior to that year. The pre-1961 pipelines would be grandfathered, not subject to the new standards. If not for the PUC's decision, the pipeline would have undergone hydrostatic pressure tests that very likely would have revealed the defect under San Bruno. "There is no safety justification for the grandfather clause exempting pre-1970 pipelines from the requirement for post-construction hydrostatic pressure testing," the NTSB report found.

Yet for 56 years, the PUC sat by as these grandfathered pipelines got older and more susceptible to failure. Even after another fatal pipeline explosion two years earlier, neither the Legislature nor the PUC thought to revisit the utility's grandfathered natural gas pipelines. In that incident, another PG&E gas pipeline exploded in the Sacramento suburb of Rancho Cordova on Christmas Eve and killed one person, injured five others and caused severe damage to two homes.

It's not as if PG&E isn't regulated. No, it and every other utility in California, and every manufacturer, and every homebuilder, and every farmer, and all their second cousins are up to their ears in tough regulations and eager regulators. Rather, the San Bruno catastrophe happened because the state is regulated in ways that are either corrupted or driven by questionable policies. The grandfathering of old pipelines stands as one of the more tragic examples of how influence and power corrupt California's regulatory model, just as influence and power corrupt every capitol in America and around the world.

In 1961, the influence and power was squarely in the hands of business interests, so state policy mirrored business policy, and old pipelines were exempted from costly regulations. But today, the influence and power reside with public employee unions, trial lawyers and environmentalists, explaining the current state of California's policy-driven regulations. One popular policy, which took hold in 1969, was that all schools, whether in rich or poor neighborhoods, should be equal. California succeeded splendidly at regulating equality into its school system: It simply diminished the quality of the good schools in wealthy areas.

Today the policy that most drives California state government, and that busied the PUC when it should have been thinking about how to prevent pipeline explosions, is a commitment to single-handedly saving the planet from the ravages of global warming. (In the past couple of years, of course, global warming advocates have worked tirelessly to rename it "climate change," a broader category that will keep the regulators in power even if temperatures don't rise.) Consequently, PG&E and the state's other utilities are told to stop being so reliant on cheap and dependable carbon-based energy and find ways to quickly meet 30 percent of the state's electrical demand through costly and less reliable clean energy, like wind and solar. On top of that, the utilities are now is required to pay millions of dollars annually in taxes on their greenhouse gases - and to spend millions more on equipment and personnel to monitor those gases in order to compute the taxes. That all this money obviously would be passed on to the public, and even more obviously, would be better spent on pipeline inspections and maintenance, doesn't sway policy-driven regulators from their Quixotic mission to save the planet ... instead of saving Joe Ruigomez's girlfriend and seven of his neighbors.

CATASTROPHE AS A CHANGE AGENT

The eight people who died in the San Bruno gas pipeline explosion should be immortalized for showing so well that years of control by Progressive politicians, environmentalists, unions and trial lawyers have reduced once-proud California to a collection of ongoing near-catastrophes that are beginning to erupt. The stories told in *Crazifornia* reveal a state that has become so misdirected, ungovernable and untenable that the primary driver of change has become the catastrophe. Californians saw that as the state Legislature leapt into action *after* the San Bruno explosion, quickly passing new pipeline safety bills. Californians, who just 50 years ago showed post-war America how to capture its wildest dreams, are now reduced to watching in disbelief as the state's budget, schools, economy and infrastructure teeter on the precipice, while entrenched political differences and powerful special interests keep anyone from hitting the brakes or grabbing the steering wheel. Many would welcome the crash, because it's increasingly clear that the only way to fix California may be to pick it up after everything explodes or collapses.

I was recently talking about one of California's greatest catastrophes in waiting, its water delivery system, with one of state's more opinionated water leaders, Peer Swan. I asked the long-time board member of the Association of California Water Agencies what he thought would happen in the Sacramento-San Joaquin Delta, the collapsing hub of the state's water network. The Delta is 57 islands, two-thirds of which have sunken below sea level and are protected by over 1,100 miles of levees, many built by Chinese coolie laborers over a century ago. Riddled with rodent holes and roots and built over unstable peat moss-rich soil, the levees are at risk of liquefying if the Hayward Fault, a little cousin of the more famous San Andreas fault, starts shaking. If enough levees fail, seawater will flow into the Delta from San Francisco Bay and eventually reach the big pumps that push fresh water from the Delta to thirsty cities and farm fields from the Bay Area to San Diego. Delta waters are awash with chemicals from farms and ammonia from more than a hundred upstream wastewater treatment plants. Big mouth bass, Asian mussels, water hyacinth and other non-native invasive species thrive there, displacing the natural ecosystem, including the Delta smelt, which became famous when the environmentalists' lawsuits that sought to protect it succeeded in dramatically reducing the pumping of water from the Delta.

California's water leaders have been trying for years to find a way to avoid these multiple looming disasters that jeopardize the delivery of water to the state's most fertile farmland and most populated regions, and Swan was quick to sum up the results of their efforts. "Oh, we'll fix it," he replied, waiting a couple beats before adding, "After it collapses and the catastrophe hits."

After 30 years in California public affairs, looking at the state close-up, I think he's right. The state may solve some problems proactively, but they'll be the exception and governance by train wreck is likely to become the norm.

In the pages that follow, I could lay out the next in

an ongoing series of grand proposals to save California, but what good would that be? Many books have laid out such visions in great specificity, but none of them has worked because all are predicated to some degree or another on California voters, legislators, liberal and environmental interest groups, unions and trial lawyers - and yes, Republicans - suddenly changing their philosophies and letting go of their power. Where is the evidence that will happen?

Instead, *Crazifornia* will tell you stories, many, many stories, of California's dysfunction and ineptitude, some funny, some sad, but all frustrating because a state with this much greatness really should be able to solve its myriad messes before catastrophes sink it. In the course of reading these reports of what actually goes on in the once-Golden State, I hope you will come to share my belief that what turned California into Crazifornia - and what very likely will keep it crazy - are the state's strong liberal and Progressive traditions. Even though this is much more a story book than a policy book, I hope that by shining a light on some of the more egregious acts of bad governance that tarnish California, things might start becoming more sensible in this state of my birth.

But I have to admit that my wife and I were recently checking out homes in Texas.

PART ONE

CHAPTER ONE:

HOW THE PEER AXIS TURNED CALIFORNIA INTO CRAZIFORNIA

Progressives, Environmentalists, Educators and Reporters in disservice to California

N THE NOVEMBER 1986 ELECTION, California voters passed a proposition expressing their belief that AIDS isn't actually contagious and another that found there was no need whatsoever to cap the salaries of government officials. Crowding the ballot with those measures and nine others was Proposition 65, which would require warning labels on buildings and in offices so citizens of the Golden State could be alerted to the presence of any chemicals known to cause cancer or birth defects.

My long-time friend Gary Lawrence was the pollster for the No on Prop. 65 campaign, and he could only find one thing that moved the "No" needle even a little: The proposition's language exempted state government from the regulations it would impose on business. "The exemption of state government was the one thing that polled well," he said. "I felt an exemptions message would do great, but I also felt it ultimately would not be enough. I said at the time it would freeze the linebackers, but everyone who watches football knows it still takes some fancy footwork to take advantage of a frozen linebacker, and the data just didn't give us that footwork." So, the No on 65 campaign did what it could and ran television ads trying to get people to vote against Prop. 65 because it burdened the private sector but exempted government agencies.

On the "Yes on 65" side, no polling was really needed because 39 big-time Hollywood entertainers - including Michael J. Fox, Jane Fonda, Chevy Chase and Whoopi Goldberg - were eager to tour the state in support of the proposition. Among the celebrities' talking points was that "they" - the corporations behind the "No on 65" campaign - were "killing our babies." A Los Angeles Times story filed from the celebrities' stop-over in San Luis Obispo reported, "You just about needed mirror sunglasses to handle the massed star candlepower, and rubber ear plugs to dampen the shrieks."[1]

It was no contest. Applying an incomplete understanding of the issue and its potential ramifications and a complete understanding of celebrity star power, 63 percent of the voters marked the "yes" box.

After all, the majority thought, the people have a right to know about the potentially lethal chemicals evil corporations put into their homes and workspaces just to make a buck. And more importantly, Californians believe in propositions and their inherent right to tell the state what to do - even if it's to make politically powerful trial lawyers richer than Mark Zuckerberg. It was the trial lawyers, after all, who had raised the money to qualify Prop. 65 for the ballot, and who funded the panicked ads that filled the state's airwaves to drive up the "yes" vote. They were highly motivated - not out of a will to protect people from chemicals, but because Prop. 65 let them sue and collect damages from corporations that failed to accurately list every chemical and compound on their site prohibited by Prop 65. Even today, approaching three decades later, the lawyers still push every year to expand the list of supposedly nasty chemicals so they can bring lawsuits against businesses that fail to conform with regulations to update their warning signs.

I began to understand just how sleazy all this was when, in the interim between the vote and when the law would go into effect, a prominent homebuilder called me, sounding every bit as panicked as a "Yes on 65" campaign ad.

"I'm going to have to put Prop. 65 warning signs on all my new model homes or I'll get sued," he moaned. "What do you think that's going to do to sales if people are going to have to walk by a cancer warning to go into one of my models?"

At the time, late 1986, California's economy was robust and new homes were selling like SPF 30 sunscreen in Palm Springs, and prices were crazily inflated - heck, my wife and I had just paid the utterly insane price of $255,000 for a new 2,500-square-foot home. So I told him I didn't think anything would happen to his sales, especially if his competitors were forced to put the same placards on their model homes. But I was curious why a model home would need a Prop. 65

warning. After all, a brand new home is hardly a toxic sump of the sort the Yes on Prop. 65 ads had frightened Californians about.

"Well for starters, estrogen and testosterone are both on the Prop. 65 list of known carcinogens," he told me. "So unless something other than men and women is going through my models, I'm going to have to post the signs."

It was at that moment that I realized the state of my birth was no longer California, but instead was Crazifornia, a state that was rapidly becoming a state of disaster. The years since the mid-1980s have been anything but kind to California, Californians or the nation, which is all too influenced by what goes on in what now might best be called the Tarnished State. At the time the home builder talked to me, I was still a registered Democrat. But laws like Prop. 65 opened my eyes to the dubious handiwork of liberal Democrats and their financiers, while at the same time Ronald Reagan was providing an easy-to-understand comparison to Jimmy Carter. The peanut farmer from Plains, Georgia turned out to be the last Democrat Party candidate I voted for.

Prop. 65 also illustrates a fundamental principle of Progressive politics: Get the people to accept something simple and palatable and grow it into an "enlightened" new power base controlled by technocrats who know what's best for society. The proposition started with the simple and broadly accepted principle that people should be protected from harmful chemicals. But long before the signature gathering started, an entire forward-looking plot was hatched and details were put in place. The trial lawyers and legislators behind the proposition never mentioned that there already were laws and agencies aplenty with the power to control harmful chemicals, since doing so might lead voters to deem the law redundant and unnecessary. And while they diverted attention from that fact, they laid the legal groundwork for allowing private lawyers to collect fines from a public law, defined the quasi-scientific process for designating chemicals as dangerous, outlined the regulatory framework for expanding the list of harmful chemicals and recruited appointees to the committee that would oversee the process of adding chemicals. It was an evil plot worthy of super-villains like the Joker or Lex Luthor, and it was all shielded behind a façade of care and concern for the little man, and the need to rein in the inherent evil of greedy business owners. Sixty-three percent of California voters fell for it, much to the delight of the trial lawyers and the Porsche dealers they frequent.

They had reason aplenty to be delighted. In the 20-plus years since the ballot measure passed, Prop 65 litigation mills have brought more than 16,000 actions against businesses, "earning" them nearly $500 million in settlements.[2]

THE LOST PROMISE

There was a time when California was golden, when having a bit of California come your way was considered a good thing by people in other states. But that was before California fell into a sea of political stupidity. It was back when California was at the head of the pack for all the right reasons, able to accomplish expansive goals, manage its finances well, exploit its abundant resources and have enough energy and expertise left over to save this world and explore new ones.

In the middle years of the last century, Gov. Pat Brown, Jerry's father, presided over a California that was capable of building the State Water Project - 701 miles of canals, 34 reservoirs, 20 pumping plants and five hydroelectric plants that all worked harmoniously together to supply water to 20 million Californians and 660,000 acres of cropland. It was an engineering wonder of the world, a symbol of how Big Government in California can do things right, to the benefit of the people. Another big new idea that burst onto the scene at the time in California was the nation's first freeway, the Pasadena Freeway. (The Pennsylvania Turnpike was the first Interstate-type highway in the nation, opening a few months earlier in 1940 than the Pasadena Freeway. But it was not a freeway but a toll way - hardly as enlightened and liberating.) Running from downtown Los Angeles almost all the way to Pasadena - where it ends abruptly, halted by one of the nation's first effective neighborhood anti-growth movements - the freeway signaled the start of a California road construction frenzy that inspired other states.

In the private sector, the state's manufacturers were humming, lead by a booming aerospace industry that was fresh off a big win in World War II, exemplified by the Douglas Aircraft plant at Long Beach. It had turned out 30,000 warplanes during the war, then continued to employ thousands after the war to build airliners. Other California aerospace companies built the capsule that carried John Glenn into space, followed by the Space Shuttle and the Galileo and Cassini solar system probes. And the California economy was just as strong in more down-to-earth areas. On March 9, 1959, 14 years after its founders had set up shop in a Southern California garage, Los Angeles-based Mattel showed off the first Barbie. The scaled-down version of a professional gal with a 39-inch bust, 18-inch waist and 33-inch hips would go on to sell more than a billion copies globally. Seventeen years later, in 1976, the California product incubator was still toasty, as Steve Jobs and Steve Wozniak showed off their Apple I computer kit to the Homebrew Computer Club in Silicon Valley.

But that was all then. Today, environmentalists have crippled the State Water Project with lawsuits and there's not enough money in the state budget to keep the roads in a decent state of repair. California's hefty gas tax - the highest in the nation - is being tapped and spent on social welfare programs, the one thing the state still has in abundance. Manufacturing industries are fleeing the state after being nearly pummeled to death by high taxes, onerous regulations, litigation like that brought by Prop. 65, and energy blackouts that all the windmills and solar panels in the state can't eliminate. The old Douglas Aircraft plant is gone, now just an empty field awaiting development when the economy turns around. Mattel sold its Los Angeles manufacturing plant 20 years ago. Apple builds its iPad in China, and even Google, a most-Californian leader of the high-tech economy, no longer has a single server farm in the state.

The tarnish runs deep on this state that just a

generation ago remained justified in calling itself "golden." There are more welfare recipients in California than in the next eight states combined, three times more than the state should have, given its population.[3] Gasoline costs, on average, 30 cents more per gallon in California than in other states, thanks to the bane of tougher-than-average environmental regulations and higher-than-average taxes.[4] And as California's first-in-the-nation greenhouse gas cap and trade program goes into effect, today's gas prices will be a fond memory of better times. The state's debt, at a stunning $361 billion as *Crazifornia* goes to print, is almost 20 percent greater than the debt of New York, the second most indebted state.[5] It's no surprise, then, that California has the worst credit rating of any state, according to most credit-rating agencies.[6] And in the current recession, Californians' income has fallen nearly twice as much as the national average[7] and more people lost jobs, more homes were foreclosed upon, and more big banks went belly-up in California than in any other state.[8] Of course, California is also the most populous state, so it has more jobs, more homes and more banks than any other state, making those statistics less surprising. But even with that excuse, two-thirds of California voters believe the state is moving in the wrong direction, and 72 percent don't trust the state's elected officials to do the right thing.[9]

IN THE GRIP OF PROGRESSIVES

California became Crazifornia when it was turned into a laboratory for liberals, a proving ground for environmental extremists and the Petri dish of hyperactive regulators. Much of its core-deep dysfunction began as liberal politicians handed the keys of the state over to the unions that had gotten the politicians elected. In California, the old-line blue-collar unions representing private sector workers never held the sway they did in the Midwest and Northeast. It's the public employee unions that have the clout, granted to them by Jerry Brown, who gave them collective bargaining rights when he signed the Dills Act in 1977 during his first round as governor. He's now in his second round, thanks to the strong union support that funded his 2010 campaign.

The 295,000-member California Teachers Union, the California chapters of the Service Employees International Union - especially Local 1000 in Sacramento, which alone represents 95,000 of the state's 250,000 employees - the 86,000 members of the California Nurses Association, the 30,000 members of the California Correctional Peace Officers Association and a host of other local and state-wide public employee unions have become the state's leading power brokers. Their clout is out in the open today, as they're cashing in on their election backing that helped Brown defeat Republican billionaire Meg Whitman. Now the unions are keeping him from proposing anything but the most minor pension reforms. Even so, their efforts to assert their agendas are by themselves not enough to turn California into Crazifornia.

A key factor in the demise of California is the state Legislature's determination to dodge accountability for the negative effects its progressive actions have on the state's residents and businesses. To do this, the state

Senate and Assembly have effectively turned California into a technocracy - a government ruled by educated elites who know what's best for the people. It is these technocrats in the state's many large and powerful regulatory agencies, commissions and boards who actually impose the will of the Legislature through obtrusive and costly regulations and fines that were at best approved only in vague concept by California's elected representatives. As technocrats, carrying degrees in environmental science, urban planning, public administration and the like, they know a lot about how people ought to live and care little about how they want to live. The technocrats have a better feel for Utopia than they do about the actual mechanisms of an economy. This is but one reason why only 17 percent of the state's voters are satisfied with the Legislature's performance.

California's robust and powerful environmental movement has played a prominent role in the state's journey to the precipice, bringing lawsuits, backing legislation and creating coalitions ready to halt progress in the name of Progressivism. The environmentalists have taken full advantage of the move from democracy to technocracy by becoming a major supplier of the technocrats who fill California's regulatory agencies, from boardroom to cubicle. It is the environmental movement's considerable influence on state policy that led California to set diesel engine standards the state's own existing truck fleet couldn't meet. That forced small trucking companies out of business and in-coming trucks to stop at the Arizona, Nevada and Oregon borders to transfer their loads to trucks that comply with the state's new air standards.

The environmentalists' influence made it possible for California to impose a greenhouse gas cap-and-trade system while other states that had signed onto the scheme deferred, citing a desire to nurse their wounded economies back to health. California's environment-first governance style seemingly protects it from fears of what the cap-and-trade system's start-up burden of $1 billion a year will have on its already distressed businesses. Even the cap-and-trade system's supporters admit it will have no significant effect on the global climate, but they hope against the evidence that other states and nations will follow California's lead, so eventually the Earth Mother will thank California for ratcheting back atmospheric carbon. Questionable policies like these reflect the will of the elite, not the mainstream, and are put into effect by appointed technocrats, without so much as a motion or second from California's elected representatives, who merely passed the broad enabling legislation.

Unlike elected politicians, who actually have to face an angry public, the powerful appointed board members at California's regulatory agencies are well insulated from such bothers. This is best evidenced by the California State Water Resources Control Board, where state law forbids anyone with business before the unelected board to speak to board members privately, even though the board regularly imposes impossible rules on those it regulates. One such example is the board's acceptance of a technocratic determination that pristine rainwater becomes toxic the instant it touches the ground, an action that triggered massive new expenditures in the capture and treatment of rainfall before it can run off private property. Those wanting to talk to board members about such silliness are only permitted to talk to the technocrats on the agency's staff, who decide what the board members see, and what appeals will go forward. Is it any wonder that appeals that would further the environmentalists' agenda tend to advance and those that would make it easier on business or cheaper for taxpayers make it onto the board's agenda much less frequently?

Towering over the unions, environmentalists and technocrats in the ruining of California are the state's wealthy and engaged Progressives and Liberals. In universities, they teach the new generation of school teachers to live out and teach progressive concepts of class, subjugation and privilege. And the universities feed well-indoctrinated grads into positions in Sacramento's regulatory agencies. The state's wealthy Progressives use their campaign contributions to control the Democrats, who have controlled the state Senate every year since 1971 and the Assembly every year since the mid-1990s, keeping the state at the forefront of liberal legislation.

Reflecting on how all this affects those who dwell in California's fallout zone, Pat Mulroy, the dynamic head of the Southern Nevada Water Authority, recently complained to a group of Southern California water leaders, "It's hard being next to California. You're so big, so powerful ... and so crazy."

THE PEER AXIS

Together, California's unions, legislators, environmentalists, technocrats and teachers form what I call the Progressive-Environmentalist-Educator-Reporter axis - the PEER axis - which functions to ensure each generation has enough progressives in and out of government to guarantee the ongoing success of the movement.

To get a feel for the Progressives that form the "P" of the axis, take a look at Hollywood financier and political money man Steve Bing. A trust fund baby, Bing inherited an estimated $600 million when he turned 18, wealth earned by his grandfather, Leo S. Bing, who worked hard to build a fortune in New York real estate. Steven Bing's greatest notoriety comes not from his financing of films - *Polar Express, Beowulf* - but from an on-again, off-again affair with Liz Hurley, regarded as one of the most beautiful actresses in the world. He fathered a child with Hurley and, despite his millions, tried to dodge any child support resulting from that liaison, until a paternity test proved him the father. Bing duplicated the Hurley episode of fatherhood, denial, DNA testing and eventual payment of child support with Lisa Bonder Kerkorian, who for one month had been the wife of billionaire Kirk Kerkorian.

Not nearly as well covered by the tabloids is Bing's political life, where his reported contributions to Democratic political campaigns exceed $10.7 million. Benefactors include Bob Casey, Jr., who unseated incumbent GOP senator Rick Santorum in Pennsylvania in 2004; Al Gore, the 2000 Democratic nominee for president; Hillary Clinton, who ran for president in 2008; John Kerry, who ran for president in 2004; and Californians Rep. Nancy Pelosi of San Francisco and U.S. Sen. Diane Feinstein. A dedicated funder of environmental causes, Bing reportedly dumped almost $50 million into the 2006 campaign for Proposition 87, which would have jacked up gasoline prices through a new $4 billion tax on oil production to fund the development of alternative fuels. It failed by 10 percentage points, 55 percent to 45 percent. In 2008, he pledged to match all contributions to defeat Proposition 8, the measure that made gay marriage illegal in California. It passed despite Bing's millions, by 52 percent to 48 percent, although it is being challenged in federal court. And perhaps most indicative of Bing's Progressive leanings, when the William J. Clinton Foundation released its list of contributors, there was Bing, credited with giving, rather vaguely, somewhere between $10 million and $25 million. The Daily Beast reports the contribution was "on the high end of that scale."[10]

The powerful environmental movement - the first "E" in the PEER axis - promotes a pro-big government, anti-business agenda on a global scale, but was spawned in California's battles over timber production, proposed dams and housing development. The premier cheerleader for these battles was Berkeley native (surprised?) David Brower. Like any top-tier environmentalist, Brower can claim bragging rights for protecting some beautiful land, like Redwood National Park on California's North Coast. But his greatest commitment was to increasing the reach and power of the environmental movement. He was the first executive director of the Sierra Club (a post he held from 1952 until he was expelled for mismanagement and being overly autocratic in 1969). Then he founded the League of Conservation Voters and Friends of the

Earth. Finally, in 1982, he founded the George Soros-funded Earth Island Institute. Brower explained the ever-increasing radicalism of his career track to E Magazine: "The Sierra Club made the Nature Conservancy look reasonable. I founded Friends of the Earth to make the Sierra Club look reasonable. Then I founded Earth Island Institute to make Friends of the Earth look reasonable. Earth First! now makes us look reasonable. We're still waiting for someone else to come along and make Earth First! look reasonable."[11]

In an era that supposedly celebrates tolerance and inclusion, Brower told the Christian Science Monitor, "I'd like to declare open season on developers. Not kill them, just tranquilize them."[12] Such thinking - which he repeated regularly in lectures to college students - took hold, as environmentalists now frequently call for Grand Inquisitions against skeptics. The message apparently reached at least one environmental apparatchik at an environmental agency one of my clients was trying to get a permit from. In an employee parking space in the agency's parking lot, there was a Volkswagen bus that sported a government parking decal and a bumper sticker that said, "Developers, Go Build In Hell."

Brower also worked hard to program his acolytes to always put the earth well ahead of mere humans, saying, "While the death of young men in war is unfortunate, it is no more serious than the touching of mountains and wilderness areas by humankind." And, "Loggers losing their jobs because of Spotted Owl legislation is, in my eyes, no different than people being out of work after the furnaces of Dachau shut down." For views like this, California Sens. Dianne

Feinstein and Barbara Boxer introduced legislation in 2008 to rename North Palisade Peak in the Sierras after Brower, who died in 2000 at the age of 88. The bill failed following an outcry from locals who didn't want a perfectly fine mountain to be named after someone who for decades had tried to sequester their property for inclusion in the growing land inventory of California and the federal government.

Brower's intense focus on indoctrinating college students shows how important educators are as the second "E" in the PEER axis. California is, and always has been, full of teachers eager to indoctrinate the next generation in progressive principles. There was Berkeley's first president, Benjamin Ide Wheeler, who told the school's students in 1899 to discount any teaching that hews to the traditional way of looking at things. Seventy-five years later there was an unnamed Los Angeles public school teacher who encouraged one of his students to start dealing cocaine. The student, "Freeway" Ricky Ross, went on to be one of the leading instigators, and beneficiaries, of the crack cocaine epidemic.

I asked Lance Izumi, the senior director of education studies at the Pacific Research Institute, if educators deserved their own "E" in the PEER Axis. He agreed emphatically. "If you look at the teachers who are coming into the system, you'll find that a lot of them have gone through the state universities' schools of education, where they have been taught a lot of progressive teaching methodologies that deemphasize the older, tougher instructional methods such as drill, practice, memorization, rote learning, testing, assessments and being accountable for performance.

All those are bad things in the eyes of progressive faculty, and certainly in the eyes of progressive professors at schools of education," Izumi said.

"These teachers care primarily about not damaging the self-esteem of your child or anybody else's child," he continued. "They think it's more important to preserve their mental state than whether they can actually work with their brains. What they fail to understand is that the empirical evidence shows very conclusively that the thing that causes kids to have better self-esteem is not to tell them that they have better self-esteem or that they're great people, but that by their achieving better scores on tests, they're learning more. When kids are able to grasp their subject matter, the self-esteem comes along with it. These teachers are so wedded to progressive teaching traditions that it's almost like religion to them." As a result, California's schools turn out new generations steeped in progressive concepts - not just teaching concepts but all the other progressive thinking their teachers picked up on the way to their teaching certificate.

There have been so many California educators working so hard to churn out future generations of Progressives that it's difficult to pick one to exemplify the many. So instead I'll point to another unnamed Los Angeles Unified School District teacher who was photographed sitting on the back of a Volvo convertible during a 2007 gay pride parade. In the photo, he is holding up a hand-written sign urging everyone to "Teach Respect." That's ironic because he's wearing a black T-shirt proclaiming in large block white letters "BUCK FUSH." The photo, which ran without comment in Teachers United, the organ of the United Teachers of Los Angeles union, shows how thoroughly indoctrinated the susceptible targets of the PEER axis have become. These molders of the next generation believe respect is something given only to people aligned with the Progressive social agenda, and tolerance is not something to be extended to people who "aren't like us."

The reporters making up the "R" in the PEER axis acronym include the classic ink-stained liberal reporters of print media, like George Skelton of the Los Angeles Times, who has covered California politics for 50 years. He recently revealed just how closely he cleaves to the California model of big government and high taxes when he published a list of the top five stories of his career. It included, for all the wrong reasons, both Ronald Reagan and Proposition 13, the 1978 proposition that is the favorite of fiscal conservatives because it stopped government's endless ratcheting up of property taxes and mandated a two-thirds legislative vote for tax increases.

Reagan, he said, was guilty of a "drumbeat that 'government is not the solution, government is the problem,'" that "promoted anti-government cynicism and paved the way to Proposition 13." Skelton doesn't praise Prop. 13 for keeping a lid on government, but rather, blames it for "a lack of badly needed tax reform" - with reform meaning, in this case, increases to support bigger and bigger government. He didn't mention that before Prop. 13 passed in 1978, the Democratic-controlled Legislature and Jerry Brown - who also was governor at the time - repeatedly refused to pass tax reform on its own, forcing the people to take matters into their own hands at the ballot box.

The "R" in PEER includes more than the George Skeltons of the world under the heading of reporter, however. It represents the entire class that reaches a vast audience via the media: the bad news babbling bubblehead bleach blondes of broadcast, made famous by Don Henley in the Eagles song "Dirty Laundry," the emerging social media moguls and mavens and the biggest California influencer of all: Hollywood.

It was Hollywood that took out-of-work, Michigan-born, California-based journalist Michael Moore and bankrolled him into one of the most successful documentary film makers of all time. In 1989, Warner Bros. gave Moore $3 million for the distribution rights to his first film, the pro-worker, anti-management "Roger & Me," an unheard of amount for the first film from an untested documentary director. In 2002, Hollywood gave him an Academy Award for the pro-gun control "Bowling for Columbine." And in 2005, it honored him with A-list celebrity treatment at the Academy Awards show - seating him next to former president Jimmy Carter - when his anti-Bush, anti-corporate America, anti-media, anti-war "Fahrenheit 9/11" was up for the best picture award.

Hollywood also propelled global warming activism to the top of the international agenda when it gave an Academy Award to an out-of-work former Tennessee senator, Al Gore, for the inconveniently untruthful film, "An Inconvenient Truth."

The PEER axis of Progressives, environmentalists, educators and reporters is responsible for ensuring there will be a continuing flood of newly emerging

Progressives pouring into each element of the axis. From the universities of Los Angeles and the Bay Area, these recent graduates of environmental studies, public administration, law, education, journalism and film enjoy a direct channel into city and state office buildings, environmental group headquarters, classrooms and new and old media outlets. There, thanks to the PEER axis, they are greeted by like-minded alumnae ready to show them the ropes so they, too, can influence and implement policy, bring lawsuits, and mold the next generation with appropriate political and environmental doctrine.

CALIFORNIANS WITH A PEER

To understand how California's PEER axis helps to drive the Progressive agenda nationally, look no further than Hilda Solis, President Obama's Secretary of Labor. Solis, who grew up in an East Los Angeles union household, is the proud holder of a 99 percent "liberal quotient" from Americans for Democratic Action and a two percent "conservative quotient" from the American Conservative Union from her time in the U.S. House of Representatives from 2001 to 2009. She graduated from La Puente High School in the Los Angeles Unified School District, then went on to California Polytechnic University under California's progressive Educational Opportunity Program. There, she prepared for public sector work with a political science degree, then moved on to the University of Southern California, where she picked up the degree coveted by all feeders at the public trough: a Masters in Public Administration.

Solis has never spent a working moment in the private sector. Instead, she worked first with another program for disadvantaged students wanting to go to college - California apparently needs at least two such programs - before winning her first elected position, on a college district board. Her subsequent legislative career, first in California, then in Washington, reads like a Progressive's check list: pro-illegal immigrant, pro-union, pro-regulation, pro-abortion, anti-business and anti-gun. No wonder she caught Nancy Pelosi's eye and became vice chair of the Democratic Steering & Policy Committee, then caught Obama's eye as he looked for someone to fill his last remaining cabinet seat, Secretary of Labor.

Some of the first rumors of her appointment to the cabinet came from the Communist Party USA's People's Weekly World, which may not be surprising, since the party had backed Solis when she first ran for Congress in 2000.[13] The Red rag reported that Solis' name was put forward by Service Employees International Union president Andrew Stern,[14] which explains why the nomination was seen as a big win for unions and evidence of pro-union things to come from the Obama administration. Republicans held the nomination up for months, in part because she was not forthcoming in her answers about her support of the Employee Free Choice Act, which would have reduced free choice in union elections by eliminating secret ballots. The nomination was also slowed because she was caught in the same net as so many Obama nominees: failure to pay taxes. In Solis' case, it was her husband who didn't pay. But the revelation still was damaging, and the cause of more than a little political lampooning. The news of tax-dodging broke about the time the Federal Aviation Administration released tapes of Capt. Sully Sullenberger's radio chatter as he safely landed US Airways Flight 1549 in the Hudson River, a juxtaposition that caught the eye of Los Angeles Times "Top of the Ticket" blogger Andrew Malcolm, who made up this phone conversation out of thin air:

> *Hilda Solis: We had a problem on takeoff. Flew into a flock of liens.*
> *White House: Of what?*
> *HS: Liens. Tax liens. My husband has more than 6,000 in unpaid business taxes.*
> *WH: That's a lot of faxes!*
> *HS: No, not faxes. Taxes. You know, like money. That regular people pay to government.*
> *WH: We've heard of that.*
> *HS: It was an accident. An unintentional oversight.*
> *WH: We've heard of that too.*
> *HS: For about 16 years.*
> *WH: Oh.*
> *HS: Yes.*
> *WH: How long have you been in public office?*
> *HS: For about 16 years.*
> *WH: Oh.*[15]

Flocks of liens notwithstanding, Solis' nomination finally made it through the Senate. Since then, she's extended unemployment benefits, added 250 investigators to the department's Wage and Hour Division and directed them to crack down on what few employers in the country still have employees, loosened restrictions on "immigrant labor" put in place by President Bush and issued the largest OSHA fine in U.S. history. The Democratic Socialists of America, the U.S. affiliate of Socialists International, is pleased as Red punch by Solis, writing in 2010:

> *Those who voted for "change you can believe in" in 2008 have found many reasons since Obama's inauguration to be disappointed with the new White House. But there have been some bright spots in the administration's first year as well - positive steps that illustrate the difference that a progressive-minded administration can make when it stands up to corporate interests and is unafraid to act in the public good. One well worth acknowledging ... is the work of the Department of Labor under Secretary Hilda Solis.*[16]

Another product of the PEER axis, although he doesn't yet enjoy the national influence of Solis, is Los Angeles mayor Antonio Villaraigosa, whose career trajectory is still upward despite running a city that has a $600 million deficit and having trouble keeping his trousers zipped up. Already the father of two illegitimate children from his college years, and busted by his wife in 1994 for philandering while she struggled with thyroid cancer, Villaraigosa was caught in 2007 having yet another affair, this time with Telemundo news anchor Mirthala Salinas, who covered his administration. Still (or maybe because of the scandals), the mayor is said to have "impeccable progressive credentials."[17]

Like Solis, Villaraigosa is a product of the Los Angeles Unified School District, where he landed after being expelled from Catholic schools for fighting. He then latched onto an Upward Bound program and attended East Los Angeles College, where Chicano Studies has its own department, but history and African-American studies are in the school of Social Sciences. He then transferred to the University of California, Los Angeles, where he received a very progressive indoctrination into U.S. history while pursuing a BA in the field. One of his teachers there was likely Juan Gomez-Quinones, a classic cog in the PEER axis education machine. Gomez-Quinones taught history and Chicano studies, and got much of his academic esteem for being a founder of the Movimiento Estudiantil Chicano de Aztlan (MEChA), which calls for Chicanos to rise up and take back California and most of the West, creating a new Marxist-Leninist state within Mexico. America has California to thank for MEChA, by the way. In April 1969, more than 100 Hispanic activists, including Gomez-Quinones,[18] converged on another California liberal institution of higher learning, the University of California, Santa Barbara, and out of that session came MEChA.[19]

Villaraigosa was no academic star at UCLA, but he was a rock star in radical politics, delivering fiery speeches as a MEChA campus leader. The highlight of Villaraigosa's college career came with MEChA's takeover and vandalizing of UCLA's Chicano Studies Center. Another MEChA member, Arturo Chavez, said of Villaraigosa, "He was one of the guys that would go out there and start the slogans because he was the loudest one. He was one of the people who would make sure people were riled up."[20] Years later, when a few brave radio talk show hosts dared to bring up his days as a MEChA activist, Villaraigosa clammed up, calling the question inflammatory.

After graduating, Villaraigosa studied law at the suitably progressive but unaccredited People's College of Law, but gave up becoming a lawyer after four failed attempts at the bar exam. He became a union organizer and president of the ACLU's Southern California office, the perfect credentials for a successful run for California Assembly, representing East Los Angeles. He became speaker of the Assembly in 1998 and left office in 2000 due to term limits. When he returned to Los Angeles and became mayor, his appointments read like a Who's Who of Progressive politics: community organizer and former UCLA professor Larry Frank as deputy mayor; Mexican American Legal Defense and Education Fund attorney and USC adjunct professor Thomas Saenz as legal and policy advisor; UCLA grad and gay and lesbian activist Torie Osborn as special advisor; and activist environmentalist and affordable housing advocate Cecilia Estolano as head of the Community Development Agency. The radical magazine Dissident gushingly described the appointments, saying, "Villaraigosa signaled his political loyalties by appointing some of L.A.'s most effective activists to key positions in the mayor's office, as department heads, and as members of powerful boards and commissions."[21] Many of these appointees will graduate from Los Angeles to posts at the state and federal level, ensuring California's continuing role as an engine for American Progressivism.

A LABORATORY FOR LIBERALS

As a laboratory for liberals, California has become tax-crazy, imposing the nation's highest unemployment tax and personal capital gains tax rates. And it's near the top on income tax rates, corporate tax rates and corporate capital gains tax rates. Despite its excellence in collecting taxes, the state's services continue to deteriorate, even as stiff fees are added for the joy of interfacing with grumbling bureaucrats who are counting the days until they can collect their budget-busting pensions. How stiff are the fees? One of my homebuilder clients recently was told that until he paid $275,000 to the California Coastal Commission, its staff would not start processing his permit for a subdivision - even though the California Coastal Act limits such fees to a "moderate" $100,000.

Because of all this and so much more, about 150,000 Californians have been fleeing the state each year lately.[22] In fact, Los Angeles alone has lost more households than New York, Miami and, incredibly, the economically decimated city of Detroit ... combined.[23] More Californians have fled to Texas and Oklahoma in the last few years than came from those states to California during the Dust Bowl years of the 1930s. But as awful as all this is, more frightening by far for people living in other states is this: Crazifornia is coming to you soon. As Glenn Beck reminded his viewers recently, "As California goes, so goes the nation."[24]

President Obama certainly thinks that's true. In a

speech given shortly after his election, he warned America what he had in mind, saying, "Consistently, California has hit the bar and then the rest of the country has followed."[25] In other speeches, the president has held up California's environmental regulations and its approach to providing healthcare to the poor as models for the rest of the nation. But he holds his highest praise for California's aggressive push to save the planet from global warming, and he makes no bones about how much he wants other states to follow California into the happy green economy. In a campaign speech, he said, "In states like New Hampshire and California, people are taking the lead on producing fuels that use less carbon. It's time we made this a national commitment..."[26]

His commitment to following California's lead is one of the rare campaign promises he has kept. Shortly after his election, the new Obama EPA announced an about-face from the position it held during the Bush years and dropped its opposition to California's efforts to impose automotive fuel economy standards that are much more stringent than their federal counterparts. In return, California agreed to adhere to the national standard - as long as the national standard was basically its standard. This change in policy allowed California to go ahead with its technocrats' demand that new cars and trucks in the state must achieve 40 percent better fuel economy by 2016 - a fleet average of 35.5 mpg. When the announcement was made, 13 other states and the District of Columbia were cued up to follow - even though the standards are predicted to raise the price of a car by $1,300[27] and, in the opinion of many experts, would lead to more highway driving deaths because cars would be lighter, and therefore less safe.

INMATES RUNNING THE ASYLUM

Maybe California should be cut some slack. After all, running the state well is quite possibly an impossible challenge. Just consider the sheer numbers of the place: 8 million students from kindergarten through high school (that's equal to the entire population of Virginia), a quarter million prisoners and parolees, well over a million people on welfare,[28] 16,662 miles of highways[29] carrying 19.8 million registered cars (only five states have more registered vehicles than does Los Angeles County alone),[30] 53,000 teenage pregnancies each year[31] and $10.5 billion spent annually on services to illegal immigrants.[32]

Californians haven't ignored these problems. They've done something far worse: They've tried to fix them through ballot initiatives. Californians can't stop themselves from trying new ways to fix the mess, amending California's constitution 512 times in 130 years, or almost four constitutional amendments each year, year in and year out, since the state was founded. Many amendments were written by the state Legislature. But between 2000 and 2009 alone, 71 constitutional amendments grew out of California's out-of-control initiative process, which allows anyone with a hefty bank account to get a constitutional amendment on the ballot. Each general election cycle, 50 or more new initiatives are filed with the state attorney general and begin working their way toward the upcoming ballot.

These propositions bring negative consequences so frequently that Californians' obsession with the process can be likened to the Alcoholics Anonymous definition of insanity: doing the same thing over and over again while expecting a different result. Proposition 98, for example, in 1988 locked in a formula for school funding at about 43 percent[33] of the state's annual general fund expenditures. Even though per-pupil funding has increased 30 percent since its passage, California's elementary school rankings have plummeted. It is 48th among the states in reading and 49th in science. Despite this dismal performance, Prop. 98 ensures that dollars continue to flow into schools, having no discernible effect except to limit the Legislature's ability to balance its budget.

If that seems insane, consider California's recent mental health proposition, Proposition 63, voted into law in 2004 by a 54 percent to 46 percent margin - with almost 75 percent of San Francisco voters thinking it was a terrific idea. Thanks to the vote, Californians with gross incomes over $1 million now must pay an additional 1 percent state income tax to raise $1.8 billion a year, to be spent on improved mental health services for the poor. "My God," said Troy Senik of the Center for Individual Freedom after the vote, "If you're a millionaire and you're still living in California, you need mental health services."[34]

Similarly, it may be insane to stay in California if you're a Republican. After losing races for every state-wide office and failing to pick up seats in 2010, like Republicans did in every other state except for New York, the future of the California GOP is looking bleak indeed. And that is perfectly OK with the state's Progressives, who would just as soon not be bothered with troublesome political minorities, especially ones that continue to insist on paring down government to balance the state budget. Like many California liberals, Monterey-based left-wing historian and blogger Robert Cruickshank sees California's current political landscape as permanent and has decided the GOP might as well not even bother showing up:

> *California has changed, and its political system and parties ought to change with it. If a party refuses to change and adapt, then that party should rightly suffer the consequences at the ballot box. That's exactly what has happened to the Republicans.* **And that means they have lost any claim to playing a role in the governance of this state.**[35] *[Emphasis added]*

Maybe a proposition that would outlaw taking any action against the Progressive agenda for California will be next.

CHAPTER TWO:

REDS IN THE GOLDEN STATE: CALIFORNIA AND THE BIRTH OF PROGRESSIVISM

California's political and cultural climate has always been conducive to the growing of fruits and nuts.

BARACK OBAMA WOULD NEVER have been elected president were it not for some turn-of-the-century French restaurants in San Francisco. It was a reaction to the political corruption behind those restaurants that birthed California's Progressive movement, which to this day vitalizes the big government, liberal movement in America.

Certainly, the slaughterhouses of Chicago that inspired Upton Sinclair's 1906 reformist novel *The Jungle* deserve some credit since it fueled a backlash against unregulated business. Some credit for The Jungle goes to California, though, because John Rudolph Haynes, a millionaire Los Angeles socialist, and Kate Crane-Gartz, a Pasadena plumbing heiress, helped finance Sinclair's work.[1][2] Also deserving some credit is the prairie populism of Wisconsin, which nurtured Robert La Follette, who ran as the Progressive Party's candidate for president in 1924.

But as with so many bad ideas that trace their roots back to California, modern Progressivism, with its promotion of expansive government, its distrust of the free market and its fondness for big spending on social and environmental programs, would have had a much different flavor were it not for California. The state's modeling of Progressive legislation and policies and the sheer number of Progressives churned out by its schools and universities has given Progressivism staying power, both in the state and across the nation. California would probably lead the nation in left-wing intellectual exports, if such a thing were tracked.

SCANDAL IN SAN FRANCISCO'S "DINING BEDROOMS"

President Obama frequently taps into rich reserves of campaign cash by holding $1,000-a-plate political fundraisers in San Francisco, a city that by the early 1900s had already earned a reputation for Progressive politics - and fine dining. It was a certain class of French restaurants with names like Delmonico's, the New Poodle Dog and the Pup that played a key role in the spawning of California's Progressive movement, not because of what was served in the dining salons on the first floor, but rather, what went on in the upper floors. While innocent patrons enjoyed affordable dinners on the ground floor, the real business of these places was the not-so-innocent patrons in the "dining bedrooms" on the floors above. Patrons there enjoyed rich meals smothered in creamy sauces, washing it all down with wine and topping it off with brandy and cigars - cigars that were rarely smoked down to the stub because dining bedrooms came with a dessert, in the form of lace-clad ladies on feather mattresses.

Even in Baghdad by the Bay, as San Francisco was broadly known, prostitution was technically illegal, and this was definitely prostitution. When one of the establishments suffered the somewhat unusual misfortune of being busted, 1,600 prostitutes were arrested.[3] And when that happened, the city's mayor, Eugene Schmitz, and his top aide, Abraham Ruef, saw opportunity. Ruef and his client, the politically powerful Southern Pacific Railroad, had run Schmitz for mayor as someone who could get the vote of the increasingly rebellious working class while remaining beholden to the railroad's interests. When Schmitz won, Ruef turned the mayor's office into mob headquarters, as evidenced some years later when a Grand Jury indicted Schmitz and Ruef, laying out the restaurant scheme as but one of many:

> *The Ruef-Schmitz organization, recognizing how easily such illicit enterprises could be made to pay tribute, devised a plan to obtain a share of their profits. ... The Mayor inspired ... the Board of four commissioners, who had absolute power to grant or withhold liquor licenses, to commence an attack on the system and to threaten refusal to renew the licenses. The restaurant keepers soon discovered it was necessary to employ Ruef as an attorney to defend them before the Board. ... Ruef was paid large "fees" by the restaurant proprietors, and the licenses were renewed at their expiration.[4]*

It was graft, plain and simple, and San Francisco under Schmitz and Ruef was full of it, as Ruef collected bags stuffed with cash from businesses in need of the city's services or protections. It was all going along well until a new breed of Californians came along, shocked that evil politicians were not behaving in ways befitting the splendor of California, but instead were committing crimes in pursuit of evil profit to the detriment of the working class.

Ruef met his match in Rudolph Spreckels, an anti-corruption Progressive with a sterling Progressive pedigree - he was a trust fund baby, heir to a fortune someone else had earned. Spreckels' father, Claus, grew and processed sugar beets in the San Joaquin valley and built the San Francisco & San Joaquin Railroad to ship his sugar and other Central Valley produce to the world. Son Rudolph chose San Francisco over Fresno and played with his father's money until he was approached by Ruef with a scheme to rig a bond sale to Spreckels' and Ruef's advantage. Wrote the Grand Jury:

> *The day his proposition was made, Mr. Spreckels met Mr. Thomas Driscoll and Mr. Edward Tobin at luncheon and told them of his experience with Ruef and of his intention some day to organize and drive such men out of power in the city, and, by perfecting a good government organization, keep them out. Up to this time Mr. Spreckels had taken no special interest in civic affairs, but the boldness of Mr. Ruef and the viciousness of his proposition opened his eyes to the duty of men in his position to use their influence for better city government. It*

was this incident, he says, which turned his mind away from a career devoted exclusively to business.

Spreckels kept his promise, funding an investigation undertaken by another Progressive, William H. Langdon. Ruef had run Langdon for district attorney in an effort to shore up Schmitz, who was increasingly unpopular, in his third run for mayor. It worked, as Schmitz was re-elected. Langdon's election to DA would prove to be a grave tactical error, however, because the attorney saw himself as a reformer and set out to work with other early Progressives to bring down Ruef, who ultimately was sentenced to 14 years at San Quentin State Prison. As he left the courthouse after his conviction, Ruef quipped that he was "trading in his pinstripes for zebra stripes."[5]

That the Schmitz administration was corrupt and Ruef deserved prison is beyond refute. Just as irrefutable is how clearly the scandal illustrates the hold the Progressive movement was beginning to have on California. The Grand Jury report read like something written by Van Jones - who a century later found initial success in his career as a radical in the Bay Area - an indication of how Progressive thought in California had already advanced far beyond mere anti-corruption efforts. The report used language loved by Jones and other Progressives, blaming "bitter class antagonism" for Schmitz's rise to power, saying he was carried into office by the "oppressed and exploited class," but then turned against them.

HOTBEDS OF LIBERAL THOUGHT

California has always attracted people wanting to let go of convention. In the 1960s and 1970s, it was people like Charles Manson, the Rev. Jim Jones, the original "drink the Kool-Aid" guy, and William and Emily Harris of the Symbionese Liberation Army, all of whom, strangely enough, fled Indiana for California. In the late 19th century and the early 20th century, some new Californians let go of convention to go into a capitalist frenzy, becoming railroad tycoons, land speculators and newspaper publishers. Others let go into a populist frenzy, becoming social crusaders, union organizers ... and newspaper publishers.

Central to both sides was the Southern Pacific Railroad, the SP, which had funded Ruef and Schmitz along with many other politicians and hacks. The SP had first connected the far-flung towns of California, then united the state with the rest of the nation as the second trans-continental railroad in 1881, helping to spur the state's economic and population growth. The railroad created fortunes for many, who then ensured its continuing dominance through graft and clout. They, under the umbrella of the SP, ran Sacramento as if the capitol were the SP's own internal public affairs department. The railroad's grip on state government so infuriated the sensibilities of California's emergent Progressives that fighting the SP became to them what fighting slum lords, robber barons and factory owners was to Progressives back east. Distaste for the corrupt political practices of the SP was well placed, but many who were offended by the dirty relationship between business and government at the time would have been even more offended by how the spark that fired California's Progressives grew to a conflagration of anti-business policy that continues in California until today. The first great Progressive victory in the state, the election of Hiram Johnson as governor in 1910, didn't just effectively end the SP's longstanding political dominance of state politics; it enshrined in Sacramento a Progressive-dominated government that has either run the state or influenced the state, and the nation, ever since.

It should come as no surprise that California's universities were hotbeds of Progressivism in the same era, given the reputation California universities have today for leaning left. Berkeley's first president, Benjamin Ide Wheeler, made sure the school promoted liberal thought and discounted conservatism, saying in his 1899 inaugural speech, "All teaching which does not deal in fresh new visions of the truth, truth seen and felt each time it comes to expression as a new and vital thing ... is a dead and hopeless exercise."[6] Not exactly a strong endorsement for hewing close to biblical teachings and the precepts of the Founding Fathers!

Across the bay in Palo Alto, Stanford University president David Starr Jordan established California's fixation with progressive thought, and its export of it back east, in an 1898 article in The Atlantic Monthly. He wrote that Californians were obligated to govern themselves better in order to honor the state's stunning natural resources, a precursor to the earth-worshipping that later spawned the environmental movement. "Everywhere the landscape swims in crystalline ether," he wrote, "while over all broods the warm California sun. Here, if anywhere, life is worth living, full and rich and free."[7]

But Jordon's essay wasn't simply a celebration of California's gorgeous vistas and good life; it was also a condemnation of a society that would allow evil to live in a place of such magnificent landscapes, presented with a Progressive's flair for finding darkness under every rock. He scorned San Francisco's "saloon-keepers, and keepers of establishments far worse, toward which the saloon is only the first step downward." Also in his sights were lawyers, politicians, crooks, clairvoyants, gamblers and other scoundrels "that feed upon the life-blood of the weak and foolish"[8] - those weak and foolish souls who needed the protection of enlightened, elite overseers then, as they do still today.

California's premier historian, Kevin Starr, credits the widely-read essay with cementing in the minds of Californians that they were indeed different: stronger, more *progressive* than those less enlightened, less adventurous souls who clung to old ways back east. Published just 49 years into statehood, Jordan's essay made the case that California needed to transform itself from its robust "anything goes" philosophy and set about the serious business of reform.

THE SOUTHERN CALIFORNIA SOCIALIST

The true significance the Ruef trial to the Progressive movement wasn't only that it was an attack on corruption in business and government; it was, rather, who was doing the attacking. The initial prosecutor, Francis J. Heney, was quickly disposed of in one of the most sensational events in a highly sensational trial, when he was shot in the courtroom by one of Ruef's deputy bagmen. That act changed California forever, because stepping in to fill Heney's shoes was an up-and-coming attorney, Hiram Johnson, who quickly leveraged the fame he gained with Ruef's conviction into a successful 1910 run for governor.

The thought of Johnson as a reformer was probably met with considerable cynicism by Californians who remembered his father, Grove Lawrence Johnson, a one-term U.S. congressman who left office after being charged with one of the most creatively wicked political schemes of all time. Facing certain defeat at the polls, the elder Johnson somehow saw to it that invisible ink was used on the already-printed ballots to print his name over his opponent's, and vice versa. The invisible ink lasted just long enough for the ballots to be marked, then disappeared, so all the ballots marked for his opponent appeared to have been marked for him.[9] But the son proved to be a dyed-in-the-wool Progressive firebrand.

Hiram Johnson's progressive streak probably would never have come to fruition in Sacramento were it not for a hardworking socialist in Los Angeles, John Randolph Haynes, a millionaire developer and doctor who was in many ways the predecessor of today's Silicon Valley and Santa Monica liberals. While Northern California progressives of the day were fixated on the workers' struggle against capitalist domination - their primary mouthpiece, author Jack London, signed his letters, "Yours for the Revolution!"[10] - the Los Angeles Progressives, perhaps mellowed by the warm sunshine, adopted the principles of the Fabian Socialist movement, advocating gradual reform through the political process rather than manning barricades. To draw a current comparison, the Northern Californians were Occupy Wall Street and the Southern Californians were Obamacare. Johnson's political power came from his ability to use the raw emotional intensity of the Northern California revolutionaries to move the political agenda established by the Southern California reformers, all while not appearing to be too far removed from the political mainstream.

Haynes, while practicing medicine and building his portfolio, had been a Chamber of Commerce type, keeping a low political profile while he grew his net worth investing in the city's expansion and its infrastructure projects. But in 1897, he attended a lecture by a Christian socialist, the Rev. William Dwight Porter Bliss, and his days as a Progressive began. In 1898, Haynes financed the losing gubernatorial campaign of Job Harriman, who ran on the Socialist Labor Party ticket,[11] and in 1899 he immersed himself in a popular Progressive political trend of the day, direct legislation - the incorporation of initiatives, referenda and recalls into city charters and state constitutions in order to shift the balance of power to the people. In 1902, he succeeded in making Los Angeles the first government entity in the nation to adopt direct legislation, giving its citizens the right to recall elected lawmakers, as well as to make laws through initiatives and overturn them through referenda.

Haynes then paid a team of lobbyists to promote direct legislation in Sacramento. But in session after session he was defeated by the Southern Pacific's lobbying might. Finally, in 1910, Haynes aligned with a group of Republicans running on an anti-Southern Pacific reform ticket under Johnson's umbrella. He promised to deliver Southern California Progressives if Johnson would commit to moving direct legislation through the Legislature. The resulting platform united anti-SP radicals, social reform Progressives, pro-direct legislation factions in both parties and mainstream Republicans, giving Johnson the governorship. Johnson did not garner a majority, though, as 12.4 percent of voting Californians that year chose socialist J. Stitt Wilson, with 46 percent going to Johnson, 40 percent to Democrat Theodore Arlington Bell and 2 percent to Prohibition Party candidate Simeon P. Meads.

REPUBLICAN IN NAME ONLY, CIRCA 1910

In his inaugural speech, Johnson must have given some of his mainstream Republican supporters the willies when he said, "The system - that is but corporate interest seeking its own gain and advantage allied with politics - is the gravest menace and danger today threatening our Republican institution," and, "Insurgency means opposition to the looting of the people by the unholy alliance between big business and politics."[12]   Johnson's rhetorical prowess was noted by a writer for the progressive LaFollette's Magazine, who wrote the new governor was able to fire up in his audiences with "a moral fervor fusing the assemblies into almost a spiritual frenzy."[13]

In a special election in November 1911, Californians accepted direct legislation, with its referenda, initiatives and recalls, by a vote of 168,744 to 52,093. The state has never been the same. Today, California's ability to balance its budget is complicated by voters who have used propositions and initiatives to mandate how money should be spent. For example, as mentioned earlier, 43 percent of general fund revenues must go to education because of one successful proposition, Prop. 98; and other propositions have crowded prisons through mandated tougher sentences for criminals, or driven up health care costs for California's uninsured children and its aging population through mandated coverage. As a result, even a fiscally conservative Republican legislature and governor - if one could imagine such a thing in California - wouldn't have the flexibility needed to deal with budget deficits.

Nine states had preceded California's 1911 approval of direct legislation - all except Michigan were west of the Mississippi - but in California, the process helped to bring a Progressive governor to office. So, 60 years after its formation, California became a Progressive state, armed with the "people's vote" and headed by a very independent and driven governor determined to reform California away from its rambunctiously capitalistic, free-market roots. Johnson expressed just how progressive his politics were in a 1912 speech that sounds as if it could be given at Berkeley today:

> All of us know that this nation must control its big business. We know that we must conserve that which belongs to the nation. All of us today

understand that there must be a fairer division of the wealth which is the product of labor; that wealth in this nation must be made the servant rather than the master of the people.[14]

In Johnson's day, the tie between Sacramento politicians and the SP was the same sort of crony capitalism that infuriates so many today as the Obama administration showers taxpayer funds on the alternative energy companies that backed his campaign, and uses government's heavy hand to endanger their fossil fuel competitors. In a Progressive maneuver Obama would appreciate, Johnson used a simple thing most could agree on - the wrongness of government and business enriching each other at the expense of the citizenry - and used it to dramatically grow the size and power of government. In the process, he made California the most Progressive state in the nation, a goal he claimed he achieved during his eight years as governor.

He attacked wealth and big business at every turn, creating institutions that ultimately would go far beyond solving the problem statement that started it all, that business and government had become too close. He first created a railroad commission that ultimately curbed the power of the Southern Pacific over Sacramento and followed that success by establishing more unelected but powerful commissions made up of members of the Progressive elite who set about finding and curbing corporate abuses wherever they were perceived. They fixed wages and work days, mandated working-condition improvements (many of them needed at the time), established conservation as a state mission and increased the power of state employees. It can be argued that each of these was a rational, even laudable, reaction to a pendulum that had swung too far in one direction. But Johnson and the Progressives that followed him used the reforms to create a big-government political mindset that sent California down the road toward ever more extensive and expensive Progressive policies and, ultimately, an inability to compete with other national and global markets.

Hiram's Legacy

When Johnson moved on to the U.S. Senate in 1916, the Progressive movement in California shifted from policy-driven improvements for the working man to infrastructure-driven improvements that provided continuous work for blue collar voters and the growing public sector. The movement culminated in the governorships of Republican Earl Warren and Democrat Edmund G. "Pat" Brown, who was governor in 1964 when California passed New York to become the nation's most populous state.

Warren attended the University of California, Berkeley during Hiram Johnson's governorship, and was highly influenced by Progressive thought, something he was particularly susceptible to since his father worked for the notorious Southern Pacific until being blacklisted after participating in a strike. Brown, who like Warren rose to the governorship through the state attorney general's office, continued Warren's old-school Progressivism. When asked by his son, Jerry, what he hoped to accomplish as governor, he said, "I told him: essentially to make life more comfortable for people, as far as government can."[15]   Making government responsible for the comfort of the individual is a very Progressive take on the Founding Fathers' vision of individuals being free to pursue happiness.

Many of today's leading California Progressives grew up on Pat Brown.   Los Angeles liberal Rep. Henry Waxman, a Democrat famous for his investigations of just about everything conservative and his crusades for cap-and-trade and against smoking, was elected to the Assembly just three years after Pat Brown handed over the statehouse to Ronald Reagan in 1967.   Nancy Pelosi's comrade in arms, Rep. George Miller, D-Concord, a long-time labor advocate who recently became infamous for choosing fish over farmers in the California water wars, was just 21 and a student at San Francisco State University when Brown left Sacramento. Miller's father was a liberal Democratic state senator allied closely with the governor, so Miller grew up on Progressive politics, Brown-style. As for Pelosi and U.S. Sen. Barbara Boxer, D-Calif., both were 26 when Brown left office, but neither moved to California until a few years later, when both quickly became active in Bay Area Democrat politics and must have been regaled with stories of the great Brown years and angry diatribes about the dark era that Democrats believed followed Reagan's election.

California may be on the verge of becoming a failed state, but it has been extremely effective at promoting the Progressive cause and spreading Progressivism's various ills nationally.   Up until the 1970s, California was a national leader in the areas where government most touches taxpayers - schools, highways, water, power. But profligate spending on welfare, social justice and public employee salaries and pensions, combined with a decidedly anti-business bent by the state government, has left schools, highways, water and power buried under debt and regulatory burdens. Still, Californians continue to elect liberal majorities to the legislature, where the Progressive legislators dutifully press forward, fighting cuts to entitlement programs and public employee pensions and passing more laws to make the state less business-friendly.

Across the country, most legislators, but hardly all, can see in California's financial meltdown reasons aplenty to shy away from any impulse to parrot the state's policies and repeat its mistakes. That should provide some comfort to conservative voters in other states. But conservatives should remember that, while politicians don't last forever, bureaucrats, academics and journalists do, and are in it for the long term, making sure the Progressive movement isn't bothered too much by the whims of mere voters. Count on it: California's progressive policies will continue to take root elsewhere.

CHAPTER THREE:

PROGRESSIVISM'S LEGACY: JERRY BROWN'S SECOND CENTURY

California's governor is still a Moonbeam - and still an oil baron.

EVEN THOUGH THERE WERE 135 candidates on the ballot, it was an easy decision to vote for Arnold Schwarzenegger for governor in the exciting 2003 election that accompanied the recall of then-Gov. Gray Davis. After all, the two other prominent actors on the ballot - child star gone bad Gary Coleman and porn star gone worse Mary Carey - just didn't seem to have Schwarzenegger's gravitas.

Just six years later, Californians, myself included, were fed up with the fallen superhero. Schwarzenegger had promised his charisma was sufficient to break down the boxes that hobble Sacramento, but he left with the boxes all pretty much intact, and some very troubling bright green new boxes to boot. The Governator was no Gipper; rather, he was more like Hiram Johnson, the Republican governor of the early

19th century who had ushered in an age of Progressive politics in California that continues to today. Schwarzenegger's legacy isn't the governmental and budgetary reform he promised; it's Assembly Bill 32, the Global Warming Solutions Act of 2006, California's hysterical, egotistical plan to single-handedly save the world from global warming. It is estimated AB 32's mandated cutbacks in greenhouse gas emissions will cost California as much as $180 billion a year in higher energy costs and lost jobs.[1] The law is an example of Progressivism at its worst - meddling, costly and based on highly suspect justifications provided by politicized, not pure, science.

Schwarzenegger's commitment to an expensive green agenda despite its inherent unfriendliness to most businesses turned most California Republicans against him. But, as he should have expected, the state's progressive greens weren't swayed to stop being against him. One of the state's most prolific green journalists, Dan Bacher, gave a typical Schwarzenegger snub upon hearing that the former governor had commissioned three heroic bronze statues of himself. Bacher, tongue in cheek, recommend the statues' design be modified to commemorate what the left really thinks of the former governor's vaunted green legacy.

The first statue, the "Fish Terminator," would portray the "action hero" standing triumphantly in a pile of thousands of dead Delta smelt, longfin smelt, Sacramento River chinook salmon, Central Valley steelhead [sic], Sacramento splittail, green sturgeon and other fish species. This statue would commemorate Schwarzenegger's leadership role in killing millions of imperiled species in the state and federal Delta pumping facilities by exporting record amounts of water to southern California water agencies and corporate agribusiness from 2004 to 2006.

The second statue, the "Green Governor," would feature Schwarzenegger and Catherine Reheis-Boyd, president of the Western States Petroleum Association, shaking hands as he congratulates her on her appointment as chair of Schwarzenegger's Marine Life Protection Act (MLPA) Initiative for the South Coast. The statue could either be a sickly green or oil brown color to celebrate the green-washing that occurred under Schwarzeneggger's [sic] marine "protection" fiasco...

The third statue, "Arnold, the Canal Builder," would depict Schwarzenegger outfitted in a hard hat, with a shovel in one hand and a copy of the water policy/water bond package that he rammed through the Legislature in November 2009 in the other. Schwarzenegger would be addressing a rally of the agribusiness Astroturf group, the Latino Water Coalition, at the State Capitol to campaign for the construction of the peripheral canal to divert more Delta water to agribusiness and southern California. [2]

Schwarzenegger's drive to push AB 32 through may have earned him a grudging nod from the state's eco-regulators, since it pretty much guarantees them full employment. It certainly endeared him to California's masters of green industry cronyism. But it was not enough to appease California's Progressive base, which doesn't see Schwarzenegger as a Republican in the style of Hiram Johnson, as many California conservatives do. No, they forever will see him as just another Republican.

As the Republican vacated the governor's office and took down his smoking tent, Democrat Jerry Brown quickly put on the Progressive mantle. Brown signaled his Progressive intentions on January 1, 2011 - two days before he was sworn in - when his office leaked the news that former Assemblyman John Laird, D-Santa Cruz, would be his Secretary of Natural Resources. Laird had co-authored AB 32. Having him in charge of one of the state's most powerful regulatory agencies ensures that natural resources, not resourceful humans, will continue to be the focus of California state government. The leftist YubaNet.com reflected the mood of many Progressive California voters when it declared the Laird appointment "sets off green fireworks."[3] Ironically, as detailed in Chapter Seven, the environmentalists who supported Brown, Laird and AB 32 have been busily engaged in a campaign to prohibit most firework displays in California, green or otherwise.

JERRY BROWN, OIL BARON

Early in 2010, the year that would see Jerry Brown once again elected governor of California, long-time Sacramento Bee political columnist and Jerry Brown watcher Dan Walters explained his view of the man once known as Moonbeam to me, saying,

> *He's the perennial ... not a perennial politician so much as he's kind of a perennial college sophomore. This is his alternative to actually getting a real job. It's a game to him; he enjoys the play. And since he has his family's Indonesian oil money, he doesn't have to earn a living, and he can play. So he's kind of a perennial dilettante in many respects.*

Wait a minute - his family's Indonesian oil money? Yes, it's true: Brown's strong environmental and populist stance is not without equally strong oil-fueled irony. Brown was very effective during the campaign at projecting himself as just a poor public employee, trying to hold his own in an America plagued by an unjust disparity between rich (2010 GOP candidate for governor Meg Whitman) and poor (Brown and his union friends). He set this workingman tone from the outset, holding his first official fundraiser as a candidate for governor in the simple apartment he lived in the last time he held the office, after famously shunning the more opulent governor's mansion. While politically expedient, this image of Jerry Brown as everyman is patently false.

Brown has a lot of money - how much exactly is not public. And like many who enjoy the guilty pleasures of inherited wealth, especially inherited tainted wealth - he hides his considerable bank account behind a wall of liberal politics. Unhappily for his environmentalist and global warming alarmist supporters, Brown's fortune comes from that most dreaded of natural resources: oil. Even more unhappily, it's oil money from Indonesia, a country whose radical Islamists spawned the Bali nightclub bombings in 2002, killing 202 people, and the beheadings of many Christian schoolgirls.

Walters spent months researching the story of the Brown family's oil wealth, and ran the story in his column on October 15, 1990. The Brown family has never contested Walter's story, which he shared with me in his small office crowded with family pictures, cattycorner from the Capitol.

After Brown's father, Pat, left the governorship in 1967, Walters recounted, he joined a law and lobbying firm where he was quickly introduced to the Indonesian generals who had just overthrown the country's post-colonial dictator, Sukarno. The generals were international pariahs, having killed somewhere between 500,000 and two million citizens in the process of seizing power. Pat Brown's job was to tote one of the junta's generals around America, introducing him to big bankers, a job he excelled at, cobbling together a consortium of banks that lent the junta $12 billion. "That was a lot of money in the late 60s," Walters noted. The banks were interested in the immense Royal Dutch Shell petroleum holdings in Indonesia, which the Junta now controlled.

Once the $12 billion was in hand, the Indonesians set up two trading firms, one in Hong Kong and one in California, that arranged the shipping of the oil and were rewarded with a fee for each barrel they handled paperwork on - "a little taste, as they might say in the Mafia," Walters said with a chuckle. In return for securing the loan, Brown was given 100 percent ownership of the California trading firm and a half interest in the Hong Kong office. The deal was a very lucrative one because only the light, sweet crude oil from Indonesia could meet the low-sulfur requirements California's early clean air standards set for the fuel burned in the state's power plants.

Three of Pat and Bernice Brown's children, Barbara, Cynthia and Kathleen, were cut in on the deal, but Jerry wasn't - although the Junta did contribute $70,000 to his first gubernatorial campaign, in 1974.[4] Still, it was probably the family ties more than the campaign contributions that led Jerry Brown to protect the Indonesian oil monopoly in California power plants when it was threatened by Alaskan oil upon the 1977 completion of the Alaska Pipeline.

California's largest company and largest employer, Chevron, had made a big commitment to Alaskan crude by expanding and updating its refinery in El Segundo so it could produce fuel oil with lower sulfur content to compete against Indonesian crude for the California power plant market. Before the El Segundo facility could refine a barrel of North Slope crude, however, the California Air Resources Board, headed by Jerry Brown's former campaign manager, Tom Quinn, passed a tighter standard for sulfur that was just barely too high for Chevron to meet with Alaskan oil. That cemented the Indonesian junta as the only oil provider to the California power industry. And in return for this favor, when Jerry Brown left the governorship, Pat Brown rewarded him with his own cut of the family oil business.

"To this day, Jerry's very sensitive about it," Walters told me. "He just hates the idea that people will bring it up because what it is, is the Brown family is in partnership with these corrupt, murderous dictators. I mean, they killed two million people after the coup!" (Some estimates are lower - 500,000 to a million - but Walters still makes a good point.)

So it turns out that despite his pauperish public persona, Jerry Brown was just as capable of self-funding his gubernatorial campaign as was Meg Whitman. But Brown wasn't about to show his wealth to California's Democratic and Independent voters, who are notoriously dismissive of wealthy candidates, so he turned instead to the public employee unions for campaign cash - $30 million of it.

A Full Moonbeam Rises

That indebtedness to labor along with Brown's decades-long pro-union psyche is proving to be a problem for California, because the focus of his governorship isn't going to be something lofty. It's going to be the budget, debt and the ever-widening public-employee pension funding gap. Many thought Brown's independent streak could lead to a "Nixon in China" moment, envisioning the man who gave public employee unions collective bargaining rights in 1977 standing up to them and fundamentally changing the state's political and economic landscape. Unfortunately, that's proving to be untrue. At a community meeting I recently attended in a rural firehouse near Lake Matthews in western Riverside County, the county's district attorney, Paul Zellerbach, said that Brown had told him public employee pension reform is "off the table." He quoted Brown saying, "There's no way I'm going to disband my [union] army." It's true; meaningful reform seems just about impossible under Brown, as Orange County Register opinion columnist Mark Landsbaum wrote:

> *Considering their clout, if public employee unions had a better candidate to run for governor, wouldn't they have run him? Why didn't they? Because Jerry Brown's candidacy was their dream come true.*[5]

Even while Brown was working dually as a candidate for governor and California's attorney general, he was busy doing the unions' work. When the California Chamber of Commerce ran ads highlighting Brown's record against business during his Moonbeam governorship, Brown personally called the CEOs of Safeway, Bank of America and other Chamber board members with a threat: If they did not stop underwriting the Chamber of Commerce's television ads, he would sic his union buddies and the attorneys under his command on their businesses. His GOP opponent, Meg Whitman, responded:

> *It is clearly over the line if the Attorney General in his official capacity was pressuring Chamber members to pull from the airwaves any issue advocacy ads that disrupt his current political ambitions. We are told these calls were made, and in many cases he was irate.*

> *These threatening telephone calls raise significant questions about the Attorney General's use of his*

office and its powers to support a purely political agenda. We call on Attorney General Brown to release the specific details of these phone calls. We understand the company leaders he telephoned to threaten include a labor-dependent retail company, as well as a financial services company that is directly regulated by Brown's office. If what we have been told is true, Attorney General Brown's conduct demands an immediate and impartial investigation.[6]

Of course, no investigation followed. Who would have initiated it, California's sitting attorney general?

Once Brown was elected, the first indication of his continuing dedication to his union supporters came in his first days in office, when he named Marty Morgenstern, a labor activist who worked for Brown during the first go-round, as secretary of the Labor and Workforce Development Agency; and Ronald Yank, a retired labor attorney who had represented the powerful California Correctional Police Officers Association, as director of the state's Department of Personnel Administration. Three months later, Brown signed off on a new prison-guard labor contract that can only be seen as a thank you gift to the union, which gave $2 million to Brown's election campaign.

For all his faults, Schwarzenegger had refused for four years to approve a contract for the 32,000-member-strong guards union. But after a quick round of negotiations with Yank, the Brown administration gave the guards a contract that carried most of their fat benefits package forward. The new contract dodges having a cap placed on vacation days, so Californians can look forward to an ongoing display of pension spiking that will add millions of dollars to already extravagant pensions. It allows the guards to pocket anywhere from $780 to $1,560 a year if they have a physical exam, a benefit that will cost Californians a minimum of $25 million a year. Just lugging their fat wallets around should be exercise enough for the cosseted prison guards. Another five contracts approved in the spring of 2011 did more of the same, setting Brown hundreds of millions of dollars behind the level of cuts he promised during the campaign he would negotiate from the unions.

One year after his election, Brown finally addressed pension reform, admitting the state is "not on a sustainable path." He offered up a package of proposed reforms that would, among other things, impose a cap that would limit pensions to 75 percent of salary, increase the retirement age, create a hybrid pension with Social Security and a 401(k)-style retirement account and reduce pension spiking. When Democratic legislative leaders and public employee union heads reacted coolly, the cynicism of Brown's proposal became evident: He could appear to be concerned and decisive by offering up a lot of proposals he knew were destined to go nowhere. In the unlikely event the reforms that truly pained the unions managed to get through the Legislature, they would be challenged in the courts, where judges waiting for their own lucrative state pensions would rule on the cases.

Even if everything Brown proposed were to become law - and it won't - it wouldn't be enough. Daniel Borenstein, a mainstream Bay Area columnist who has been at the forefront of the California's public employee pension story, said the package "doesn't stop the transfer of hundreds of billions of dollars of debt to our children."[7] Reed Royalty of the Orange County Taxpayers Association, a prominent anti-tax leader in the state who has been worrying about unfunded pension liabilities for years, told me that, at best, if the package passed in its entirety, it would do about a quarter of what needs to be done.

For Brown to be a leader on his father's legendary scale, he will have to turn his back on the unions, fight the tax-and-spend Democrats in the legislature and embrace a fiscal revolution in California. If he doesn't - and his first two budgets have failed to address the problem in any substantive manner - he'll be just another in a long chain of governors who have seen their dreams swamped by a series of convoluted and contentious budget-balancing exercises, and California will be none the better when his term is over. There is a precedent for Brown to repent his ways: He embraced Proposition 13 after fighting it tooth and nail before the 1978 election. But so far he seems content to be the engineer of a train that is running full-bore toward a massive wreck, espousing Progressive platitudes along the way. Sounding a lot like another Progressive 3,000 miles to the east, in the weeks preceding his inauguration Brown said of his budget objectives:

> Income redistribution that's occurred upward from the middle class and below is now at a level comparable to pre-Depression 1920s. So what we are facing is not only a budget deficit? We're facing a societal crisis, and we will only resolve it

as we understand it and we work not only to exercise a discipline, which has been sadly lacking, but also a fairness that enables everybody to feel they have an honest stake in the whole society.[8]

Still, Brown has a fan in an unlikely source, Arthur Laffer, the economist credited with the trickle-down theory immortalized in Ronald Reagan's economic policy. Laffer shocked attendees at a Pacific Research Institute dinner when he said, focusing on Brown's economic policy the last time he was governor, "Jerry Brown is the best governor California ever had. He did a great job of implementing Proposition 13. He indexed personal income tax in the state; instituted the Gann spending limit [on the state budget] during his tenure and killed the estate tax."[9] Brown also campaigned for a flat tax during his failed 1992 run at the presidency.

But then, Laffer fled California and settled in Tennessee, which has no state income tax and is much friendlier to business. Increasingly, it seems there will be no "Nixon goes to China" moment for Brown, and his term will end as another gubernatorial disappointment, should the state's economy even survive it.

CHAPTER FOUR:

MORALITY IN PLAY: CALIFORNIA'S CULTURAL REVOLUTION

Sex, Drugs, Rock and Roll!
Oh, and Holly-weird and the gay agenda!

ABOUT THE TIME Pat Brown entered his second term as governor in 1963, a new wave of anti-establishment Progressivism that would rock America's moral fiber was being born in California, thanks to, of all things, the Central Intelligence Agency. In the late 1950s and early 1960s, a highly classified CIA-funded program, MKULTRA, was active at the Menlo Park Veterans Hospital in the San Francisco Bay Area, charged with researching the viability of mind-altering drugs as interrogation tools. MK meant it was sponsored by the CIA's Technical Services Division and ULTRA was a special secrecy classification left over from World War II.[1] Among MKULTRA's volunteer test subjects were two Stanford University students, Ken Kesey and Stewart Brand.

Kesey was attending Stanford on a graduate

scholarship program that might catch the attention of Glenn Beck fans: a Woodrow Wilson National Fellowship. Wilson has become synonymous with Progressive governmental overreach, and it was exactly that sort of overreach that basically took artistic struggle out of the writing of Kesey's first novel, *One Flew Over the Cuckoo's Nest*, since taxpayers paid him to write it. Brand was just wrapping up his biology degree at the time, which preceded subsequent studies at the San Francisco Art Institute and San Francisco State University, leading ultimately to his publication of *The Whole Earth Catalog*, the lifestyle manual of the hippie movement. Together, Kesey and Brand tripped into, and at, the Menlo Park veterans' hospital, an experience Tom Wolfe chronicles in *The Electric Kool-Aid Acid Test*:

> *It was all nicely calcimined and clinical. They would put [Kesey] on a bed in a white room and give him a series of capsules without saying what they were. One would be nothing, a placebo. One would be Ditran, which always brought on a terrible experience. Kesey could always tell that one coming on, because the hairs on the blanket he was under suddenly look like a field of hideously diseased thorns and he would put his finger down his throat and retch. But [LSD] - the first thing he knew about it was a squirrel dropped an acorn from a tree outside, only it was tremendously loud and sounded like it was not outside but right in the room with him and not actually a sound, either, but a great suffusing presence, visual, almost tactile, a great impacting of ... blue ... all*

around him suddenly he was in a realm of consciousness he had never dreamed of before and it was not a dream or a delirium but part of his awareness. He looks at the ceiling. It begins moving. Panic - and yet there is no panic. The ceiling is moving - not in a crazed swirl but along its own planes its own planes of light and shadow and surface not nearly so nice and smooth as plasterer Super Plaster Man intended with infallible carpenter level bubble sliding in dim honey Karo syrup tube ...[2]

Well, you get the idea. It goes on for a couple more pages, describing real and hallucinated events that occurred in California a full two years before Timothy Leary and Richard Alpert started "french-frying the brains of Harvard boys" with LSD, in Wolfe's psychedelic vernacular. So, in their quest for the perfect interrogation drug, or maybe torture drug, the CIA created in California, in Kesey and Brand, the prototypes of the American hippy movement that would soon be birthed in San Francisco.

Kesey defined the "smoke it, drop it, and have fun going where your mind takes you" side of the movement, a path that had an influence on popular music that has far outlived the hippies themselves. Kesey frequently rocked out to the Grateful Dead on his La Honda, California farm, although the band was then known by the much less groovy name, The Warlocks. The Bay Area had already spawned the precursor of acid rock in the folk music phenomenon of the late 1950s, which started in two Berkeley coffee houses, the Jabberwock and Cabale Creamery, and in

New York City's Greenwich Village. Cabale Creamery entrepreneur Chandler A. Laughlin III, who wore long hair and gaudy Elizabethan clothing long before it became *de rigueur* hippie wear, went on to become a rock entrepreneur, introducing not just the Grateful Dead, but also Jefferson Airplane, Big Brother and the Holding Company (Janis Joplin's band), Quicksilver Messenger Service and Iron Butterfly to San Francisco's growing hippie movement - more than four years before Woodstock.

Brand also was involved in the early promotion of acid rock music through The Trips Festival - which was credited with creating the Haight-Ashbury hippie community. He defined the "smoke it, drop it, and become the intellectual father of the green movement" side of the hippie saga. Some of the credit for the first Earth Day can go to Brand because of his aggressive petitioning of NASA to release the first photo of the "Whole Earth," which had been taken during a satellite's moon orbit. In 1968, he succeeded, and two years later the first Earth Day was held. The same year the photo appeared, Brand put it on the front cover of *The Whole Earth Catalog*, a publication that embodied the formational DNA of the environmental movement in its celebration and facilitation of going back to the earth, eating whole foods and holding natural things in higher regard than technological things.

In all of this, and in his two years as a special advisor to Gov. Jerry Brown during the Moonbeam years, Brand was establishing the Progressive green philosophy that continues to exert a heavy influence on California and the world 50 years later. To his credit, more recently Brand has scolded Greens for opposing nuclear power and the genetic modification of plants and for continuing to fret about population growth when they should be stressing about population decline.[3]

Brand also has credited California's hippie movement he helped to launch with the success of the Internet, writing in Time Magazine in 1995:

> *Newcomers to the Internet are often startled to discover themselves not so much in some soulless colony of technocrats as in a kind of cultural Brigadoon - a flowering remnant of the '60s, when hippie communalism and libertarian politics formed the roots of the modern cyberrevolution. At the time, it all seemed dangerously anarchic (and still does to many), but the counterculture's scorn for centralized authority provided the philosophical foundations of not only the leaderless Internet but also the entire personal computer revolution.[4]*

In justifying this argument, Brand said three principles born from the hippie generation apply to the philosophy of the Internet as well: All information should be free; mistrust authority and promote decentralization; and access to computers should be unlimited and total. Years later, Obama's Federal Communications Commission chairman, Julius Genachowski, parroted Brand when he defined access to broadband an entitlement.[5]

More familiarity with Brand's thesis might have diminished the shock many felt as LSD resurfaced when Apple founder Steve Jobs died in October 2011. One would think Haight Ashbury's hallucinogenic culture might be far removed from the Silicon Valley because complex tasks like designing computer circuits and writing code are best done with an unaddled mind. But that was hardly the case, according to this passage in the New York Times obituary of Jobs:

After dropping out of Reed College, a stronghold of liberal thought in Portland, Ore., in 1972, Mr. Jobs led a countercultural lifestyle himself. He told a reporter that taking LSD was one of the two or three most important things he had done in his life. He said there were things about him that people who had not tried psychedelics - even people who knew him well, including his wife - could never understand.[6]

One of the two or three most important things he had done with his life? Assuming founding Apple, launching Macintoshes (with the spectacularly foreboding "1984" Super Bowl ad), iPods, iPhones, iPads, Pixar and whole digital revolutions must count as things he sees important, along with such normal things as having children (in and out of wedlock), that makes tripping on acid a pretty significant part of what made Jobs tick.

Jobs was just 12 years old when the Summer of Love descended on San Francisco, with its estimated 100,000 young people, many with flowers in their hair and most with drugs on their minds - or in them. In its coverage of the Summer of Love, Time magazine defined the hippy code as, "Do your own thing, wherever you have to do it and whenever you want. Drop out. Leave society as you have known it. Leave it utterly. Blow the mind of every straight person you can reach. Turn them on, if not to drugs, then to beauty, love, honesty, fun." Time, like so much of the media, had drunk the electric Kool-Aid California was mixing up, and was telling the world about it. Kesey, Brand and the Merry Pranksters, their circle of proto-hippies celebrated by Wolfe in *The Electric Kool-Aid Acid Test*, had spawned a movement that claimed it would change the world, a goal it didn't entirely miss. Many of those hippies went into government jobs and many more into teaching, where they toiled to turn out new generations of like-thinking kids. Because so many of them held onto the drug culture's identification with the counter-culture and its distaste for "the man," they helped turn California's once old-school Progressivism, with its "let the state create great things" sensibilities, into a new-school Progressive force, in a "let's use the state to exert great control on everything" sense.

THAT KIND OF SMOKE-FILLED ROOM

If the CIA had decided to run its MKULTRA program in Des Moines or Birmingham instead of Menlo Park, a drug culture surely would still have burst onto America in the late 1960s. Quite possibly it would have grown in New York's Greenwich Village or in Boston, where Timothy Leary was doing everything in his power to foment the culture from Harvard. But more likely, the 1960s drug revolution still would have come out of California, even without Kesey, Brand and the Merry Pranksters.

The state already had a rich drug history - opium dens, marijuana farms and, in 1962, a crackdown of pharmacies in San Francisco that first alerted the nation to amphetamine abuse.[7]   Perhaps California became the epicenter of the drug revolution just because its weather is more pleasant than New York's or Boston's. Perhaps it's because the inventors of acid rock, the Grateful Dead and Jefferson Airplane, were regulars at the Avalon Ballroom and the Fillmore Auditorium in San Francisco. Or perhaps it was because, as Hunter Thompson wrote in his novel *Fear and Loathing in Las Vegas*, first serialized in Rolling Stone magazine in 1971:

> *San Francisco in the middle sixties was a very special time and place to be a part of. Maybe it meant something. Maybe not, in the long run ... but no explanation, no mix of words or music or memories can touch that sense of knowing that you were there and alive in that corner of time and the world. Whatever it meant ....*

> *My central memory of that time seems to hang on one or five or maybe forty nights - or very early mornings - when I left the Fillmore half-crazy and, instead of going home, aimed the big 650 Lightning across the Bay Bridge at a hundred miles an hour wearing L.L. Bean shorts and a Butte sheepherder's jacket ... booming through the Treasure Island tunnel at the lights of Oakland and Berkeley and Richmond, not quite sure which turn-off to take when I got to the other end (always stalling at the toll-gate, too twisted to find neutral while I fumbled for change) ... but being absolutely certain that no matter which way I went I would*

*come to a place where people were just as high and
wild as I was: No doubt at all about that ....*[8]

As early as 1967, though, four years before Fear
and Loathing was published, LSD had already sunk its
roots deeply into California's youth. In that year,
researchers asked California high school students
whom they would trust as the narrator of a hypotheti-
cal anti-LSD movie, and the majority answered, "No
one."[9] Two years later, in 1969, the film *Easy Rider*
debuted, telling the tale of two Harley-riding
California cocaine smugglers; it went on to become the
best drug movie of all time, according to High Times
magazine. The magazine ranked Cheech and Chong's
Up in Smoke, 1978, the best marijuana movie ever. Its
stoned-out story takes place mostly in Los Angeles.
And Ridgemont High was in the San Fernando Valley,
not Topeka or Orlando. It's no surprise, then, that the
state was pivotal in the subsequent drug waves that
spread across America.

The wildly destructive crack epidemic, for
example, has "Freeway" Ricky Ross of Los Angeles to
thank for its genesis. It started on tough streets Ross
controlled in South Central Los Angeles and spread
from there around the nation. At the peak of his crack
empire, Ross claimed he was purchasing $21 million
worth of Nicaraguan cocaine a week - almost half a
ton. He made more than $600 million ($1.6 billion in
2010 dollars) off others' crack addictions before being
sentenced to life in prison in 1996. He walked out of
prison in 2009, thanks to his good behavior - even
though his crack cocaine has been blamed for doubling
the murder rate of young black men in American cities

and essentially stopping African-American economic progress for a decade. It was a California institution, Hollywood, that introduced Ross to cocaine, in the 1972 hit movie *Superfly*, which told the story of a cocaine dealer's last big score. When Ross needed a little more motivation, it was a Los Angeles Unified School District teacher who encouraged him to start dealing.[10]

Following crack cocaine was America's methamphetamine addiction, which I first learned about from Peter Templeton, a trim, well-dressed land planner from Newport Beach I've worked with on many occasions. Templeton makes his living drawing up plans for new communities, and often is tasked with presenting those plans to the people who lived around the various project sites. On one such assignment in the early 1990s, he had left his trendy suits and Italian loafers in the closet, put on a pair of jeans, sneakers and a causal shirt, and headed to the high desert to a community meeting where he would introduce his client's plans for a new subdivision. Even dressed down, Templeton felt conspicuously over-dressed and ... well, healthy ... compared to the rough audience he faced. Nevertheless, he plowed into his presentation, focusing on the one big benefit the proposed subdivision would provide its neighbors - a new, paved road, replacing the washed-out, wash-boarded track that served the area's far-flung houses and trailers.

Templeton had just energetically told the crowd about the faster emergency response times they would enjoy when he noted with more than a little confusion that the promised improvement was met with a concerned shaking of heads and many whispers in neighbors' ears. Sensing hostility from the crowd, he wrapped up the presentation as quickly as he could. As he was packing up his projector and site plans, a man in his forties, with long, silver-streaked hair, a three-day beard and weathered skin approached him.

"We're not too keen on that new road," he said quietly to Templeton. The man looked around the room before continuing, "You see, we've got a lot of meth labs up here and we're really not that interested in faster police response time."

By then, meth had been around a long time, in inhalers for asthma patients, pumping up soldiers in World War II and fueling a lot of beatnik poetry. San Francisco, unsurprisingly, suffered through its own meth waves, first in the 1950s, then again with the Summer of Love in the late 1960s. Enough kids were becoming addicted to it that a meth clinic opened in Haight Ashbury, but the drug's presence was obscured by the media's attention to psychedelics and marijuana. The Oakland-based Hells Angels motor-cycle gang became significant manufacturers of it in the 1970s, but it remained a second-tier drug as cocaine gained in popularity among upper-takers.

That all changed in the late 1980s when cheap, smokable meth began to find a broad market. How broad a market America discovered in March 1989, when hundreds of federal, state and local law enforcement officers launched a coordinated raid in San Diego that resulted in the seizure of 29 meth labs and 830 pounds of ephedrine - meth's primary precursor - and the arrest of more than 100 meth cookers.[11] With San Diego suddenly off limits, meth production moved to the high desert communities in San Bernardino and Riverside counties, which quickly became designated the "meth capitol of the world," a title the media also bestowed at various times on Philadelphia, Chattanooga, Tulsa, Jackson County, Missouri, and dozens of other places.[12]

Today, California continues to influence the nation's thinking about drugs in its role at the forefront of the marijuana legalization movement. In 1996, the state's voters made California the first state in the nation to approve propositions legalizing medical marijuana, leading to today's scourge of marijuana clinics - about 1,000 in California alone, more than all the Starbucks coffee shops in the state. In 2010, the ballot offered up Proposition 19, which would have legalized marijuana use. Even though it failed at the polls, more California voters backed it than voted for GOP gubernatorial candidate Meg Whitman. Like earlier society-bending propositions on the California ballot - gay marriage and global warming, most recently - the measure opened a broad societal dialog, in effect blazing the trail for a national movement. After the vote count was tallied, Ethan Nadelmann, executive director of the pro-legalization Drug Policy Alliance, put it this way:

> *California's Proposition 19 may not have won a majority of voters yesterday, but it already represents an extraordinary victory for the broader movement to legalize marijuana. Its mere presence on the ballot ... elevated and legitimized public discourse about marijuana and marijuana policy. The media coverage, around the country*

and internationally, has been exceptional, both in terms of quantity and quality.[13]

Still, for every campaign California has led down drug use's slippery slope, it's led another slog up the slope toward tighter controls. Particularly ironic is that the same city that gave us Haight-Ashbury also gave America its first anti-drug law.

The year was 1875 and San Francisco was awash with opium dens. Worse still, opium dens were awash with Chinese, and San Francisco's white population was about as fond of Chinese as Mississippi's white population at the time was fond of blacks. Opium use was not illegal then, so San Francisco's white establishment responded by passing the Opium Den Ordinance, which very specifically banned only the smoking of opium in opium dens. While some white opium addicts favored the dens, most of them tended to get their fix in a more civilized, European manner, by drinking Laudanum, an elixir that was 10 percent powdered opium by weight. The ordinance let San Francisco's law enforcers clean out the Chinese opium dens while leaving the white population largely unbothered.

Then, in 1907, California became the first state to declare war on drugs. The campaign was pushed by California's powerful Progressives, who even then felt comfortable dictating how others should live. Their effort to make the sale or use of opium, cocaine, cannabis and other drugs illegal was clandestine - the quiet passage of some amendments to the existing state Pharmacy and Poison Act without press coverage or public debate[14] - but the effect was very public. The

California Board of Pharmacy's own agents, like the IRS revenue agents that would enforce prohibition a few years later, fanned out across the state busting pharmacies and opium dens with a diligent cadre of journalists in tow to make sure the busts and perp walks received considerable coverage.

Seven years later, 39 years after the Opium Den Ordinance, Congress followed California's lead and passed the Harrison Narcotic Tax Act in 1914, regulating for the first time the importation, production and distribution of opiates. It was the birth of America's long war on drugs, conceived in California - just as California decades later would help nurture a drug culture in America.

HOLLYWOOD AS BABYLON

Another child of California, the Hollywood movie industry, has also seen a tug-of-war between those who endorse a hands-off approach, despite Hollywood's long history of excesses, and those who want to impose controls.

When movies first became popular, ministers immediately noticed a drop-off in church attendance. Maybe it was that formerly faithful parishioners were just too tired to go to church on Sunday morning after Saturday night at the movies ... or maybe Hollywood, even in its earliest years, was already having a profoundly negative effect on America's morals. Some ministers responded by showing movies in church, justifying it by saying Jesus had entertained the masses with stories.[15] But the more common response was for church leaders to align with other socially conservative forces and demand a higher moral standard from Hollywood.

That Hollywood became the center of this long-running controversy is ironic given the town's genesis. Two early wealthy Southern Californians, Harvey and Daieda Wilcox, created Hollywood in the 1880s on their 160-acre ranch, declaring the town would be, "a peaceful and sacred oasis" where they and other devout Methodists could "practice abstinence and other virtues" in what they viewed as the moral capital of Southern California.[16]   When the film industry descended on Hollywood in the early 1900s, the conflicts that occurred as party-throwing movie stars moved in next door to fervently religious neighbors mimicked the nation's conflict, as the forces of morality fought the forces of film's "illicit lovemaking and iniquity," in the words of a study commissioned by President Teddy Roosevelt.

Fearing legislation to force censorship on the industry, film producers began to cut potentially offensive scenes from their movies through an informal "Don'ts and Be Carefuls" list of 11 subjects to avoid and 25 more to handle carefully. Thankfully, one of the "don'ts" still holds today - the depiction of children's sex organs - and some reflect a society we are glad has changed, like the prohibition on showing relationships between blacks and whites. But the loss of most of the "don'ts" is mainly an indication of how promiscuous, sacrilegious and unpatriotic Hollywood has become. Consider that all of this was once absolutely off-limits in American film:

1. *Pointed profanity - by either title or lip - this in-*

cludes the words "God," "Lord," "Jesus," "Christ" (unless they be used reverently in connection with proper religious ceremonies), "hell," "damn," "Gawd," and every other profane and vulgar expression however it may be spelled;

2. *Any licentious or suggestive nudity - in factor in silhouette; and any lecherous or licentious notice thereof by other characters in the picture;*

3. *The illegal traffic in drugs; Any interference of sex perversion;*

4. *White slavery;*

5. *Miscegenation (sex relationships between the white and black races);*

6. *Sex hygiene and venereal diseases;*

7. *Scenes of actual childbirth-in fact or in silhouette;*

8. *Children's sex organs;*

9. *Ridicule of the clergy;*

10. *Willful offense to any nation, race or creed;*[17]

Possible gruesomeness, sympathy for criminals, men and women in bed together (even if married) and the quaintly coined "first-night scenes" - what happens in the bedroom after the wedding ceremony and reception - were among the 25 "be carefuls." The list was voluntary, and since there was no enforcement mechanism, the tension between the America of traditional values and an America increasingly portrayed by Hollywood continued until finally, in 1930, the Motion Picture Producers and Directors Association agreed to a code of standards. The code was flouted until 1934, when the Production Code Administration was established, granting a certificate to approved movies.

But codes alone couldn't stop Hollywood from exposing the glamour-hungry American public to stories traditional America found distasteful. As gossip columnists filled newspapers and radio sets with stories of off-camera drunken orgies, marital affairs, homosexuality, drug use and socialistic political rants, filmdom's strong influence on morals - deliberate or not - took off and hasn't stopped yet. Woody Allen took nude photos of his wife Mia Farrow's adopted daughter, had sex with her and later married her. At least Dan Akroyd's worst known moral transgression is only imagined: He wrote in 2008 that a man having sex with a dog or cat would be perfectly fine with him as long as the dog or cat consented.[18] The wildly popular show Glee has been widely condemned for its harsh lampooning of conservatives and Christians, which contrasts sharply with its sympathetic portrayal of gays. And, of course, Hollywood is at the forefront of promoting environmental activism and liberal causes, in films like *The Day After Tomorrow*, *Erin Brockovich*, *Wall-E* and Al Gore's Academy Award-winning *An Inconvenient Truth*.

David Mamet, who received Oscar nominations for the screenplays for *The Verdict* and *Wag the Dog*, said of Hollywood, "We Americans have always considered Hollywood, at best, a sinkhole of depraved venality. And of course, it is." Marilyn Monroe said it even better: "Hollywood is a place where they'll pay you a thousand dollars for a kiss and 50 cents for your soul."

To many, Hollywood has sold America's soul for 50 cents, increasing public awareness and acceptance of new social norms that are much different from the American morality of the pre-Hollywood era. Many Americans argue this is a good thing, that Hollywood has helped America progress toward becoming a more tolerant society, while others argue that it has made America too tolerant of too many things best left untolerated. Some radical Islamists go further, arguing that Hollywood's effect on their traditional values is justification enough to attack America. But on this, all sides will agree: Hollywood has influenced the nation's, and the world's, values.

IF IT FEELS GOOD

In the mid-1950s, David Alberts had a little business in Los Angeles. He would advertise his wares, orders would come in through the mail and he would fulfill them. It was simple enough, and Alberts made decent money in return for the plain brown envelopes he mailed out, stuffed with magazines featuring, in the words of subsequent court cases, pictures of "nude and scantily-clad women." He peddled pretty tame stuff by today's standards, but it was much too ribald for Los Angeles in the 1950s, so one day the law came along and charged him with violating a California law forbidding the advertising or selling of "obscene or indecent" materials.

Alberts received little fame for his role in spawning the subsequent booming of the global pornography trade because he was eclipsed by a fellow mid-50s purveyor of dirty materials, Samuel Roth. Roth was a New York bookseller arrested at about the same times as Alberts and charged under a federal statute prohibiting the mailing of "obscene, lewd, lascivious or filthy" materials. Perhaps because what he peddled was more palatable - he was busted for selling *American Aphrodite, A Quarterly for the Fancy-Free* - Roth's name, not Alberts', is forever assigned to the resulting Supreme Court case that set new rules for what constitutes pornography, Roth vs. United States.

Roth, as the case is universally known, deemed a material could be declared obscene only if its "dominant theme taken as a whole" would appeal to the "prurient interest" of the "average person, applying contemporary community standards." The court also found that pornography was not protected speech under the First Amendment, a point that met dissent from Justices Hugo Black and William O. Douglas. The curious result of Roth was that the justices, excluding Black and Douglas, who refused to participate, would sit down for a weekly screening of pornographic films, in a selfless effort to better describe what constitutes obscenity.

The screenings came to an end with another California case, Miller vs. California. By now, it was 1973 and magazines like Penthouse, along with scores of Los Angeles-based movie makers, were hard at work on the edges of accepted community standards. Marvin Miller was among them, running one of the country's largest mail-order distributors of sexually explicit material. He made the mistake of mailing five unsolicited advertising brochures copiously illustrated with explicit photographs and drawings to a Newport Beach restaurant. After the restaurant's manager opened the mailing in front of his mother, exposing her to brochures for the books *Intercourse, Man-Woman, Sex*

Orgies Illustrated and *An Illustrated History of Pornography*, along with one for the film *Marital Intercourse*, Miller wound up charged and ultimately convicted of the misdemeanor of knowingly distributing obscene material.

The Miller case found its way to the Supreme Court, which sought to apply what it had learned during all those film viewings. The court decision established three criteria, all of which had to be met for a material to be deemed obscene: The same "average person, taken as a whole, community standards" test of Roth; that the work depicts or describes in a patently offensive way sexual or excretory functions; and that, as a whole, it lacks serious literary, artistic, political or scientific value. The court also found "inherent dangers" in trying to regulate expression and cautioned states that their statutes limiting obscenity had to be "carefully limited." The court stopped reviewing obscenity cases after Miller, so successful convictions increased for a while as lower-court convictions stood with no chance for further appeal. But over time, the three-pronged test Miller established and the court's cautions about regulating obscenity gave pornographers' lawyers plenty to work with in their increasingly successful defenses of their clients.

A third Californian, Harold Freeman, would bring the case that ultimately created the modern porn industry. He was arrested in 1987, when California was trying to squelch a rapidly growing porn movie business, and charged with pimping when he hired actors for adult films. Freeman's case, California vs. Freeman, is a bit messy. He was convicted of pandering, not producing pornography, and lost on appeal. But the trial judge thought jail time was unduly harsh for the crime and refused to follow sentencing guidelines, giving Freeman probation. The state appealed that, but lost.

So Freeman, free on probation and maybe feeling a bit emboldened by the judge's response, appealed his conviction to the California Supreme Court, which found the roles the actors were hired to play to be explicit but not obscene. The final stop for Freeman was the U.S. Supreme Court, where Justice Sandra Day O'Connor reviewed the case and determined it would go no further, writing that California's prosecution of Freeman "must be viewed as a somewhat transparent attempt at an 'end run' around the First Amendment ...." Freeman was a free man, and the making of porno films had for all intents and purposes become legal in California, leading to the jocular renaming of Los Angeles' San Fernando Valley as the San Pornando Valley.

Three Californians, Alberts, Miller and Freeman, had helped open the door to the expansive, largely unregulated pornography industry we know today. Twelve thousand Californians are employed in the porn industry today and pornographers pay more than $36 million annually in taxes.[19] It is estimated that 90 percent of America's pornographic films are either filmed in the San Fernando Valley, or produced by companies headquartered there.

FIRST OUT OF THE CLOSET

Just as California created the hippies, it also was the birthplace of the gay movement, which can be traced back to the formation of the Mattachine Society in Los Angeles in 1950. The short-lived Society for Human Rights, formed in Chicago in 1924, preceded Mattachine by several decades, but it didn't spawn a movement, as Mattachine did. Mattachine's founder, Harry Hay, took the name from a Medieval French secret society of men who masked their identity, and therefore were able to criticize the French monarchy with impunity.

Under Hay, the gay movement started with a leftward leaning that continues to this day. He was active in the Progressive Party in 1948, when its presidential candidate, Henry Wallace, was endorsed by the Communist Party USA. Indeed, the society's first name was the quaintly closeted "Bachelors for Wallace." Hay had been active in the Communist Party, and as Mattachine's work became more public, it caused the Reds some concern since the Party did not allow homosexuals. Instead of expelling him for being gay, however, they booted him for being a "security risk" - an action that mirrored what happened to homosexuals when they were found out at the FBI, the Communist Party's nemesis. Still, the Communists declared Hay a "Lifelong Friend of the People." Mattachine also tied the gay movement to fashion, a tie that continues today as any viewer of cable television's Bravo channel knows. The group's cofounder and financial underwriter was designer Rudi Gernreich, famous for introducing the topless bathing suit - something straight men can appreciate seeing, but only a gay man could get away with designing.

Another Mattachine founding member, Dale Jennings, is largely responsible for the birth of gay activism in America. In 1952, Jennings was arrested and charged with soliciting sex from a Los Angeles police officer in a MacArthur Park toilet. At the time, such cases were usually quickly settled, but Jennings decided to fight it in court, creating a much-publicized battle that became the first cause célèbre of the emerging gay rights movement. Mattachine spurred the case on through the formation of the Citizen's Council to Outlaw Entrapment, which promoted Jennings' battle nationally. Media attention to the emerging notion of rights for gays only grew as Jennings was acquitted by a Los Angeles jury, 11-1.

The visibility was good for Mattachine - certainly not the last time the media have fostered the growth of the gay movement - and it grew to more than 2,000 members by mid-1953. The group opened offices in San Francisco, New York and Washington, D.C., all dedicated to a fairly mainstream approach to establishing a gay rights movement in America. The group achieved considerable success before its influence faded with the onset of a more rebellious form of gay activism following New York's Stonewall riots in 1969.

Meanwhile, in 1955, the Daughters of Bilitis, the first lesbian rights organization in the country, was founded in San Francisco by two Berkeley graduates, Phyllis Lyon and Del Martin. Fifty-three years later they would become the first gay couple married after gay marriage was declared legal by San Francisco Mayor Gavin Newsome (now California's lieutenant governor). They named the group after the lead lesbian in the Pierre Louys poem, *The Songs of Bilitis*, and started it as a social club where women could dance together, free from police harassment. Later, the group began advocating for lesbian rights through new offices in Los Angeles, New York and Chicago, and the group's newsletter, *The Ladder*, became the first nationally distributed lesbian publication in America. True to the leftist roots of the gay movement, the ACLU was a featured presenter at the Daughters of Bilitis' first convention, in 1960.

The gay movement's political effectiveness was proven when San Franciscans elected Harvey Milk in 1978 as one of the first open homosexuals to hold a major public office in the country. (Openly lesbian Elaine Noble was the very first, taking a seat in the Massachusetts state Legislature three years earlier.) When Milk was assassinated during his first year in office, it further crystallized the gay movement in California and the nation. In 1984, Berkeley adopted the first same-sex domestic partnership ordinance in America, giving gay and lesbian employees of the city and school districts the same partnership privileges straight couples enjoy. In 1999, California became the first state to adopt a statewide domestic partnership ordinance, which first just extended hospital visitation rights, but subsequently grew incrementally until it covered nearly all the state benefits married couples enjoy.

More recently, two California legislators, state Sens. Sheila Kuehl of Los Angeles and Mark Leno of San Francisco, led the way in the introduction of gay curriculum in schools, which is covered in Chapter Seven. And while other states have preceded California in the legalization of gay marriage, the herculean legal battles over the issue in the state - first over Proposition 22 in 2000, which defined marriage as being between a man and a woman, then over Proposition 8 in 2008, which outlawed gay marriage in the state, and through the many lawsuits that ensued - will likely establish much of the legal foundation for whatever direction the states takes on this contentious issue. As was the case with Prop. 19, the marijuana legalization proposition, just having the issue on the ballot in California has helped proponents of gay marriage. Polling now shows a slim majority of Californians support it, a dramatic movement since 1977, when a California poll showed only 28 percent supported gay marriage.

HOPE FOR SALVATION?

Anyone driving from the Tijuana border crossing to Disneyland along Interstate 5 is tracing the route of the El Camino Real, the rough dirt road Spanish missionaries built between 1683 and 1834 to connect missions from La Paz on the Baja Peninsula to San Pablo, north of Oakland. The missions were a hard one-day ride from each other, allowing monks on donkeys to have a place to rest as they traveled California, intent on spreading the Word of God. Today, except for a small run of the original dirt road preserved near the mission at the town of San Juan Batista near Monterey, California's old El Camino Real is paved over, buried beneath interstates, state highways and surface streets that often carry the name Mission Street, if not El Camino Real.

The strong moral fiber that has always underlain California finds a symbol in today's Mission Streets and El Camino Reals - busy thoroughfares lined with churches and synagogues, as well as strip joints and massage parlors - that follow the very routes monks once took. California's strong religiosity is also evident in the quaint naming of the state capitol Sacramento, or Holy Sacrament. While much attention is given to the state's ability to erode the national character, California also has played a big role in furthering traditional moral values.

The Catholic Church's once-singular hold on California, which remains strong with a third of the state Catholic today, began to slip after the state became a U.S. territory. There were 32 Protestant churches in San Francisco by 1855; and by 1900, Protestants accounted for 674,000 of the state's 1.5 million population. True to Californians' penchant for individualism, however, the Catholics, Methodists, Presbyterians and other mainstream faiths couldn't be counted on to reach every esoteric, goofy Californian's need, so Firebrands for Jesus, the Psychosomatic Institute, the Mystical Order of Melchizedek, the Infinite Science Church and other made-to-order faiths took some small root in the state in the early 20th century.

Much more successful than these were the Pentecostal denominations that got their start when a one-eyed black minister from Houston, William J. Seymour, was invited to preach in California, arriving in Los Angeles in February 1906. Seymour settled into a dilapidated building on Azusa Street in downtown Los Angeles. Soon as many as 1,500 were attending the services, which ran pretty much round the clock and featured spontaneous singing, speaking in tongues, healings and - perhaps most unusual for the day - intermingling of races. The Los Angeles Times, showing its long history of religious skepticism, was not impressed:

Meetings are held in a tumble-down shack on Azusa Street, and the devotees of the weird doctrine practice the most fanatical rites, preach the wildest theories and work themselves into a state of mad excitement in their peculiar zeal. Colored people and a sprinkling of whites compose the congregation, and night is made hideous in the neighborhood by the howlings of the worshippers, who spend hours swaying forth and back in a nerve racking attitude of prayer and supplication. They claim to have the "gift of tongues" and be able to understand the babel.[20]

Despite criticism like this, the Azusa Street Revival spun off scores of churches and missionaries, and is seen today as the beginning of the Pentecostal Movement, which counts more than 500 million believers. The Pentecostals were followed by the revival that grew out of Aimee Semple McPherson's Angelus Temple in Los Angeles, which itself grew to a network of 240 Foursquare Gospel Churches, thanks in part to the emergence of radio as an evangelical tool. The 1960s brought Zen Buddhism, Eastern mysticism and the New Age movement, which got its start at the Esalen Institute in Big Sur. But the expansion of eastern religions was dwarfed by the explosion of Christianity that occurred in California at the same time.

Pastor Chuck Smith started preaching to hippies in Calvary Chapel in Costa Mesa in 1965, after breaking away from the Foursquare Gospel churches. He didn't realize it at the time, but he had started the Jesus Movement, which expanded with the House of Miracles, also in Costa Mesa, and the Children of God in the next-door town Huntington Beach, both in 1968. The Jesus Movement attracted hundreds of thousands of young people from both the hippie and straight communities (in the day, "straight" had to do with morality, not sexuality). It lives on in many churches today, including Calvary Chapel, which now has more than 1,000 congregations worldwide, its own Bible college and numerous radio stations. Then, on Easter Sunday in 1980, Rick Warren started Saddleback Church at Laguna Hills High School. Unknown to Warren or those at the service, they were present at the birth of perhaps one of the most successful and influential examples of the community mega-church phenomenon. Saddleback now attracts 20,000 worshippers every Sunday and tens of thousands of pastors have been trained through its Purpose Driven Church curriculum.

So, even though California's culture certainly can be seen as the devil, drug dealer or porn producer who is standing on society's shoulder, whispering persuasively about sinning in one of America's ears, the strong Christian beliefs that have been a part of California since the padres walked El Camino Real make up the angel standing on the other shoulder, whispering - praying - in the other ear.

PART TWO

CHAPTER FIVE:

GOVERNING: EXCELLENCE AT BUREAUCRATIC INEPTITUDE

*California gives too much power and too much
money to too many people who are too
incompetent.*

GROUND ZERO for what makes California Crazifornia is the state's capital, which is named for the Holy Sacrament, even if whatever there that's sacred is buried under mountains of sloth, avarice, greed and incompetence. (Of course, I need to disclaim at the outset that there are hard-working, honest government workers as well in Sacramento. I've worked with many of them.) In office buildings around Sacramento, many of the state government's nearly quarter-million employees toil away for some 380 state agencies, from the California Alternative Energy and Advanced Transportation Financing Board and the Structural Pest Control Board to the California Office of Binational Border Health and the Board of Guide Dogs for the Blind.

These departments, agencies and commissions have shown astonishing creativity during the current financial crisis ... in that they have effectively bent fiscal reality, going on as if money were as abundant as ever. While California's private sector shrinks, new state employees continue to be shown to their awaiting cubicles and corner offices. As the state lost 759,000 private-sector jobs from mid-2008 to mid-2009, state government lathered itself with 3,600 new workers. Many of these new public servants immediately got to work creating new ways to collect taxes, drive away businesses and assess fines and fees against the citizens they serve. To keep all its workers busy and assure continuing support from state employees and their unions, Gov. Brown proposed a 7 percent increase in state spending in his fiscal 2012-2013 state budget, even as recession-whipped Californians were figuring out inventive new ways to cut their household expenses.

Brown's 2012 budget announcement highlighted the dramatic: A pledge to cut 3,000 state jobs. That made for some good headlines, but the state had 226,931 employees when Brown made the pledge, so he was only paring the headcount by 1.3 percent. That's like a small business with 10 employees, facing a prolonged recession and continuing massive losses, laying off one employee's arm.

MILKING PROPOSITION FUNNY MONEY

Thanks to the ubiquitous ads from California's dairy farmers, we all know California cows are happy cows - but how unhappy it must be to be a California fish! Or maybe they're just as happy as the state's cows; it's hard to tell if the work of the state's bureaucracy is your source. A look at the 2004 California Ocean Protection Act (COPA) tells us that 98 percent of California's bays and estuaries are unfit for aquatic life and 96 percent produce fish that are unfit for consumption. But the same document tells us, "California has some of the most productive, diverse, and unique ocean life in the world."

Which is it? Are California's beaches and offshore waters a cesspool on the brink of collapse, or one of the most fabulous aquatic environments in the world? COPA and its spawn, the California Ocean Protection Council, ultimately weigh in on the side of the cesspool, even though the state does more to control pollution in its offshore waters than required by the federal government's stringent rules. The Ocean Protection Council caught my eye recently when I saw it was poised to approve nearly $2.5 million in grants at one of its monthly board meetings in 2010. For a state that was looking down a budget hole of $25 billion at the time, that seemed like a pretty lush garden of bucks. And indeed it is. It turns out that the council doled out $10,438,316 in 2009; of that, $1.7 million was funded by the federal government and the remainder was paid for out of bonds California taxpayers put themselves on the hook for when they passed Proposition 50 by a 55 to 45 percent margin in 2002.

Prop. 50, the Water Quality, Supply and Safe Drinking Water Projects Act, authorized $3.4 billion in additional bonded indebtedness so California would have higher quality water. The last time I checked, drinking ocean water was not considered healthy, so why is the Ocean Protection Council getting any of these safe drinking water funds? Most of those who voted for Prop. 50 probably thought the funds would go to make their water, not fishes' water, safer, but the proposition's fine print allows "competitive grants for water management and water quality improvement projects" without specifying whether that water is saltwater or fresh, and that's all the Council needed to raid Prop. 50 coffers free of the public scrutiny of the legislative process.

So, what are Californians getting for their money, which costs them $227 million a year just in interest payments? For starters, the bureaucrats that serve as the council's staff engineered a quarter-million-dollar grant to a Portland, Oregon outfit called Ecotrust to develop a pilot program for a seafood market at San Francisco's Fisherman's Wharf that would be filled with "regionally sourced" seafood. Talk about inept. Any visitor to Fisherman's Wharf can tell you free market enterprise has already filled the place with fishmongers hawking regionally sourced seafood. That doesn't keep Sacramento's eco-bureaucrats from subsidizing an Oregon group's seafood stand on the Wharf, even if it has nothing to do with the clean water voters thought they were voting for when they passed Prop. 50.

The Nature Conservancy (TNC) also fared well at the Ocean Protection Council's November 2010 meeting, collecting a $455,356 grant to assess the impacts of trawl fishing on the critters that live on the ocean floor. TNC contributed more than $500,000 to the Yes on Prop. 50 campaign;[1] and with this grant it had received about $1.5 million back from the council -

quite a return on its investment. The newest grant is a celebration of California's bureaucratic ineptitude, since it's a grand example of the principle of "fund first, think later." The grant came five years after TNC succeeded in getting 3.8 million acres of ocean floor near San Francisco placed off-limits to fishermen who use trawling gear. Now, the council was handing them nearly a half million dollars to find out if their anti-trawling activism was warranted in the first place, or if it hurt California's fishermen for no reason. As was the case with the grant to Ecotrust, TNC's grant was awarded without competitive bids, a violation of Prop. 50's requirement of competitive grants.

The Ocean Protection Council is but a gnat on the back of the California bear. The $10.4 million it doled out in grants in 2010 is a minuscule fraction of the money California's agencies, commissions, councils and boards expend every year on their own equally questionable grants programs. The California Energy Commission paid out $86.5 million for electricity and natural gas research in 2009, funded primarily by surcharges on the utility bills of whipsawed California taxpayers.[2] Among the things the money went to were California's very own climate change research center (as if there weren't enough of those already), research into carbon capture technology, and grants to underwrite the cost of solar energy installations, since solar still isn't capable of competing with Industrial Era power energy sources.

The California Air Resources Board's Air Quality Improvement Fund grabbed $40 million of the state's General Fund revenues in 2011, spending it on programs that supposedly will clean our air, such as:

$5 million for rebates on clean vehicles, $3 million on a pilot project for an off-road hybrid vehicle and $25 million to promote hybrid trucks and buses.[3] On and on it goes - millions of dollars spent to subsidize costly green technologies that can't compete in a free market, millions more to promote local fisheries while funding research that could lead to more local fishing areas being placed off limits, millions more to figure out how to bury carbon - the single endeavor of the global warming movement most likely to cause future generations to scratch their heads in perplexed awe at the ridiculousness of it all.

The Ocean Protection Council, the Energy Commission, the California Air Resources Board and all the other hundreds of state functionaries that routinely approve these expenses fill their staff reports with justifications for them, and add pages that show how the appropriations are legal. But they never explain how this spending orgy makes any sense at all. Consider the $5 million a year CARB is spending to encourage people to buy clean vehicles like electric cars. These vehicles niftily avoid the 65 cents in taxes Californians pay on every gallon of gasoline they pump into their cars - the highest gas tax rate in the nation - so every electric car the state subsidizes with taxpayer money will mean less gas tax revenues going to the state. The state is a snake eating its own tail, paying to change behaviors in ways that will yield less money to spend on changing behaviors that will yield even less money to spend on changing behaviors - evidence that California technocrats can generate a lot of rationales, but not a lot of economic sensibility.

CAN'T WAIT TO WASTE

The frivolous and possibly illegal grant-giving by the Ocean Protection Council is at best a minor league rookie in the major leagues of California bureaucratic ineptitude. Achieving big-league incompetence and waste is a real challenge in a state where bureaucrats consistently turn in world-class stats in the game of failing to account intelligently - or honestly - for public funds entrusted to them.

- *The Administrative Office of the Courts recently spent $2,500 to have a closet painted, and hundreds more to replace ash trays in California's courthouses. Hundreds of dollars is mere "budget dust," for sure, but why spend even a penny on ashtrays if smoking is prohibited in public buildings? Dumb as those expenditures were, they are brilliant compared to what the court system has spent on a new court computer system, which in turn is eclipsed by the run-away costs of California's new courthouse construction program. More detail on both of those disasters follows.*

- *A doctor for the Department of Corrections is so incompetent he's not allowed to care for the rapists, thieves and murders he's supposed to treat, so the state pays him $400,000 a year to work in the prison mail room. Fire him? Not in California, where the correctional officer's union wields great power in Sacramento. The Department of Corrections also employs the* *highest-paid nurse in the state, Lina Manglicmot, who hauls in $253,530 a year ... albeit down from her 2008 record of $331,346, which included $211,257 in overtime. For comparison, the director of nursing for the entire Texas prison system makes $165,000 a year.*[4]

- *The California Emergency Management Agency failed to distribute $135.6 million in federal stimulus funds, even though it had a year to do so. According to the state auditor, it has no organized strategy, policies or procedures to distribute the funds, and could be forced to return the money. It seems one of the state's 3,600 new hires could have been tasked to avoid this waste.*

- *In 2010 the Department of Education spent almost $1 million on conferences. Taxpayers should thank them for being so frugal, since the Department of Motor Vehicles spent $1.73 million on new furniture, and four state agencies together spent $18.1 million on shiny new cars and trucks.*

- *EdFund, part of the California Student Aid Commission, paid $2.6 million to lease an office building for two years, without ever actually moving into it. When a TV news crew showed up to shoot some film of the building, they were met by a state attorney who threatened to call the police if they didn't* *leave - an interesting take on government transparency.*

- *Even though they have more experience imposing taxes than bureaucrats in nearly every state, California's bureaucrats are the nation's worst at state tax administrative practices, according to the Council on State Taxation.*

Sacramento is not alone in ineptitude. Its cities stumble and bumble as well. Los Angeles' Recreation and Parks Department spent $237,000 on refrigerators, stoves, televisions, microwaves, computers, printers and even a deep fat fryer, then stored them away, unused. Its Transportation Department spent $85,000 on unused equipment and another $2.5 million on contract overages for an automated vehicle locator system that is only 11 percent implemented after 10 years. The city of La Quinta spent $93,000 on a sculpture, only to spend another $15,000 to remove it following years of complaints from residents who said it was blight, not art. And the city of Rocklin gave generous early retirement bonuses to a number of its senior employees, then hired them back. The deal is a gold mine for these public servants; for example, former city manager Carlos Urrutia is now taking home $309,000 a year, compared to his former base pay of $230,000.

Then, of course, there's the City of Bell, the plundering target of its senior staff and city council members for years. But Bell is worthy of a book of its own. Here's just one example of how colorful the Bell story is: Robert Rizzo, the city's shamed city administrator, actually filed a wrongful termination lawsuit against the city, choosing Halloween of all days to file the lawsuit, which stands as testimony to just how horrifying the story of Bell is.

Rizzo, who's about as big around as he is tall, was paid almost $800,000 a year to run the poor, blue collar city of 37,000 residents. And since that wasn't enough to satisfy him, he tapped the city for another $250,000 in benefits, then had the mayor sign a false contract to cover up his true income, according to charges against him. He apparently also spent a fair amount of time figuring out ways to play the California Public Employees' Retirement System (CalPERS) to boost his retirement benefits, which for a while were pegged at $650,000 a year. That would have made him the highest paid retiree in the state by about $120,000 a year. Bruce Malkenhorst, who managed the nearby and equally corrupt city of Vernon, had held the No. 1 slot prior to Rizzo's quick retirement, with an annual pension of $530,000. To keep it, he's going to have to overturn the state's successful challenge of his nest egg on the grounds that Malkenhorst had illegally padded it. As a result, the 77-year-old retired city manager found his pension slashed to a paltry $150,000 a year. In announcing that he will appeal the decision, Malkenhorst termed the state's slashing of his pension "elder abuse."

Rizzo faces a similar challenge with his pension. When CalPERS discovered he had gamed the system, his pension was cut - not to zero, as he deserves - but to $50,000 a year. Rizzo is appealing. Bell's retired police chief, Randy Adams, still has one of the highest pensions in the state, $265,000, but even so is pushing the city to pay his legal fees for the various corruption investigations initiated as a result of his alleged actions while on Bell's payroll.

In Rizzo's lawsuit, which he filed as his own attorney, he claims the city lacked cause to fire him since he "has not been convicted of a felony or a crime of moral turpitude, or at all." And besides, the city council failed to give him the 90-day notice his contract required - which contract exactly, the real one or the cover-up one, isn't clear.

DOES NOT COMPUTE

The fact that California can claim bragging rights as the world's foremost incubator of computer innovation has been lost on Sacramento. Sure, Apple, eBay, Google and uncounted other technology giants grew in the capital-rich Silicon Valley. But somehow all that innovation sinks into a morass of incompetence, corruption and over-spending as soon as it's drawn into Sacramento's sphere.

California began to learn just how bad its government agencies were with computers as the 21st century dawned in Sacramento. At the time, computer giant Oracle was foreseeing California saving as much as $163 million over the next six to 10 years thanks its new $95 million contract with the state. The contract, which was awarded without competitive bids, was supposed to lead to 270,000 state employees working more happily and efficiently, as they used new Enterprise 8i software provided by the Bay Area-based computer giant. Some $75,000 in campaign contributions to Democratic Gov. Gray Davis and Democratic Attorney General Bill Lockyer may have helped seal the deal, especially since a survey of more than 100 government departments two months before the contract was signed suggested few workers wanted or needed the Oracle product. A few years later, after four senior California technology officers had resigned in a scandal, the state was not looking at $160 million in savings, but a bill for $41 million in software licenses it would never need. California didn't understand its own computer needs at all, and grossly over-estimated the amount of software licenses it needed. Bad as it was, the Oracle scandal, as it is known throughout the information technology world, was a relatively modest affair, compared to the computer debacles that would follow.

Take CalPERS, the manager of the most of the state employees' pensions. It recently unveiled myCalPERS, its new $507 million computer system that is supposed to track the retirement plan contributions and benefits of its 1.6 million members. The launch was a mere one year late, which is about as close to delivering on time as a California state agency can hope for, but the system cost almost twice as much as originally estimated. Besides being late and over-budget, it is also not very good, so it will be phased in slowly because the agency anticipates initial instability and admits that users will find it difficult to work with. Meanwhile, CalPERS CEO Anne Stausboll, at whose desk the myCalPERS buck stops, was given a $96,638 bonus.

The Employment Development Department, which manages unemployment insurance, is five years behind on its computer upgrades. The original estimate is but a memory, exceeded by more than $133 million: the $53 million EDD counts today and another $80 million in previous computer upgrade cost over-runs the agency has decided to no longer count. The state's champion at incompetence, the Legislature, has its own computer nightmare. It started its 21st Century Project in 2004 with the goal of getting an up-to-date computer system capable of handling the state's payroll and human resources data. The system's main contractor was fired in 2007. Now the system, which was supposed to be done in 2010 at a cost of $185 million, won't be ready to go until 2013 at the earliest. The estimated price tag is now at least $305 million - $120 million over budget.

In education, the problem isn't that the computer system performs poorly and upgrades are behind schedule and over budget. It's that the system doesn't even exist. When Stanford University pulled together nearly 40 researchers at the call of Gov. Schwarzenegger to learn all they could about the state's education financing and governance systems, to find ways to improve the state's poor education performance, the researchers concluded:

> [W]ithin California we have a worse situation than in many other states or nations. Our information systems are so inadequate, that even if we implemented reforms that were particularly effective, we might not realize it. Similarly, we cannot be confident that we can recognize and weed out programs that are ineffective at improving student achievement. To date, we have had

very little data available on students, teachers, schools, and districts that link them together over time in ways that would allow us to assess the effects of policy interventions.[5]

The lack of a statewide education data system doesn't stop California educators and lawmakers from churning out a steady stream of new programs, mandates and methodologies, blindly throwing them into a system the Stanford study claims is untestable.

Against even these deplorable examples of cyber-incompetence, the California Court Case Management System stands head and shoulders above the rest, as the worst computer debacle in the state. It was originally going to cost $260 million, but somehow things got a little messed up and it's now estimated it will cost $1.9 billion - an astonishing $1.6 billion over estimate. Courts participating in pilot tests of the system had such a bad experience that they're reluctant to even try to use the CCMS package when it was estimated to come on line in 2015 or 2016 - seven years late. Once it is complete, an additional $1 billion will be needed to actually deploy the system in 400 court facilities around the state. Two of the courts that thought about not installing the computer after participating in the pilot tests - Los Angeles and Sacramento - are so important to the state's court system it's difficult to imagine a statewide courts records system moving forward without them.

An audit by the California State Auditor recommended that the whole CCMS endeavor be stopped and reconsidered because it is so far behind schedule, so far over budget and so at risk of quality problems when it finally is implemented. The saga is so convoluted and rich in troubling detail that the auditor's report required 143 pages to lay it all out.[6] One of the audit's most troubling findings is that of California's 51 superior courts, 32 said their existing systems would last them for the foreseeable future. Only 12 of the courts support CCMS, and none of those experienced the horror of pilot testing. So the question needs to be asked, albeit $1.9 billion too late: Why did the bureaucrats behind the curtain of California's courts undertake this project in the first place?

Maybe the question never will be asked. At the end of March 2012, the California Judicial Council pulled the plug on the entire system. The council is composed of judges and court representatives from throughout California and is presided over by California Supreme Court Chief Justice Tani Cantil-Sakauye. One council member, Yolo County judge David Rosenberg, said after the decision, "I believe that 10 years ago, a case management system was a farsighted vision, but a statewide connected system is just not feasible in the current climate and in the foreseeable future. It's just too expensive."[7] That's what happens when your project comes in so unfathomably over budget.

As bad as the CCMS $1.6 billion cost overrun is, it's hardly the Administrative Office of the Courts' most sensational example of bureaucratic ineptitude. That dubious honor goes to its $5.6 billion plan to build new courthouses all over the state, to be funded by bonds that in turn will be repaid by mind-numbing increases in criminal fines and court filing fees. For that $5.6 billion, California will get 41 courthouse improvement projects, or a median cost of $137 million per project. Put another way, the courthouses are going to cost as much as $747 per square foot to build. That's what the estimate came in on for a one-room courthouse in Lake Tahoe, and it's only for the construction. Land is extra and will push the price to $900 per square foot. Courthouse News Service reported that the second-highest cost for courthouse construction is in New York, at about one-third the cost of the Lake Tahoe project: $269 per square foot.[8]

CALTRANSYLVANIA

Anyone who's had to deal the state's transportation department, Caltrans, knows that a big conference room is a necessity. When Caltrans shows up for a meeting to discuss a road project, it brings an army. And it's not because Caltrans bureaucrats are particularly eager to work. It's because the department is overstaffed by as much as 15 percent, according to the Legislative Analyst's Office.

Thirty-year Caltrans veteran Manus Thananant documented as much in his final years before retirement, when he was posted in the Office of Pavement Design. It requires a dozen or so high-priced engineers to design pavement in California, not because there's such an abundance of pavement to be designed nowadays, but because Thananant's colleagues spent much of their work day conducting personal business, sleeping at their desks or not showing up at all. He calculated their average real work time to be about 24 hours a week, although they were paid for 40 hours, and estimated the cost of these practices in his department alone to be $500,000 a year. In the two years after filing the documentation of his complaints, all Thananant has seen is one letter from the Bureau of State Audits telling him not to bother them with requests for progress reports.[9]

The snoozers and no-shows at the Office of Pavement Design are model employees, however, when compared to another Caltrans employee, Duane Wiles. Wiles' job in Caltrans' Foundation Testing Branch is much more critical to California drivers than the mere designing of pavement; he's tasked with conducting tests to determine the structural integrity of bridges. One of his assignments was the $6.3 billion reconstruction of the Oakland Bay Bridge, which was damaged in a 1989 earthquake. (Yes, it took more than 20 years for Caltrans to repair it.) A Sacramento Bee investigative report found that Wiles failed to properly conduct tests on the Bay Bridge's new span and dozens of other bridges, fabricated results on at least three Caltrans projects, often discarded his raw data files and inflated his overtime pay.[10] Perhaps all this was merely the side effects of personal problems Wiles was experiencing at the time, as he faced felony charges for a sex crime against a child.

Other employees in the department had raised concerns about Wiles three years earlier, but Caltrans failed to take action until after a reporter from the Sacramento Bee called, armed with materials provided by a whistleblower. It took another three weeks for Caltrans to shuffle Wiles off to a less visible place where there was less risk that he would harm the public. But just two days after the story became public, Wiles was fired, along with his supervisor, who not only had tolerated Wiles, but also had used Caltrans workers to do work on property he owns. Reasonable people must question how many other supervisors are ignoring how many more test fabricators and overtime falsifiers at Caltrans. Should it really require negative publicity for the agency take action?

Even if it has difficulty testing bridges and firing dangerous employees, the agency responsible for transportation in the Golden State should be able to keep track of its own cars. But this elementary task also is beyond Caltrans' management capabilities. In a 2009 expose, the Sacramento Bee reported that the agency has spent more than $4 million on cars and trucks that sat in parking lots for months or even years, unused. Worse, Caltrans had purchased extended warranties for many of these vehicles, a waste if the vehicle spends its life parked. Under pressure, the agency confirmed that over 12 percent of the vehicles it purchased were not being driven two years after they joined the Caltrans fleet. To excuse themselves, Caltrans officials blamed the mandated furloughs of their mechanics, and said that it could take up to three years to ready a truck for Caltrans duty.[11] Pity the poor private-sector truck converter who was equally incompetent.

In fairness, I've never had a custom bed put on a truck, though, so I don't know how long it typically takes. To learn, I called John Schatz, the former general manager of Santa Margarita Water District, which has a small fleet of service trucks with all sorts of custom beds. "There's no way it should take more than a few weeks or a month at the most to have the vehicle rolling," he said. "If the service body or other equipment that's going to be attached to the truck requires a longer lead-time, then obviously those parts should be ordered first and the purchase of the trucks should be timed accordingly, not the other way around." Schatz said it was obvious, but it appears that oblivious is the operational word at Caltrans.

Still, Caltrans can be forgiven for some of its bureaucratic incompetence because it is, after all, just trying to do business in California, so it, too, has to modify its trucks to meet tough new standards set by the California Air Resources Board. If it rolls out a truck that hasn't been adequately modified, it faces a fine of $1,000 a day. And it, too, is under the thumb of public employee unions. So when administrators tried to job out some truck conversions to private shops, state employee union bosses whispered a word or two in an ear or two and all the work stayed in-house.

Caltrans is not alone in vehicle mismanagement. The Department of General Services paid $1.2 million for 50 Toyota Priuses in 2009, when the car was selling at or above sticker, then left them on the roof of a parking garage for eight months. When confronted with this ineptitude (again by the Sacramento Bee, whose investigative reporters appear to have a job akin to shooting fish in a barrel), the agency explained that it was waiting for federal stimulus funds so the cars could be converted to plug-in hybrids. "In retrospect," an agency spokesperson said, "it would have been a good idea to put them in the ... fleet."[12] The governor-appointed bureaucrat in charge of this operation was paid $106,800 a year for her skills. Not to be undone by a mere 50 Priuses, the California Highway Patrol bought 51 vans for $881,565, then let them sit unused for two years, paying another $90,385 in interest payments while the vans collected dust.[13]

As bad as Caltrans is at managing its fleet, it is even worse at managing its real estate portfolio. The agency owns many buildings it has condemned for road construction projects that never moved forward. Included in its housing inventory are more than 500 homes it purchased in Pasadena and South Pasadena decades ago in anticipation of the Pasadena Freeway actually reaching all the way to Pasadena - something that never happened due to Caltrans' mishandling of neighborhood opposition to the project. The Los Angeles Times recently reported the agency spent nearly $2.4 million reroofing 33 of these homes, or an average of $70,944 per job. The most expensive cost taxpayers $171,508.[14] The story came to light when Caltrans spent $103,472 to replace a roof, even though the tenant said the old roof worked perfectly. After the work, the tenant told the Times, the roof leaked and bees came in from the attic "like a plague."

Roofers who were asked to review the contracts said Caltrans had paid four to five times what a private homeowner would pay for a similar roof. Caltrans attempted to blame the high cost on the historic nature of the homes, but the State Historical Preservation Office reviewed the Caltrans work documents and declared the agency's excuse to be, in the jargon of historic preservation, "bogus."

THE DIMMEST BULB OF ALL?

California made national headlines in 2000 as rolling blackouts and brownouts swept across the state.

Many think the blame for the California energy crisis lies with Enron and other energy speculators, and certainly, speculators didn't help the problem. But the real blame can be laid at the feet of the California Public Utilities Commission (PUC), the agency charged with protecting energy consumers and providing reliable utility service at reasonable rates, a goal it fell far short of accomplishing during the energy crisis. Energy production in the state was already in disarray before the PUC acted in 1999 and 2000, because environmental regulations were making the construction of new power plants next to impossible. Energy prices were rising, and instead of making it easier to build power plants, the state blamed the utilities and began imposing new regulations on them under the guise of deregulation.

The PUC had forced utilities to sell their power plants (more "deregulation"), thinking it would spur competition. The utilities were transformed from energy producers to energy buyers, and were doing what they could to deal effectively with rising energy costs by negotiating long-term contracts to buy power at locked-in prices. But the technocrat "experts" on the PUC staff didn't like these long-term contracts because they were convinced consumers would be stuck with higher rates when energy prices fell. They believed it inevitable prices would decline from the five cents per kilowatt hour the utilities were getting on five-year contracts. To discourage long-term contracts, the PUC added a performance clause requirement. Jim Brulte, the top Republican in the state Senate at the time of the energy crisis, described the performance clause to me, saying, "The PUC basically told the utilities, 'You can do those contracts, but understand that at the end of the contract, we're going to look back with the information we have then and we're going to decide then whether the decision you made years earlier was prudent.' If it wasn't, the utilities would be penalized. So why would they enter into long-term contracts under those conditions?" They didn't.

As it turned out, no penalty would have been imposed if the utilities had stuck with their contracts. At the peak of the energy crisis, the spot market price for a kilowatt hour rose to 35.5 cents, more than seven times the old long-term contract rate; and even when prices fell back to earth, they settled in at 7.2 cents. Instead of protecting consumers, the PUC had stuck them with higher energy bills.

Still, many will point to energy speculators like Enron as the cause of a spike that was beyond the PUC's ability to foresee. That's far too simplistic. The PUC was meddling not just with energy purchase contracts and power plant ownership, but also with driving the conversion of California's oil-fueled plants to natural gas. The switch was made, of course, to reduce carbon emissions - the task California's regulatory agencies seem to be most focused on. The utilities, frightened of huge penalties from the new performance clauses and forced to buy natural gas instead of oil, started buying natural gas almost exclusively on the spot market. As it turned out, the winter of 2001 was a cold one, which drove up the spot market price of natural gas just as the state became significantly more dependent on it. Then, to make matters worse, at the peak of the pinch, Caltrans shut down a critical natural gas pipeline so repairs could be made to an adjacent freeway, which drove up the cost of what natural gas was available. Next, the possibility of buying cheaper hydroelectric energy was foreclosed on because a drought precipitously cut hydroelectric output in the Northwest. By this time, 71 percent of the state's energy came from natural gas, thanks to PUC pressure, compared to 51 percent nationally.[15]

All in all, by December 2000 the price of wholesale power soared to 11 times higher than it was one year earlier. Pacific Gas & Electric filed for bankruptcy as San Diego Gas & Electric teetered on the brink, and Californians paid the price of bureaucratic foolishness every month on their power bills.[16] Some have tried to blame population growth for the power reliability problems in 2000 and 2001, but just a year before California breezed through the summer with almost no power interruptions. So the population argument is a red herring. It was regulation under the guise of deregulation that brought a summer of brownouts and rolling blackouts in 2000. And matters just got worse in 2001, when nearly 160 power emergencies were declared. The energy crisis began winding down only after the Davis administration stepped in and started buying power ... under the very sort of long-term contracts the PUC had previously attacked as too high-risk.

Looking back on such a crisis, one would think that a state would go about fixing its power deficiencies, kick-starting the construction of new power plants and easing up on environmental regulations that make power generation in the state more difficult and costly. Instead, California has launched a series of initiatives to make things worse.

First among many missteps is Assembly Bill 32, the California Global Warming Solutions Act of 2006. The bureaucrats responsible for enacting AB 32 have been busy spewing out regulations, covered extensively in Chapter Eight, to save the planet from their greatest fear, the ravages of SUVs and other signs of comfortable life. Among the regulations are a new mandate that 33 percent of the state's energy come from clean - and expensive - alternative energy sources by 2020. Earlier, the mandate was set at 20 percent by 2010, and the increase to 33 percent alone is expected to double the cost to consumers of the earlier mandate. The new price tag: $114 billion.[17]

California's powerful eco-crats are also imposing more barriers against purchasing cheaper, albeit dirtier, energy from other states, an action sure to further drive up energy costs. Until AB 32, the state's environmentally sensitive residents were satisfied pretending California was becoming greener, while much of the power needed to power their computers and charge their electric cars came from coal-burning plants in Utah, New Mexico, Nevada - even as far away as Montana and Colorado. Together, these plants have traditionally supplied up to 20 percent of the power in California's electric grid. That's coming to an end as the Brown administration works to reduce purchases of conventionally generated electricity from out of state, in favor of alternative energy sources that aren't yet ready to fill in the gap.

It looks like California is due for a new, bigger energy crisis that will make the last one seem quaint and even a little friendly by comparison.

HIGH SPEED FAIL

It is becoming increasingly clear the 2000 California energy crisis won't stand long as the biggest display of bureaucratic ineptitude California has ever seen. The California High Speed Rail Authority is overtaking the energy crisis at high speed - hopefully the only high speed maneuver it will ever be allowed to execute. The Rail Authority got its start with a proposition, 2008's Proposition 1A. Like many propositions, its title was a hint of what was promised with all the surety a political campaign can muster: the Safe, Reliable High-Speed Passenger Train Bond Act for the 21st Century. I suppose that would be SRHSPTBA21C for short.

Prop. 1A's promise was futuristic and optimistic, calling to mind Donald Fagen's song I.G.Y., in which the Steely Dan founder mocked futurists by singling out their woefully wrong mid-20th century prediction for rail. They had foreseen that by 1976 "graphite and glitter" trains would be gloriously whisking passengers under the sea from New York to Paris.

Glorious indeed! The high-speed rail advocates proclaimed that for just $9.95 billion (Heaven forbid that it should be $10 billion!), California would be on its way to a sexy high-speed rail line connecting San Francisco to Los Angeles. Passage of the proposition, voters were told, would trigger matching federal funds, and this $19.9 billion would get the core route built. The entire system would cost a mere $34 billion. Happy voters dreamed of the day in the not too distant future when they would no longer have to hang their heads in shame whenever the high-speed rail systems of France's TGV and Japan's Shinkansen were mentioned at chic cocktail parties.

Even as it passed, Prop. 1A was already behind schedule, which is not a good thing for a railroad. The measure was originally slated for the ballot four years earlier, in 2004, but was delayed when Gov. Schwarzenegger pulled most of the project's initial funding from an earlier bond. Unfortunately, he left enough money to keep High-Speed Rail on life support, and it resurfaced for the 2006 election, only to be pulled again out of fear an even larger revenue bond on that ballot - Proposition 1B's $19.9 billion in bonds for general transportation funding - would diminish the chance the rail bond would pass. Finally, in 2008, Prop. 1A made the ballot with a $2.6 million campaign bankroll behind it, funded by unions and private companies well positioned for future rail contracts. One of those companies, AECOM Technology Corporation, gave $50,000 to the campaign[18] and has won Rail Authority contracts totaling at least $70 million to date, a tidy return. Opposition to the rail proposal hadn't yet solidified and no substantive campaign was run against the measure. It passed 53 percent to 47 percent.

It turns out the original, $34 billion cost promised by in Prop. 1A was a bit too low for all that graphite and glitter. By 2009, a year after the measure's passage, the Rail Authority said the cost would actually be almost one-third higher, or $43 billion. Then, just after Halloween 2011, it released a frightening new estimate that more doubled the two-year-old estimate, to $98.5 billion ... or maybe $117.6 billion, who could really tell for sure? At about the same time, a report by the California Transportation Commission found a $294 billion deficit in funding needed to maintain the state's existing transportation infrastructure over the next nine years - or more than $30 billion in shortfall annually.[19] While the high-speed rail pot of money is separate from the general transportation pot, its deficit emphasized the dubious sanity of continuing to pursue the costly, new and shiny when the future viability of the state's established and dull system of roads and rail is in such bad shape.

To keep their new estimate under $100 billion (or maybe a little over it), the Rail Authority staff stealthily redefined the project, whacking out Sacramento and San Diego. Oh, they'll still get their promised stops on the high-speed rail route, but not until some ill-defined future phase, which could add another $80 billion to the price tag. The Rail Authority's November 2011 revised business plan shows a total of $15.55 billion available to build the core route - the original bond, $3.3 billion in federal matching funds and $3.25 billion in federal stimulus funds - which we're told should be just enough to build the much-anticipated 160-mile route from just outside Bakersfield to somewhere outside Merced in the Central Valley. No other route could be built for that little, given the high cost of purchasing or condemning private property along more populous segments of the proposed route. Under the Rail Authority's latest plan, most riders would have to wait until 2033 to experience a segment of the train line that actually travels between two points significant numbers of passengers are likely to travel.

The Rail Authority also says the finished route will

be profitable - with a definition of profitability only a government employee would be comfortable with: A profit will be declared if the train covers its operating and maintenance expenses. Never mind the $100 billion or more it will cost to build it; that doesn't count under California's proposed definition of high-speed rail profitability. The profitability projections are based on ridership projections of 28.6 to 37.1 million passengers a year. Prop. 1A was sold to the voters on projections of 90 million riders a year, so the Rail Authority is being more honest than it once was. But it is still a long way from being able to make any claim of honesty. If California's high-speed trains end up capturing the same ridership levels enjoyed by Amtrak's most successful train, which services the highly populated, rail-friendly run from New York to Boston, it would transport about five million riders annually, not 28 or 37 million. Even so, the Rail Authority's PR firm, Ogilvy, assured Californians the system will be profitable - right up until they resigned their $9 million contract. The Rail Authority's spokesperson explained that Ogilvy resigned to avoid being fired as criticism of the contract amount and their performance grew.[20]

So far, the Rail Authority has only exceeded expectations in the area of incompetence - failing to identify a route that makes sense, failing on all its projections and failing to be open with the public (it prohibits its vendors from discussing their contracts publicly, for example). Unless high-speed rail is killed - and it might be, as public opinion turns against it - the Rail Authority will no doubt go on to show even greater levels of bureaucratic ineptitude as it tries to actually build and operate a railroad.

CHAPTER SIX:

BUSINESS: ROLL UP THE RED CARPET AND CALL THE MOVING VAN

"Detroit, only with sunshine."
- Investor's Business Daily on California's business climate

ALIFORNIA MAY DO a great job of attracting welfare recipients through more generous benefits, or featherbedding the pensions of state employees, but it has been recognized as the bottom-dweller of business friendliness every year since at least 2009. That's when the readers of Chief Executive magazine first decided running a business in California was even crazier than trying it in New York, Illinois, New Jersey or Michigan.[1] "Sacramento seems to take perverse delight in job-killing legislation," the magazine wrote. California state senator Ted Gaines, R-Roseville, was more colorful in his description of the state's approach to business, writing in a Sacramento Bee op-ed: "I am tired of my constituents and other business owners here being treated like piñatas by regulators and politicians who smack them around until some fine or penalty falls out."[2]

Whether you call it a perverse delight or piñata-smacking, the result is the same: Legislators, regulators, lawyers and environmentalist have driven up the cost of doing business in the Golden State until it has become 30 percent greater than in the neighboring states. Those states are actively wooing California businesses - and the impact is showing. Through Ronald Reagan's governorship, California attracted millions of people from all over the country for the simple reason that they could make more money in the Golden State than anywhere else in the Union. Now it's a business black hole. Jerry Brown started it in 1975 with his anti-growth policies that stopped infrastructure construction and started many of the state's environmental regulations. He was so successful that by the end of his governorship, just eight years after Reagan left office, the state had become the fourth least business-friendly in the nation.

The result of 40 years of anti-business policy is evident in a major reversal for California: It now has a declining standard of living. California's median household income plummeted by 9 percent - nearly twice the national average - between 2006 and 2010, according to the U.S. Census Bureau. By late 2011, not even half the state's population made enough money to be categorized as middle class, the direct result of California losing 26 percent of its manufacturing jobs and 35 percent of its high-tech manufacturing jobs between 1990 and the start of the recession in 2008.[3] When mid- and post-recession numbers start being reported, expect the state's standard of living to drop even more, since it lost 1.2 million jobs between 2008 and 2010. In the same period, Texas added 165,000 jobs.

This state, that over time has tempted millions to leave their dusty towns and rusty cities for the California promise; that once inspired an entire nation with its gutsy embrace of the future; that birthed Hollywood, aerospace, Apple and eBay and their seemingly countless high-paying jobs, is now the state that leads the nation in gloominess. In 2010, at least 204 companies said goodbye to the state, exactly four times more than fled in all of 2009.[4] The exodus surged to more than 280 companies in 2011, when they left the state at a clip of 5.4 companies per week. And that's only the companies that let people know they're pulling out. Company relocation specialist Joe Vranich says that, for every one departing company he tracks, five companies probably leave surreptitiously. By that calculation, as many as many as 1,400 companies could have left the state in 2011, leaving more joblessness and economic gloominess in their wake. And for every company that actually packs up and leaves, dozens more move assembly lines, processing centers and entire divisions elsewhere, while executives stay behind to enjoy one thing California does excel in - a pleasant climate.

But even those palm trees, ocean breezes and balmy nights might not be enough. John Watson, the chairman and CEO of the highest-ranking California company on the Fortune 500, Chevron, recently wrote that 84 percent of business owners in the state now say they wouldn't locate here if they were starting over. As for Chevron, which invested $7 billion in its California operations between 2004 and 2009, Watson said:

> We would invest more if we could. But it is difficult to make the economic case when construction permits take years to approve and are then thrown into the courts, where they are delayed even longer. We are experiencing this gridlock directly at our Richmond [Calif.] refinery, costing the community millions of dollars in economic support and more than a thousand jobs. Companies large and small across California could tell similar stories.
>
> California needs to get serious about adopting rational reforms to a regulatory apparatus that is smothering business and destroying jobs. The seemingly endless restrictions are not just increasing the cost of doing business but also adding to the uncertainties. Many businesses feel they can't control their own destiny in California, so they look elsewhere.[5]

CALLING THE MOVING COMPANIES

Vranich is one Californian who won't be packing a moving van any time soon. The Irvine-based business relocation coach, whose expertise has made him a guest on all the national television networks, has been a very busy man lately, helping California companies study the financial ramifications of relocating to a more business-friendly state. Oh, occasionally he works with CEOs from elsewhere who still fantasize about setting up shop in La Jolla, Santa Barbara or some other California paradise. Those jobs, he recently told a group of mayors and city council members, usually don't last past the comparison of housing costs, when the CEO realizes that a dream house on the coast is well outside his reach.

Vranich developed a "Top Ten Reasons Why California Companies are Calling the Moving Companies" list after realizing just how strong his outgoing relocation business had become. His most recently updated Top Ten, in the typical David Letterman order, is:

10. *Unprecedented Energy Costs;*
9. *Severe Tax Treatment;*
8. *Worst Regulatory Burden;*
7. *Dreadful Legal Treatment;*
6. *Most Expensive Business Locations;*
5. *Provable Savings Elsewhere;*
4. *Downright Unfriendly;*
3. *Uncontrollable Spending;*
2. *Excessively Adversarial;*
1. *The "Outpouring" of Poor Rankings Continues.*[6]

So many facts support Vranich's list no one ever tries to rebut him. For example, on his 10th point, ever since California vowed to fix its energy mess after the state's energy crisis in 2000, it has only succeeded in driving up costs, driving down reliability and inventing new ways to make its energy picture worse. On No. 9, taxes, only New York is worse in its overall business tax burden, according to the Tax Foundation.[7]   Sure, the state's tax rate on millionaires, 10.3 percent, isn't the worst in the country. Two states tax the successful more progressively.   (California's middle-class wage-earners, earning $48,000 or more a year, are treated the way other states treat millionaires. Actually, they're treated worse - their 9.3 percent state tax rate is higher than the rate paid by millionaires in 47 states.[8]) Any wishful thinkers who hope that the California Legislature would ease up on reason No. 8, the regulations that make it so dreadful for businesses, shouldn't hold their breath.   California regulators continue to create new regulations, even though they're already costing California businesses almost $500 billion a year - which translates into almost 4 million jobs. Hand-in-hand with overregulation, the state's legal system, No. 7 on Vranich's list, has been ranked the most business-battering in the nation.

And on it goes. I laughed when I saw "Downright Unfriendly" and "Excessively Adversarial" on Vranich's list because I had just had coffee with a friend from rural Kern County who recently bought a ranch in Texas' hill country. She told me how the only permit she and her husband would need to build a new home on the ranch is one verifying a successful percolation test for the septic system. "But what was even more amazing," she added excitedly, "was that when we went to the planning office, they welcomed us warmly and really helped us. I wasn't expecting that!" Nor should she have. Even Kern County, which is generally regarded as one of the most development-friendly counties in the state, has a planning staff that tends to look at every application filed as a new challenge to play a game of "Call of Duty: Black Ops."

When Chief Executive magazine again crowned California the business class dunce in 2011 - a title it bestowed on the state again in 2012 - the magazine highlighted the Green Chemistry Initiative as a model for why it's so hard for businesses to succeed in the state. A legacy piece of nightmare legislation by former Gov. Schwarzenegger, it has spawned an initial 92 pages of regulations that force California companies to manufacture their products without using compounds deemed to be just too nasty for the environment. Competing companies in other states and nations can use many of these less expensive chemicals at will, however, since their own regulatory agencies have found them to be perfectly acceptable. This being California, unacceptable chemicals will be defined largely by unelected green-leaning regulators influenced heavily by environmental group lobbyists who in turn are funded by trial lawyers - the same lawyers who subsequently will bring costly lawsuits against those manufacturers, importers, and even retailers that aren't marching in exact lockstep with the Green Chemistry Initiative.

And this being California, the initiative is envisioned as a model the rest of the world should rush to adopt. Schwarzenegger's Secretary for Environmental Protection Linda Adams wrote of it:

> *The GCI proposal presents a new way to look at chemicals in our society, unleashing the creativity and innovation of our scientists and engineers to design and discover the next generation of chemicals. ... These landmark policy options will continue California's environmental leadership*

and foster a new era in the design of a new
consumer products economy - inventing,
manufacturing and using toxic-free, sustainable
products.[9]

Those scientists and engineers are going to cost money, driving up the cost of doing business in California. And worse, the products they're forced to fabricate are going to impact sales because the new toxic-free, sustainable chemicals routinely make the products they're in less effective. Californians knew this long before the Green Chemistry Initiative came about. For years, many of them have risked fines of several thousand dollars as they smuggle in gallon cans of superior oil-based paint from Arizona, since California's air quality czars restrict its sale. The regulators are concerned about the effect of evaporating solvents, but it's not as if Californians were keeling over dead because of the chemicals in their paint. In fact, Arizonans, who still are allowed to breathe in fumes from oil-based paint, live on average about six months longer than Californians. Nevertheless, at least eight states now have imposed or are planning to impose similar bans, another example of how California's regulatory fervor routinely spreads to other states.

In a Washington Examiner column, radio talk show host and early *Crazifornia* booster Hugh Hewitt quoted an attorney colleague who said of the Green Chemistry Initiative, "Take whatever you think is the worst regulatory regime out there, and expand it exponentially, and you get a glimpse of what's coming to California."[10]

Everyone knows businesses are fleeing California because of the higher costs that grow out of ideas like the Green Chemistry Initiative, yet the initiative is moving inexorably toward implementation. Even so, California's powerful environmental groups were quick to challenge the draft regulations, after language was added to require the state to prove that a chemical is indeed harmful before banning its use under the initiative. True to form, the groups demanded a wholesale rewrite. Count on the environmentalists' powerful lobbyists to crush industry lobbyists as the initiative moves forward. And count on the state's business climate once again being worsened by their zealous efforts.

SAVING THE PLANET

The law most likely to be compared to the Green Chemistry Initiative in terms of its negative impact on business in California is AB 32, the arrogantly named California Global Warming Solutions Act of 2006, which requires the state's greenhouse gas emissions to be reduced to 1990 levels by 2020. John Laird, Jerry Brown's secretary for natural resources, authored the law when he was in the Legislature, and now he has immense regulatory power to move it forward. Gov. Schwarzenegger made AB 32 his signature piece of legislation, campaigning hard for its slim passage through the Legislature and praising it at the signing ceremony, saying, "Some have challenged whether AB 32 is good for businesses. I say unquestionably it is good for businesses. Not only large, well-established businesses, but small businesses that will harness their entrepreneurial spirit to help us achieve our climate goals."

Not everyone agrees. When the Governor's Office of Small Business ordered a report on the effects of AB 32 on small business, the authors put the average cost of implementing the law at $3,857 per household, and $49,691 per small business. The report put the average loss of annual gross state output from small businesses alone of $182 billion, or about a tenth of the state's gross output. They then helpfully translated that into 1.1 million lost jobs - presumably because companies that can leave California will.[11]

The high cost of implementing the bill, which includes a cap-and-trade provision, can be blamed mostly on its effect on energy costs - an immediate increase of 20 percent to California's energy bills, which are already the costliest in the country. "Unprecedented energy costs" was the first thing listed by Vranich as a driving motivator for businesses to leave the state. They will locate to other states with air quality standards that are lower in nearly all cases than California's pre-AB 32 standards, or will move their manufacturing to China, where the standards are probably lower than California's pre-1932 standards. The net effect of the California Global Warming Solutions Act, then, will not be a solution, but rather a worsening of global air quality. The eco-regulators would have accomplished more by accomplishing nothing.

The California Air Resources Board, the agency most responsible for implementing AB 32, counters that California's climate change initiatives will save its households hundreds of dollars of energy costs. But that will occur only when the cost of alternative energy falls below that of conventional. And, CARB says, the cleaner fuels mandated by AB 32 will provide air quality improvements worth more than $4 billion by 2020. But the agency fails to note that California already has the cleanest fuels in the nation, and it doesn't say exactly to whom even cleaner fuel would be worth $4 billion.

CARB is already hitting California pocketbooks and accounting ledgers, thanks to its first-in-the-nation fee on greenhouse gas emissions, assessed at a rate of 15 cents for every ton of carbon produced by the state's utilities and businesses. The state's Legislative Analyst has determined the cap-and-trade scheme will cost business as much as $14 billion a year.[12] That should help pay for the 175 CARB staffers who are working full-time on even more climate change regulations and climate research. More than 250 different types of businesses will have to pay the fee, with an oil refinery paying about $1.3 million a year and a cement plant about $200,000. Of course, these costs will be passed on to consumers and will make California businesses even less competitive. Plus, CARB is only counting the cost of carbon credits, ignoring the cost of complying with the new fee, which will require measuring equipment, additional staff, consultants and, invariably, lawyers. As a spokesperson for the California Manufacturers and Technology Association said upon CARB's approval of cap-and-trade, "Every additional cost adds burden to our already very high cost of doing business in the state."[13]

Still, AB 32 remains popular. Voters smashed Proposition 23 in 2010, which would have delayed AB

143

32's implementation, again showing their willingness to put environmental idealism ahead of economic pragmatism. The recession has hit the popularity of the law, however, with support for it among California voters dropping from 78 percent in 2007 to 67 percent in 2011, according to the Public Policy Institute of California. Its support also comes from the hope that the law will create a boom in green jobs in California, which was the crux of the campaign against Prop. 23. That's turning out to be a pipe dream, because California's tax structure, labor regulations and environmental regulations are just as unfriendly to green companies as they are old-line manufacturers.

Voters heard the jobs argument in the heat of the 2010 election campaigns for and against Prop. 23. A green jobs industry association spokesperson said overturning AB 32 "would be the real job-killer," arguing that passage of the anti-global warming law had boosted green job growth by 36 percent from 1995 to 2008, while total employment grew by only 13 percent. Wait a minute! AB 32 was passed in 2006, so giving it credit for 11 years of purported green job growth before its passage is hype. It's also unclear whether California is getting any green job boost at all. Futurist and California critic Joel Kotkin, writing in Forbes, pointed out that California's pre-recession gain of 10,000 green jobs annually has to be measured against the 700,000 jobs the state lost when the recession kicked in. "Any net growth in green jobs has barely made a dent in any economic category," Kotkin wrote.[14]

Even if regulation and labor costs make it hard to manufacture a solar panel in California, it doesn't take away from the state's claim to being the home of the nation's green jobs spin machine. Long before President Obama picked up the green jobs theme - and hired Californian Van Jones to promote it - Gov. Schwarzenegger was promising that if AB 32 passed, California would be a magnet for green industries and the wonderful jobs that come with them. And way back in 1988, 11 years before he became Oakland's mayor, Gov. Brown suggested the poverty-torn city could become a green industry "ecopolis" with bountiful new high-paying jobs - some of the first green job hyperbole by an American politician. Oakland's unemployment rate is among the highest in the nation (16.3 percent in early 2011), so it hasn't exactly turned into a place of bountiful jobs.

The hype hasn't matched reality, as a recent study by the Brookings Institution found green jobs constitute only 2 percent of the national workforce, and only 2.2 percent of the Silicon Valley workforce - the epicenter of California's green job revolution.[15] In fact, Silicon Valley lost green jobs in the years since AB 32 passed, and in July 2011 had an unemployment rate of 10.5 percent versus the national rate of 9.1 percent. The spokesperson of one green jobs company that hires engineers and marketers in San Jose, but outsources its manufacturing to China, told the Times the prospects for green jobs in California remain bleak for reasons that should surprise no one - taxes and labor rates.

COULD CARL DO IT TODAY?

Shaking hands with Carl Karcher, the founder of the popular Carl's Jr. hamburger chain, was an unforgettable experience. Talk about a presence! I'm six feet tall and there's a bit too much of me around the middle, but Carl towered above me, to the left of me, to the right of me, all without looking like he was carrying much fat at all. And when that huge right hand of his wrapped around mine, it left my fingers searching for a grip along his mitt's outer edges, as if I were a child shaking hands with an adult. But Carl always accompanied the handshake with eyes and a smile so warm that after seeing him, I'd always feel better ... even if a little smaller.

Carl died in 2008, just shy of his 91st birthday, 67 years after he and his wife Margaret opened a hotdog stand at the corner of Florence and Central avenues in South Central Los Angeles. Back then, you'd think opening a hotdog stand would be a pretty straightforward proposition, but California was already well on its way to being inhospitable towards businesses. The company's current CEO, Andy Puzder, explained how tough California was on Carl in a column Puzder wrote marking the company's 70th anniversary:

> ... The Health Department complained that Carl's fledgling business lacked restroom facilities, so he had to persuade the owner of the gas station across the street to let his employees use the station's restrooms. The State Board of Equalization complained that Carl didn't have a sales tax permit and ridiculously claimed that he owed back sales taxes from before he bought the cart in an amount in excess of the $326 he paid for the cart.
>
> Carl hired a lawyer for $100 and argued that he

owed no tax because his customers consumed their hot dogs off premises - and he won. He then was hit with a state law requiring that he carry workers' compensation insurance, which he purchased for an additional $15.

Clearly, even back in 1941, there were issues with government and small businesses. As Carl wrote in his book, "Never Stop Dreaming," these issues caused him to wonder if his decision to purchase that hot dog cart "had been a good one."[16]

Puzder concluded that, if Karcher were starting his business in today's California, it's very unlikely it would have survived - if it had opened at all. "[T]he burdens have become so onerous that they all but destroy the businesses of tomorrow before they begin. This is particularly true in California," he wrote, citing in particular regulations that make it costly and time-consuming to open new restaurants and labor rules that mandate costly breaks and preclude four-day work weeks. He's thinking of moving the iconic California company to Texas, where it's much easier to do business. He told the Austin American-Statesman, "There's a lengthy list of regulations that you have to comply with in California that make doing business virtually impossible. If you're going to grow, you want to grow in someplace like Texas."[17]

RED-LIGHTING GREEN ENERGY

At the other end of the technological spectrum from Karcher's hamburgers are the silicon chips that power computers. California's anti-business, ultra-environmentalist policies are no more accommodating to them, making companies like Intel Corp. turn away from the state. The key motivator to driving them out is the unreliability of electrical supply in the state, and its very high cost. The latest example of how California is making its electricity even more expensive and unreliable to the detriment of business is the recent action - again by regulators, not the elected Legislature - to force multi-billion-dollar retrofits to power plants in order to eliminate the practice of taking water out of the ocean, cooling the plant with it, then returning it to the ocean in pretty much the same shape as when it left.

Environmental activists have convinced California's regulators to ban the practice - called "once-through cooling" - to save marine life that is sucked into the power plants. Even if the intakes are screened to protect fish and seals, the environmentalists bemoan the demise of fish eggs. And regulators who went to the same schools and took the same courses as the environmentalists quickly jump on the bandwagon. Eliminating once-through cooling will drive electricity costs even higher since it is expected to cost millions of dollars to retrofit each plant. Worse, the move could make brownouts and blackouts even more likely because some coastal power plant operators could shutter their plants since there is no guarantee the California Public Utility Commission will let them raise rates enough to recoup retrofitting costs, or that the California Coastal Commission will approve their projects in a timely manner.

That's not all that's making electricity costlier to

businesses that already are being wooed by other states. In 2009, already one year into the Great Recession, with a swoop of his pen, Gov. Schwarzenegger required the state's electrical utilities to boost the percentage of alternative energy sources in their grid from the 20 percent by 2010 already required by the unelected California Energy Commission to 33 percent by 2020. It certainly wasn't the utilities' better-than-expected success at incorporating alternative sources that drove the decision. In fact, the utilities were on target to hit the 2010 goal at least three years late, as the percentage of renewables in the state's power supply remained stubbornly in the low teens. (Even that number is misleading because 60 percent of the state's current renewable energy comes from geothermal sources that were online long before the mandate was set.) "Alternative energy" is another way of saying "energy that's too expensive to compete in the free market," so the estimated cost of achieving the 33 percent by 2020 goal is more than $114 billion - money that will be passed through in higher electric rates that will pose a "high risk" to the state's economy, according to state auditors.[18]   It's no wonder, then, that as far back as 2001, during the state's energy crisis and before the drive for renewables made things even worse, Intel CEO Craig Barrett said:

> *Would I OK the expansion of anything in Silicon Valley right now? Not a chance. Will I build my new facilities in Oregon and Arizona and New Mexico and Ireland, and even Massachusetts and Israel, were I can get an assured supply of power?*

Absolutely, yes, and that's where my expansion is going.[19]

Ten years later, Intel made good on the promise, announcing it would build a $5 billion semiconductor plant in Arizona that will create thousands of new high-paying jobs. The announcement wasn't made at Intel's Silicon Valley headquarters - it was made at an Intel plant in Oregon that is undergoing a multi-billion-dollar expansion.

It's not for a lack of effort by industry to provide new sources of power that California utilities are having difficulty achieving their renewables mandates. It's because California's environmental protection laws and environmental activists are getting in the way of protecting the environment. Every new wind or solar farm has to go through the same sort of rigorous environmental review California requires of conventional power plants and massive new subdivisions. When the public comment period opens and the public hearings are held, environmentalists raise a ruckus: They fight wind farms because the wind-driven generators kill birds; they fight desert solar plants because they cover habitat that's home to endangered species like the desert tortoise; they fight transmission lines to carry whatever solar or wind energy that does get produced to the cities, because the power lines induce growth. A spokesperson for the Sierra Club, a group that pushes relentlessly against fossil fuels while protesting alternative energy plants, recently told a reporter, "Of course the Sierra Club favors renewable energy in the abstract, but each project has to be assessed individually to see how green power balances against ecological damage."[20]

Solar and wind energy companies that raced to California to seize the business opportunities presented by the state's alternative energy mandates have found that all the hype about the green jobs they'll produce doesn't matter one bit when an environmental group decides their project doesn't pass that green power/ecological damage balance test. But the unions are even more dangerous, because they confront wind and solar energy producers demanding union labor be employed to build and operate the plants. If they don't, the unions make clear, progress on their plants will grind down to the pace of a desert tortoise as the unions use tactics developed by environmental groups to delay construction and drive up costs. Like the environmentalists, the unions do this by exploiting the California Environmental Quality Act's byzantine regulatory and legal processes.

According to the New York Times, one energy company that shunned the unions was hit with 144 data requests from the union, another with 143, and a third company complained to the Energy Commission that union activists were abusing environmental laws to force unionization. A fourth company that agreed to unionize its operations received no such scrutiny from the unions even though its proposed plant had similar environmental impacts. In fact, the union agreed to mediate between the company and environmental groups challenging the project. "This does stress the limits of credibility," a member of the California Energy Commission, Jeffrey Byron, said when a labor attorney aggressively attacked a proposed solar plant because of its purported environmental impacts, according to the Los Angeles Times.[21]

A HOUSE DIVIDED

In July 2011, as the nation's unemployment rate stood at 9.1 percent, California's rate climbed to 12 percent, second only to Nevada. Analysts blamed the state's high unemployment rate on the deathly slow return of its housing sector, which is really just another way of blaming California's poor economy on the state's legislators and regulators. California's housing bubble grew bigger because laws and regulations made it so difficult to build houses that supply was artificially restricted as demand surged in the mid-2000s. Then after the crash, as the recovery took hold, less regulated states like Texas came back more quickly because fewer regulations stood in the way of meeting returning demand.

Still, housing in California, particularly in the coastal regions, remains among the most expensive in the nation. The high cost of housing in California is one of the factors Vranich noted that drive away businesses, and it's remaining a problem even after the real estate meltdown has stripped equity from homes from Chula Vista to Crescent City. Worse, the state needs jobs, and each new home built creates three new permanent jobs according to the Building Industry Association of Southern California - not to mention $300,000 in economic output, and $19,000 in state and local tax revenues (great for balancing upside-down budgets!). What is California doing in response? Is it looking for ways to roll back the costs its regulatory agencies place on new homes? No, it's doing just the opposite. California's legislators and regulators are continuing to impose tougher requirements for energy efficiency, air quality, stormwater management, global warming, coastal protection, labor and insurance that far exceed those of other states and will make homes in California even costlier.

Sure, California regulates everything from the type of paint that's used in a house to the amount of construction waste that's allowed, but that's just old-school regulation that, while effective in making homes less affordable, is hardly the sort of cutting-edge regulation that California is known for. That can be found in California's newfound regulation of *where* houses can be built, not just *how* they're built.

The state's intense effort to mandate where you can and can't live started in 2007 with - no surprise here, really - Jerry Brown. That was when, as attorney general, he sued the county of San Bernardino for approving a new long-term growth plan that he felt didn't do enough to appease global warming alarmists, himself included. The county eventually settled, promising to put the kibosh on "leapfrog" developments and other sprawling housing patterns, a surrender that pushed other counties to accept the state's campaign to eliminate new suburban developments in favor of stacked lofts in dangerous neighborhoods next to noisy trains and trolleys.

Now Kamala Harris, the San Francisco district attorney who succeeded Brown as California's attorney general, is keeping the pressure on municipalities that fail to join in the goose-stepping toward forced urbanism in the name of fighting global warming. Citing AB 32 and its evil twin, Senate Bill 375, 2008's

California Sustainable Communities and Climate Protection Act, Harris recently threatened to axe 10 years of planning in Los Angeles County's Santa Clarita Valley. Why? Because, she argued, the area's new long-term growth plan didn't do enough to address global warming. If the valley's 230,000 residents did 10 percent more - or 100 percent more - to whittle down their carbon footprint, would it still be enough to actually address global warming? It's highly doubtful the globe would notice. No matter. Harris is also suing San Diego because its long-range plan did too much for highways - the transportation system people love to use - and not enough for mass transit - the transportation systems people love to avoid.

If the Santa Clarita and San Diego plans aren't changed to meet Harris' pleasure, she can use Sacramento's regulatory powers and her abundant staff of litigators to drive up the cost of housing even further by stringing out approval timelines for new developments there. For Santa Clarita, this would remove the area as an option for families that want to flee urbanized and dysfunctional Los Angeles for a safer place with cleaner air and better schools. And that's exactly the goal of the so-called "smart growth" movement that is at the heart of SB 375. The law embodies the Progressive assumption that the elite know what's best for us - in this case, city living, not suburban living. Forcing people to live where the state wants them to live is exactly what California's Progressive-dominated legislature set out to do when passing SB 375 - and it's exactly what's happening now all over California, including Harris' hometown of San

Francisco.

In their "Initial Vision Scenario for 2035," Bay Area transportation agencies and cities said that by 2035 the Bay Area's population will grow by 2 million people, who will need 902,000 new homes. Despite this projected population growth, the plan says there will be fewer cars in the Bay Area in 2035 than there are today. Two million more people and fewer cars - that means a lot of people will be standing around waiting for buses and subways, or peddling to the office like Chinese workers, instead of commuting by car, with the privacy, convenience and comfort most people still prefer. Spot quiz: Do young kids dream of the day they'll get their driver's license, or the day they'll get their bus pass?

The Initial Vision Scenario exemplifies the sort of new planning that's in store for every metropolitan area in California as a result of SB 375.

The law was authored and championed by Sacramento Democrat senator Darrell Steinberg (the president of the California senate at the time of Crazifornia's publication). He explained the purpose of SB 375's utopian planning and statist mandates in a Wall Street Journal op/ed that ran, appropriately, on May Day in 2012:

> More unmitigated sprawl, more smog, more cars on our already congested freeways - is that tarnish what Californians really want to see for the future of the Golden State? ...

> The California Sustainable Communities and Climate Protection Act (SB 375) is a rational

approach that serves as a blueprint for other states on how to turn inevitable growth into smart growth. Its provisions provide regions with a thoughtful framework to minimize expanding development, relieve roadway congestion, provide housing and working alternatives to Californians confounded by gridlock, and improve air quality.[22]

In other words, the state will make it so you can't live in suburbia and commute to work. The state doesn't care if you want your kids to be raised in the suburbs instead of the city. The state chooses to ignore that the air isn't getting dirtier; it's getting progressively cleaner because of advances in automotive and industrial technology in the face of earlier regulations.

Many of my younger friends say they prefer urban to suburban living, but will their current preferences endure? The progressive planners behind the smart growth movement seem to have forgotten that in the late 19th century, Americans fled the cities by the millions as soon as newfangled transportation systems reached the suburbs. America was a land of choice then, and people chose the suburbs, which offered a better life free of the crowded conditions and high crime rates that came with urban living.

Choice has been replaced, in California most of all, with smart growth and global-warming fighting. It's been highly effective at raising the cost of housing in California, but it's but one of many layers of regulatory burdens that have been shoved onto the state's housing market. California's Environmental Quality Act also adds another bundle. It requires costly scientific studies of all the impacts a project may cause, then mandates even costlier mitigations for those impacts. One frequent requirement is to increase the amount of open space in a project. I worked on one project, Tejon Mountain Village, that had 5,000 acres of development and 23,000 acres of open space. That's a rather extreme example, but it's not uncommon to be required to leave one-third of a new subdivision as natural open space. That means there will be fewer houses to spread the costly regulatory burden across.

The mitigations cooked up by cities and counties to offset the impact of new developments range from the routine - like requiring the developer to pay to signalize an intersection or two, at about $150,000 each - to ones that seemingly have little nexus with the actual impact. The developer may be required to give $100,000 to the library, or pay for the restoration of a park across town, or price ten percent of the units below market price for low-income buyers. (The amount of money developers lose to these affordable sales is added to the cost of the other homes in the tract, in a classic Progressive wealth transfer scheme.) Cities particularly love the sort of big developments SB 375 is attacking, because with more on the table, city planners can hold the developers hostage. If not enough goodies are promised, the environmental review process can become more difficult and more dragged out. Watching their finance charges tick up with each month's delay, most developers eventually pull out their wallets and acquiesce.

One of my clients was required to build a nature center for about $1 million - and pay for the city employees who would staff it. The city also mandated that they donate land for a fire station, pay for a fire truck, buy an ATV for the police department, and establish a multi-million-dollar endowment to pay for the perpetual maintenance of the trails they were required to build in the open space they were required to dedicate. Another client must pay for $15 million in flood control improvements that normally would be built by the county using state and federal funds. With just over 100 homes to spread that cost over, that one mitigation alone will add well over $100,000 to the cost of each home.

It's no surprise, then, that a 2008 study found all of the 20 cities nationwide with the highest cost impact from regulations are in California.[23] San Francisco's homes have the highest regulatory burden - surprised? Add the city's jungle of regulations to the state's, and $400,000 in regulatory costs is added to the price of a house there. When the study was done in 2008, the median home value in the city was $806,700, so regulatory burdens made up nearly half the cost of that median-priced home. The bursting of the housing bubble has dropped the city's median home price to $675,000, but there's been no significant lessening of the regulatory intensity, so that burden now stands at 60 percent. Oxnard, #20 in the study's ranking, adds $246,858 in regulatory costs to the price of its new homes. That means Californians pay more for regulations than the most U.S. citizens pay for a home. According to the Census Bureau, the median price for a home in the United States is just $221,800 - so for what Oxnard home-buyers pay in regulation, someone in Iowa or Oklahoma or North Carolina could buy an entire house with a brand new Hyundai Sonata, the best-selling car in America, in the driveway.

Even so, any effort to ease regulations and encourage more new housing in order to spur the economy and create jobs is greeted by bureaucratic rejection, environmentalist litigation and new legislation to ratchet up the state's regulatory prowess. That drives more businesses out of California to areas where employees can afford to live.

STANDING UP FOR BUSINESS

Lest you misjudge California, you should know that not every proposed regulation on business has an easy route to the ordinance book. When some workers in California's porn film production industry petitioned the Board of California's Division of Occupational Safety and Health in 2010, asking that condoms be required on porno film sets, Sacramento's response can be best categorized as a slow grind.

To make their case to the state, the AIDS Healthcare Foundation helpfully provided the board with 58 pornographic DVDs to view, along with quotes from porn stars supporting the ban, like this one from former porn star Jan "Meza" Merritt:

> It breaks my heart to acknowledge that during my time as a porn star, I've done a scene with 25 men and even though I was assured that all of the STD testing had been taken care of by the producers, in my heart I realize now that this was probably a lie because I never saw the tests for myself.[24]

Her heart is not the body part Merritt should be

looking to for medical evidence of whether the producers lied. Another starlet, Madelyne Hernandez, recounted a shoot in which her role called for her to do what porn stars do with 75 men, none of whom wore condoms. And at the board hearing, porn actor Darren James, who has tested positive for HIV, told the Board, "You think you're safe, but you're not. In between scenes, you don't know what the other actors are doing."[25] Nor do we want to. In California, one would expect a regulatory board to quickly get down on business in the interest of workers. But if the Occupational Safety and Health Board was shocked, it wasn't enough to break it out of its bureaucratic doldrums. Rather than stand by the porn workers, the board dodged the issue, voting instead to form an advisory committee that would consider how exactly to go about regulating the industry - probably diligently studying those 58 DVDs in the process.

Their investigation quickly lost its thrust, however, because California's Progressive proposition system acted faster than the bureaucrats in Sacramento. In Los Angeles, the first city in the nation to allow citizens to place measures on ballots, the AIDS Healthcare Foundation gathered nearly twice the 41,138 signatures needed to qualify a city initiative for the ballot that would require condoms on porn movie shoots. No condoms, no filming permit. Filming permits probably aren't something most think about when they're watching their favorite television show, heading out for the Cineplex or indulging in some of the less reputable output of California's movie industry. But Los Angeles excels at creating costly and time-consuming permitting processes that hurt the massive entertainment industry, long a leading job generator in the state.

The Milken Institute recently reported that the number of mainstream movies filmed in California dropped from 272 in 2000 to 160 in 2008. The state's share of the nation's film production jobs dropped from 40 percent to 37.4 percent in about the same period - not a surprising statistic since three-quarters of the movies made by the big Hollywood studios are now shot outside California. If the state had been able to hold onto its 40 percent share, the study reported, 10,600 production jobs would have been saved and another 25,500 jobs would have been created in other business sectors that benefit from film production.[26]

Because porn productions don't have as complex a permitting process - they typically don't require streets to be closed down, for example - getting permits hasn't been as costly a problem and the porn industry is still comfortably ensconced in the San Fernando Valley neighborhoods of Los Angeles. But the condom initiative is changing that. Faced with the successful signature gathering for the AIDS Health Care Foundation's initiative, the Los Angeles City Council voted 11-1 early in 2012 to enact the condom initiative as an ordinance, sparing the city the $4 million expense of putting it on the ballot. And what an ordinance it is - indicative of just how willing California is to lay down the law and screw business.

Under the ordinance, porn producers will have to pay a fee to the city for every production. That explains the 9-1 vote - the city, like all of California government, is cash-strapped and looking for ways to impose new fees. Exactly how much the fee will be and what it will be used for will be determined by a special committee. Early indications are that the city's health department will use revenues generated by the fee to hire inspectors whose job it will be to monitor porn sound stages to make sure condoms are always used.

People immediately started joking about the number of applications the city's health department would receive for the job, but I see it differently, and I think California's trial attorneys are with me on this. How could the ordinance ever be enforced without a great gush of employment lawsuits charging the city forced employees into a degrading work environment, that the city caused an inspector's disgusted wife to divorce him or that the city caused an otherwise perfectly normal employee to have to claim a 100 percent disability pension due to the ravages of a devastating addiction to porn flicks?

Of course, all this will backfire on the city. There is plenty of studio space available just across the Los Angeles city line, so there's nothing to keep porn producers from following their more legitimate counterparts and move production to locations where regulations don't cover quite as much. One of L.A.'s largest pornographic film producers said as much, telling the Associated Press, "Ultimately I think what [the city] will find is people will just stop shooting in the city of Los Angeles. That's a given."[27]

FROM ANTI-BUSINESS TO MEGA-ANTI-BUSINESS

As the recession clings to California, about the only shovel-ready job in the state is the ongoing installation of barriers to business, to the point where the only thing that's keeping a lot of businesses from fleeing is the recession itself. "It costs a lot of money to move and many companies just don't have it now," Vranich told me. "Once the recession lifts, I see the exodus from California really picking up steam."

A new motivation for companies to leave lies about as well hidden as a body in a very shallow grave in Gov. Brown's 2012-13 budget proposal. It is the governor's latest reaction to California's business exodus: a new mega-agency, the Business and Consumer Services Agency. Brown hyped it as an effort to downsize government through consolidation, but it's really something much more sinister: a consolidation of anti-business attitudes into a new mega-agency. One look at its structure and it's evident the Business and Consumer Services Agency will "service" businesses in the way male farm animals "service" female ones.

The agency will combine habitually anti-business state departments handling consumer affairs, "fair" employment practices and various business licensing and inspection functions, creating a concentration of the state bureaucracies that are most inclined to make things harder for business owners. Into this fetid anti-business environment Brown plans to drop, quoting from his budget summary, "the newly restructured Department of Business Oversight."[28] Restructured from what? The department doesn't currently exist, so it appears that Brown is creating an entirely new arm of government, surrounding it with anti-business zealots and charging it with increasing the amount of oversight directed at California businesses that are already suffering from acute oversight poisoning.

Meanwhile, the budget summary's description of the Business, Transportation and Housing Agency, which "includes programs that promote the state's business and economic climate," doesn't include one word about business. Instead, it references Caltrans, the state's highway department, its boondoggle High-Speed Rail Commission (which Brown proposes to continue to fund) and the lethargic Department of Motor Vehicles. The absence of any reference to business in the write-up of the department that supposedly supports business is more evidence, if it is needed, of the low regard the Brown administration has for the private sector.

It's not like business interests haven't been trying to get Brown's ear. It's not like he hasn't seen the studies and heard the arguments about how easing regulatory burdens on business would be good for California. It's just that Brown doesn't want to hear, or more accurately, doesn't believe or understand what he hears. Raised in a big government Progressive family, having lived a big government Progressive life, he believes business is something to control tightly, quash regularly, and tax steeply - not something to encourage and leave relatively unfettered.

MAKING CALIFORNIA BUSINESS FRIENDLY

Bill Hauck, the former CEO of one of California's leading pro-business groups, the Business Roundtable, told me he misses the days when the business lobby had the sort of clout in California needed to turn Brown and the Democratic Legislature around. But those days are gone, he said, as the power now resides lopsidedly with public-employee unions and trial attorneys.

Hauck also told me of a CEO who said to him, "If we can't straighten this place out, I don't want to leave, I don't want to move, but I could be forced by my shareholders to move because of the cost of doing business here and its impact on profits." Nothing substantive has changed since then, so one has to wonder if that company is still here, or if it's joined the exodus of companies leaving the state for greener pastures - financially, not environmentally - elsewhere.

Still, there are a few kinds of businesses that thrive in California. The creative high-tech companies like Google and Apple like it here because there's plenty of brainpower to draw on. And since they're rich, they can afford to have their headquarters anywhere. But of course, their labor-intensive manufacturing plants and power-hungry server facilities were moved out of California long ago. Then there are the companies that serve markets within California - the restaurants, groceries, real estate companies, service companies, food processors and manufacturers who stay in California because the state offers so many heavily populated markets to saturate.

Then there are companies that thrive on California's dysfunction, like mold on a rotting vegetable. My public affairs agency, which specializes in regulatory issues, exists simply because it's so hard for businesses to weave through the thickets and swamps of regulations planted by Sacramento. We, along with business law firms, lobbyists and all kinds of consulting firms, have learned the water, air, land and labor regulations and have found we can earn a good living moderating the pain for our clients. As a result, we are unemployable in states like Texas, where regulators are spread thin and are armed with even thinner books of regulations. On the other side, environmental groups and law firms that specialize in running litigation mills fueled by California's anti-business regulations are similarly tied to the state and would have difficulty being as successful in other, more reasonable markets.

Together, these businesses are hardly enough to support a healthy economy, and I'm not about to predict that the state's business climate will improve any time soon. Tort reform could help, as could the easing of highly restrictive and costly labor laws. And, as Meg Whitman pointed out during her 2010 campaign for governor, even a modest relaxation of regulation would lead to a surge in employment. But realistically, reforms like these will be fought tooth and nail by the unions, attorneys and big environmental groups that oppose them. So the best that can be hoped for in the short term is incremental change - a slowing of anti-business bills more than a wave of pro-business bills, the failure of anti-business propositions more than the success of pro-business ones, and perhaps even a court victory from time to time.

Besides, the Left has become arrogant in the face of California's job losses and the state revenue losses that have resulted. They believe taxes can be raised and raised and raised again, and the wealthy won't budge. Here's CaliCon, who blogs anonymously on one of California's most influential leftist blogs, on the subject:

I was really tired of hearing conservatives (like Meg Whitman in 2010) praise Texas as a model for California. ...

But the thing is, our mild climate and natural beauty can't be found or replicated in Texas. As oil is to that state, the environment is a resource to us. Its [sic] a strong enough resource in fact that the wealthy will continue to live here regardless of the tax situation (much like they live in France). ... Our environment opens the door to higher taxes on the wealthy as long as its [sic] packaged as the price to live here. ... Companies that are high tech and want to attract people that want to live the California lifestyle can afford those taxes.

Bottomline, Texas plans to attract the lowest bidder (those that don't want to pay taxes). Like Wal-mart shoppers they don't expect frills or high quality products and services. California is like (insert expensive store of your choice, I won't play favorites) it gives you high end stuff and you expect to enjoy the experience not get the deal and rush out.[29]

CaliCon may not be noticing that every year, fewer companies think the California experience is enjoyable enough to justify staying, and head out for more Wal-Mart-like environs. With the state's Progressive base ignoring the impact of their policies on business, it's hard to visualize a pro-business California. California won't stop digging its business-killing hole deeper unless the majority of voters finally react to the state's catastrophic business climate and start voting pro-business - and there's no evidence that will happen any time soon. A California electorate that has shown such passion for electing liberal politicians and passing propositions that burden business just doesn't seem like the bunch that would ever do something as sensible as an idea my wife came up with recently. "What if regulators' salaries were cut every time a business left the state?" she asked. "After all, they're causing the businesses to leave, and every time a business leaves, the state loses revenue. What do you do when you lose revenue? You cut payroll expenses."

It sounds like a ballot proposition in the making, but not one that would pass today. Public attitude rides a pendulum, however, and some day the majority of Californians will have grown sufficiently frustrated by the state's anti-business attitude to vote for such a proposition. California's business owners just hope the awakening comes quickly enough.

CHAPTER SEVEN:

EDUCATION: ALL CHILDREN LEFT BEHIND

Teaching America all about bad schools, bad teachers and bad administrators

HE WASHINGTON MONTHLY - staffed by "righteous redistributionists," according to the pro-business Forbes Magazine - recently gave a solid endorsement of California's higher education system when its 2011 college rankings placed the University of California San Diego at the top of the academic ivory tower. It ranked well ahead of Harvard, which came in sixth, behind UCSD, other University of California campuses in Los Angeles, Berkeley and Riverside, and Stanford. Poor Harvard. At least it squeaked in ahead of UC Davis, which also made the top 10. How can California's colleges be ranked at the top of the charts by Washington Monthly when the primary school system that feeds them is ranked 46th among the states in math, 48th in reading and 49th in science, out-performing only Mississippi?

The answer might be found in the title of the The

Washington Monthly's website article announcing the rankings, "Is our students earnings?"[1] This incomprehensible grammatical nightmare certainly hints that basic education may not be the grandest of the publication's ranking criteria. As it turns out, that's exactly why California's colleges were rated so highly. The publication doesn't rank colleges based on the usual metrics like student/faculty ratio or the GPAs and SAT scores of the incoming class. Rather, its first measure of a college is how well it performs as an engine of social mobility. Schools also are ranked by the number of graduates that go on to public service instead of more capitalistic endeavors. It's no wonder, then, that California colleges rank so well, since California schools are as much about leading the Progressive's education revolutions as they are about basic academics.

EQUALITY OF OUTCOME, NOT OPPORTUNITY

Marin County-based conservative blogger Bookworm of Bookwormroom.com - who hides her true identity to protect her children from bullying in Northern California's enlightened, leftist public schools - identified the cause of the decline of California's education system recently when she wrote:

> *"As Mencken should have said, 'No one ever went broke underestimating Progressives' pathological need to tax the public to obtain reparations for self-defined PC victim groups.' ... This is a weird version of the Left's obsession with equality of outcome, rather than equality of opportunity."*[2]

(She was referring to curmudgeon H.L. Mencken's quip, "Nobody ever went broke underestimating the intelligence of the American public.")

That obsession for equalized outcomes is, in a nutshell, what's driven California's schools from among the best in the nation to among the worst. Forty years ago, California was considered a national leader in education. But now its schools lag behind nearly all the rest of the country by almost every measure: student achievement, teacher qualifications, teacher/student ratios and facilities. But not all the stats are bottom-dwellers. According to the Pacific Research Institute's Lance Izumi, California has the best-paid teachers in the nation. Why is uncertain, since a comprehensive RAND Corporation study found only Louisiana and Mississippi rank lower than California on national standardized tests. Even after the state spent billions to improve its student-to-teacher ratio, it's still the second-worst in the nation, at 20.9 students per teacher, compared to a national average of 16.1.[3] Only 46 percent of the state's school districts require teachers to have full standard certification in the subjects they teach, compared to 82 percent of districts nationally.

The plummeting performance of California's schools can be traced back to the socially conscious year of 1969, when California became the first state in the nation to "reform" school finance, stripping local school boards of responsibility for their own budgets and shifting control to Sacramento, where the Legislature and education bureaucrats have since botched the assignment dismally. The move was made because Democrats were horrified to learn schools in some wealthier parts of the state spent more per student than schools in poorer regions. Surely, they thought, Sacramento could give those poor kids the same chance rich kids have, lifting everyone to a higher, brighter future in the process. They gave their initiative great prominence, naming it "Educational Equity" and placing it near the very top of the California Education Code, as Article 2 of Part 1.

The result was one of the Legislature's rare victories, as it succeeded in shrinking the gap between wealthy and poor districts across the state - a feat accomplished by dragging the better districts down, in part by lowering per-student spending overall from $400 above the national average in 1969 to $600 below it in 2000, according to RAND.

The Pacific Research Institute chronicled just how bad California schools have become in a comprehensive study, *Not as Good as you Think, Why the Middle Class Needs School Choice*.[4] The study starts by describing Alta Loma High School in San Bernardino County. It was selected because it is emblematic of the sort of school that isn't awful, but is bad enough that wealthier parents might want to move to a district with better schools. Some 22 percent of Alta Loma's students qualify for the free lunch program, and about the same percentage are classified as socio-economically disadvantaged. Alta Loma's students, like all students in the state, take standardized tests in the 11th grade, resulting in these findings: 55 percent of the 11th graders scored below "proficient" in the California standardized English exam, 70 percent scored below "proficient" in algebra and 75 percent below "proficient" in geometry.

PRI's study compared schools like Alta Loma to schools in some of the wealthiest towns in the state. Thanks to the Legislature's leveling process, schools in gold-plated towns were not as much better as one would expect. In ultra-tony Beverly Hills, where just 4 percent of high school students qualify for the free lunch program, 41 percent of the 11th graders scored below "proficient" in the California standardized English exam, 51 percent below in algebra and 59 percent below in geometry. The scores are better than Alta Loma's, of course, but who would be thrilled to pay the high property taxes Beverly Hills residents pay to support schools that are only marginally better than those in the blue-collar Inland Empire? Sun-kissed Malibu fared no better, with 40 percent below "proficient" in English, 76 percent below in algebra and 75 percent below in geometry.

In a state where voters have come to expect that the Legislature will fail at achieving its lofty goals, Sacramento has indeed achieved considerable success in its goal of equalizing school grades across the state's diverse socio-economic lines. Now, you can expect your child to get a lousy education in any public school in the state - and that is just fine in the Progressive world view, where equality is a higher value than individual achievement.

FROM HIGH TO LOWELL

Nowhere is the neutralization of excellence more evident than at San Francisco's Lowell High School, the oldest high school west of the Mississippi and the city's academic crown jewel. Lowell graduates include Supreme Court Justice Stephen Breyer, left-wing columnist Naomi Wolf, Daniel Handler, who authored the *Lemony Snicket* books - and the anonymous Bay Area conservative blogger, Bookworm. Lowell hasn't exactly fallen off the academic map, but it's plummeting. When Bookworm graduated in the late 1970s, it was ranked the ninth best school in the country; it's now ranked 68th in Newsweek's rankings - still quite an honor, but also quite a slip.[5]

Blame for part of the drop can be placed at the feet of the California Legislature, of course, not just for its leveling efforts but also because it mandates curricula for Lowell just like it does every other public high school in the state. And it burdens administrators with so many mandates it's hard for them to shift their focus from paperwork to education. (Administrators are paid well for their trouble, however. Between 2004 and 2009, their income rose 28 percent, compared to 21 percent for teachers. In the same period, the state's per capita personal income rose much less, 15 percent.[6]

Harmful as the state's efforts may be, San Francisco itself played a larger part. First, for all its liberal, inclusive window dressing, San Francisco has a rich history as a very racist city, particularly when it comes to Asians. In the 19th and early 20th centuries, city leaders lobbied relentlessly for laws restricting Asian immigration and denying rights to Asian-Americans, leading campaigns to pass the federal Chinese Exclusion Act of 1882, which halted Chinese immigration and denied them citizenship, and the California Alien Land Law. The latter targeted primarily Japanese farmers, and was passed by a public initiative vote in 1920. Backed and strongly promoted by Progressive Republican governor Hiram Johnson, it passed by over 75 percent.[7]   (The federal Chinese Exclusion Act was repealed during World War II when China was an ally against Japan, and California's Alien Land Law was thrown out by the U.S. Supreme Court in 1952.)

In the 1940s, many San Franciscans were not the least bit upset when Japanese-Americans were forced into internment camps, losing their property and businesses in the process. Anti-Asian racism continues even today, as a wave on black-on-Asian violence wracked the city in 2010. City officials tried to sweep it under the rug, saying gangs take advantage of vulnerable "small-stature" groups[8] - a hurtful state-ment that seems deserving of some politically correct curricula mandates on tolerance from Sacramento.

Prejudice against Asians is part of the downfall of Lowell. Not surprising to anyone familiar with the common Asian obsession with education, Lowell has a lot of Asians in its student body. Even in Bookworm's day, the school was so dominated by Asians and Jews that the joke was, if Yom Kippur and Chinese New Year were to fall on the same day, the halls would be abandoned.   In 1983, the school district acted to forcefully limit Asian enrollment at Lowell, imposing a grades-based quota system that required a significantly higher testing score from Asian 8th graders seeking enrollment in the school. That in turn allowed more black or Hispanic students, who had lower requirements, to get in. The quota, in one form or another, stood until 2005 before finally falling to litigation and agitation from the Asian community and anti-affirmative action groups.

But years of allowing kids with lower grades into the school wasn't the worst of it. "The city punished Lowell by giving it terrible teachers," Bookworm told me. "It had these superb students - Carol Channing, the famous Communist Irving Stone, an unusual number of Nobel Prize winners - but it was renowned for having some of the worst teachers in the city." She described her math teacher as one of the more awful. "For one thing, he looked awful. How do they let people come to school like that? He had this rank, greasy, shoulder-length hair. God knows what he was thinking - he'd wear his shirts open down to his sternum, and under them he'd wear T-shirts you could see he had ripped open so they wouldn't show under his unbuttoned shirts." He frequently would break out of the lifeless doldrums of his teaching style to loudly shame students in class or shout down kids in the hallways, where students frequently gathered. "Periodically during class he'd drop his eraser and chalk and rush out into the hallway, where you could hear him screaming, 'Get out of my hallway, you future pimps and whores!'"

Today, continuing the campaign to drive Lowell to the bottom, San Francisco Unified has imposed disproportionately deep budget cuts on the school. "SFUSD Stiffs Lowell by $400K," read the headline in a recent alumni newsletter, which goes on to say:

After years of budget cuts affecting public schools throughout the city and state, the San Francisco Unified School District has abruptly changed a long-standing funding formula that will have a disproportionate impact on Lowell .... As a direct result of this decision, Lowell will lose ... five teachers. This means that course offerings will be trimmed and class sizes will increase throughout every department.[9]

"They've always had the feeling, 'They've got the best students; they don't need money,'" Bookworm explained. But it's really more than that, and it's more than just about Lowell High School in San Francisco. So long as Lowell stands above the other schools in the city, and any California school achieves academic greatness compared to the others, California has failed to achieve legislated equality of outcome in its schools. Consequently, in California's twisted view of things, good schools can be seen more as a problem to be fixed than as an accomplishment to be celebrated.

Besides the Legislature's effort to equalize all the state's schools, the electeds and education bureaucrats of Sacramento also degrade the quality of California's schools by burdening them with a nearly impassable obstacle course of mandates and regulations. The state's Legislative Analyst's Office reported in 2010 that the Legislature has thrown so many mandates on school systems that administrators "have to perform hundreds of activities even though many of these requirements do not benefit students or educators." Statewide, school districts spend more than $400 million a year to comply with the mandates, the report stated - up from $5 million in 1992. That explains why 50 percent of California's school spending goes into administrative overhead, versus just 20 percent in Connecticut.[10]

The state is supposed to reimburse districts for these expenses. Not surprisingly, the Legislature chooses to ignore the requirement, deferring to date more than $3.6 billion in reimbursements due to the districts. Five school districts brought a lawsuit challenging the deferrals, and a Superior Court judge ruled in 2008 that deferring the reimbursements was, in fact, unconstitutional. But he also decreed that constitutional separation of powers means the Legislature doesn't have to do anything just because some judge told it to. So, in the interest of cobbling together what they pass off as balanced budgets, Legislators probably will continue to defer these payments for years to come.

BIG MONEY, BAD TEACHERS

Beyond forced leveling and overburdening mandates, a third force adds a powerful final push to California's race to the bottom: a functional inability to purge the schools of bad teachers. Behind each of these negative forces is the California Teachers Association, a fierce and wealthy advocate for teachers good and bad, and the largest player in California politics - by far. In its report, "Big Money Talks," the California Fair Political Practices Commission, an independent campaign watchdog, calculated CTA's overall political expenses for lobbying and campaigns in the first decade of the 21st century at $211.8 million. That's nearly twice the expenditures of the second-place player, the California State Council of Service Employees, and nearly five-and-a-half times more than the California Chamber of Commerce's lobbying bankroll.

CTA's clout comes from the $1,000 a year it receives from each of the 340,000 teachers it represents, who all get a lot for the money: They are the best paid in the nation. That's because the union exists to improve the lot of teachers, not the lot of students. Like any good union, it fights with bare knuckles and bared fangs for its members, with all the money it needs for a good fight. And when there's not enough money, as was the case in 2005, when Gov. Schwarzenegger tried to reform California through a series of propositions to cut spending and limit the influence of public employee unions, CTA still finds a way. For that battle, the union actually mortgaged its headquarters near Sacramento and used the money in a successful $57 million campaign to defeat the measures.

CTA traces its history back to the Civil War and claims as one of its first victories was an 1878 lobbying effort that led to a law banning the use of public school funds for religious purposes, proof that keeping God out of the classroom is nothing new in California. The union truly came into its own in 1977, when Gov. Jerry Brown pushed for legislation to give teachers and other public workers collective bargaining rights. That quickly led to higher wages and higher dues. So the CTA went looking for a way to guarantee all those teachers would make all that money in perpetuity. They found it in 1988's Proposition 98, which requires that 43 percent of the state's general fund be allocated toward education. The union calls Prop. 98 "a turning point in CTA's history," and it certainly was a turning point in the state's fiscal history. Along with the enactment of Proposition 111 in 1990, which effectively ended the Gann Limit on state spending, Prop. 98 ended a brief era of spending limits in Sacramento and replaced it with the ballot-box budgeting that leaves the Legislature with few options in its annual struggle to balance the ledger.

Arrayed against Prop. 98 were Republican Gov. George Deukmejian, every business and taxpayer association in the state, almost every newspaper in the state and a number of other public employee unions that feared the 800-pound gorilla would get all their bananas. Joining CTA was the state's Superintendent of Public Instruction, Bill Honig, who predicted - wrongly - that "the initiative will hold educators accountable for the job they do and the tax dollars they spend." Five years later, Honig was removed from office after being convicted of four felony counts of steering lucrative state contracts to a firm operated by his wife out of the Honigs' home. The felonies later were reduced to misdemeanors. The proposition squeaked through 50.7 percent to 49.3 percent as CTA spent 25 times more than the opposition. The very next year, the state's schools got $450 million in new funding - so much that plenty was left over to hike teachers' salaries. Quite a return on their $57 million investment!

Besides causing chaos in the annual budget-balancing exercise and creating a class of very well-paid teachers and administrators, Prop. 98 has accomplished little. The most comprehensive recent study of California's education system, Stanford University's Getting Down to Facts, said in 2007:

Past experience and the research we review here

*indicate with some certainty what will **not** work if our goal is to make dramatic improvements in student learning. It is clear, for example, that solely directing more money into the current system will not dramatically improve student achievement and will meet neither expectations nor needs. What matters most are **the ways in which the available resources and any new resources are used**. These studies make clear that California's education system is not making the most of its current resources.*[11]   *[Emphasis in original.]*

Nevertheless, CTA will fight any effort to reform the current spending model and Prop. 98, and will continue to use its political contributions to lead legislators through various exercises to continually improve the lot of teachers. That includes codifying the principle that being named a teacher in California is almost tantamount to being appointed to the U.S. Supreme Court - it's basically a job for life. The Legislature has written employment protections for teachers that take up a full 58 sections of the California Education Code,[12] spelling out a process so devilish in its details that it consumes 18,142 words and fills 35 single-spaced pages. No notice of dismissal or suspension can be given between May 15 and September 15, we're told. If a teacher is suspended due to drug use, then returns after rehab, he or she receives all accrued pay and vacation time. Hearing board make-up, notice periods, appeal rights and discovery are all laid out in the Niagara of words, a testament to the strength of the CTA ... and the nonexistence of a

California Students' Association. After reviewing all this, the Stanford *Getting Down to Facts* study concluded, "Strong teachers are central to student learning; yet, current policies to select, develop, evaluate, and promote or dismiss teachers are not well designed and are counterproductive in many ways."[13]

These rules made it nearly impossible for administrators to fire teachers like the greasy-haired math teacher Bookworm remembers, since he was protected by tenure. California is one of 10 states that grants teachers tenure after only two years in the classroom. But even untenured teachers can cause considerable chaos and educational harm before school districts can get rid of them. Such was the case of Michael Huang, a second-year teacher at Clayton Valley High School in Contra Costa County's Mt. Diablo School District. Among Huang's students was the daughter of Alison Moore. We don't know the daughter's identity because, ironically, it is protected by the very privacy laws that shined a bright media spotlight on her - and on the lunacy that prevails in the state's education system.

The 9th grader, like others in her class, struggled to understand Huang's thick accent, which was difficult for even the culturally diverse Bay Area freshmen. But that wasn't Huang's real problem. Students were frustrated with him mainly because he exerted little or no control over his classroom, often working in a silent sulk at his computer as the kids roughhoused and shouted around him. Just before Christmas vacation in 2008, one student stuck some Play-Doh in a microwave in the classroom. (Why California math classes come with microwaves when budget crunches make it hard for school districts to buy enough books isn't explained in the news report in the Contra Costa Times.)[14] As the room filled with foul-smelling smoke, Huang uncharacteristically took swift and decisive action: He refused to let students open the windows to air out the noxious fumes. The incident was nothing new. In other Huang class sessions, students had lit fires in trash cans, smoked cigarettes and even fired up joints, with no response from their teacher.

Appalled by the goings-on in her daughter's class, Moore lodged a complaint with school officials, who let three months pass without doing anything. As the third month ticked by, her daughter was so fed up with the situation that she used her cell phone to videotape a paper-ball fight that raged as Huang sat silently at his desk, making no effort to stop it. Another parent emailed the clip to Mt. Diablo's interim superintendent, Dick Nicoll, who, unlike Huang, knew how to deal with such situations and leaped into action. He suspended Moore's daughter for two days because videotaping a classroom without permission is a violation of the California Education Code. As for Huang, Nicoll took no action whatsoever.

Moore appealed her daughter's suspension, pointing out that the girl did not participate in the roughhousing, and should be protected from the prohibition on videotaping without permission because she was a trying to bring a problem to the attention of school leaders. "Of course she couldn't get the teacher's permission," Moore wrote in her appeal. "It was for the purpose of blowing the whistle on the teacher! The school has failed the students and the students should NOT have to suffer the consequences."

Confronted with a failing teacher and a student being punished for trying to improve teaching conditions in the school, the school opted not to provide a lesson in maturity and rational thought to its students. Instead, Principal Gary Swanson simply refused to discuss Moore's suspension. Later, Vice Principal Adeyinka Fashokun visited the class and berated Huang for his teaching methods in front of the students, in a shocking display of cultural insensitivity and bullying that ran counter to policies governing student behavior in California schools. Not surprisingly, at the end of the school year Huang left teaching. That was a good thing for future students at Clayton Valley High, because if there's one thing the California education system is good at, it's keeping incompetent teachers at the front of classrooms.

In a Los Angeles Times review of 15 years of records where tenured teachers in the Los Angeles Unified School District appealed their firing - 159 cases in all - appeals were usually upheld, even if a teacher's desk was stuffed with pot, cocaine or porn, or the teacher was involved in frequent incidents of insubordination, illegal behavior or even sexual abuse.[15] Among those who successfully fought suspension, reported the Times, was Carlos Polanco, who got in trouble after telling a junior high student who had recently slashed his wrists in a suicide attempt that the cuts "were weak." He went on, "Carve deeper next time. Look, you can't even kill yourself." LAUSD tried to fire Polanco, but a review committee didn't see the behavior as "goading or callous." Besides, LAUSD hadn't given the teacher the proper 45-day notice of the firing, so the dismissal was overturned.

The district also tried to fire 74-year-old math teacher Shirley Loftis because she didn't give directions, assigned homework that wasn't appropriate to the grade level and, like Huang, failed utterly at controlling her class. In her case, according to the complaint, students pulled down their pants, fought and threw things. The review commission was unswayed, criticizing the school district for not trying hard enough to work with Loftis. Instead of firing the incompetent teacher, they recommended her for a new job - training other teachers! "She's obviously an intelligent lady," the commission wrote in its ruling, "and such a program might well succeed." The district was not only stuck with Loftis; it also was stuck with a $195,000 bill from her attorney for defending her.

If California school districts don't try to fire incompetent teachers like Loftis, Huang or Polanco more often, it may be because they wouldn't know incompetence if it bit them in the nose. LAUSD has 30,000 teachers and recent evaluations found that 98.9 percent of the tenured ones meet standards. The district said the 1.1 percent who didn't meet standards aren't that bad - they just suffer from tardiness or attendance problems, not an inability teach or discipline. Of course, there are many, many more poor teachers in Los Angeles and throughout the state than these numbers suggest. Besides the state's poor rankings - again, it's 46th among the states in math, 48th in reading and 49th in science - there's this: One-quarter of L.A.'s public school teachers send their own kids to private schools.

FEELING GROOVY

Despite all its whacky dysfunction, educators in other states have long looked to California as a generator of exciting new approaches to teaching. The most famous - or infamous - of these started one day in 1984, when 54-year-old John Vasconcellos didn't like hearing from his cardiologist that his heart and arteries were a mess. The doctor ignored Vasconcellos' lofty position in California's Legislature, where he was a powerful assemblyman, sat him down, and treated him like any ordinary working stiff about to suffer a massive heart attack. "Cut back on your schedule," the doctor said. "Get by-pass surgery, quit smoking and change your diet."

Vasconcellos (D-San Jose) had a better idea. He told all his friends to pause at a specific time each day and imagine themselves within his arteries, on their hands and knees scrubbing away the plaque. At exactly the same time, he would visualize all of them frenetically working their scrub brushes. Then he would channel the sheer power of all that positive visualization, spike it with a surge of self-esteem sparked by having so many people working so hard to save him, and simply will the blockages into dissolving. It was a very California idea, and like a lot of California ideas, it didn't work. At his next check-up, he received the unwelcomed news that his arteries were more clogged and his heart's condition had deteriorated further, so he did what the doctor told him to do in the first place - went under the knife, quit smoking and changed to a healthier diet.

A lesser man might have questioned his commitment to New Age mumbo jumbo at that point, but not Vasconcellos. Already the second longest-serving member of the California Legislature (after the legendary Assembly Speaker Willie Brown, D-San Francisco) and chairman of the powerful Assembly Ways and Means Committee, Vasconcellos bounced back from his heart problems in 1986 with the introduction of a bill that sent shockwaves through education - and gave late-night comedians lots of side-splitting monologue material. His bill created the much-praised and much-maligned California Task Force to Promote Self-Esteem and Personal and Social Responsibility, which in turn launched a nationwide self-esteem movement that was most evident in education.

"How nice," you might be thinking, because self-esteem is held in high esteem by many. But it wasn't really nice at all, since it led to a generation of kids who felt they were just great, thank you, but had no idea how to actually be great. As radio host Dennis Prager has noted, murderers have an extraordinarily high level of self-esteem since they place their wants above the very lives of their victims. Self-esteem without a good work ethic and solid values is a dangerous gimmick, but that's not how Vaconcellos and his peers saw it. No, they truly believed anyone would do better, be they moral, amoral or immoral, if they just felt better about themselves.

Vasconcellos' bill generated a blaze of national publicity as it breezed through the California Legislature. But that didn't protect it from quickly suffering a self-esteem crushing veto by Republican Gov. George Deukmejian, who felt universities could carry out the research without a state-funded task force. The assemblyman wouldn't be stopped, however. Rather than will the governor to change his mind, the Silicon Valley Democrat sat down with Deukmejian and told him what he was proposing was a very conservative use of the taxpayers' money since higher self-esteem could turn criminals into good citizens, which would empty prisons and create better students and citizens. It was just too important to have hidden away in a university. Deukmejian asked for and got a face-saving snipping of the task force's budget, then signed the bill. I'm sure he felt very good about himself as his pen swept across the paper.

What followed was a California-spawned national phenomenon of self-esteem for the sake of self-esteem, as schools handed out trophies to every player no matter how miserably they played; every student was praised no matter how deficient in praiseworthiness he or she might be; and spelling bees, valedictorians and "most likely to succeed" couples in high school yearbooks all disappeared in order to protect the self-esteem of crummy ball players, lousy students and kids destined for anything but success. Closer to home, it resulted in one of my daughters becoming a chronically challenged speller, the hapless victim of teachers who refused to mark up her papers because they didn't want red marks to mute her budding self-worth. Some 20 years later, the result was not someone with high self-esteem regarding her spelling: She is in public relations and writes for her living, but admits to being nervous if a spell-check program isn't backing her up.

In a 1999 article, Los Angeles Times education writer Richard Lee Colvin described how California's esteem-building ideas manifested themselves, telling of a classroom at Loren Miller Elementary School in Los Angeles:

> *In daily "I Love Me" lessons, [students] completed the phrase "I am..." with words such as beautiful, lovable, respectable, kind or gifted. Then they memorized the sentences to make them sink in.*[16]

Lessons like these were exactly the sorts of classroom activities Vasconcellos thought would grow out of his California self-esteem task force. The section on schools in the final report of the self-esteem task force, "Education, Academic Failure and Self-esteem," set a course for schools where ambitiousness and competitiveness would be sacrificed so the fragile egos of the unambitious and uncompetitive would never suffer a bruise. After stating a belief (later disproved) that low self-esteem interferes with learning and high self-esteem may promote it, the report expounded that "one of the culprits" that beats down the beneficial effects of high self-esteem is "the currently accepted practice of competition to motivate students." It suggested that if competition is allowed in classrooms, then success and failure will become associated with high or low ability, and that ability itself is "an immutable factor, over which a failing student has little control."[17] Little control, that is, short of cracking a book, listening in class and turning in assignments on time.

To protect students from the horrors of competition and striving to improve, the task force recommended that every school in the state adopt the promotion of self-esteem as a goal, integrating it into the school curriculum, and requiring all educators to learn self-esteem principles. So, in no time, people in California were looking at bumper stickers like those issued by Cleveland Elementary School in Santa Barbara, proclaiming that "all children are honored" at the school. Kids at Cleveland, like kids in many other schools, sat in monthly award ceremonies, listening to their principal stressing "over and over again ... that they're all students of the month."[18] Had Grover Cleveland been exposed to such silliness, he probably never would have been elected president and subsequently had a school in Santa Barbara named after him.

Educators across the nation looked to California and liked what they saw, so in no time, students from Maine to Montana found themselves doing "I Love Me" lessons. The movement became so prevalent that in 2012, years after research confirmed that good grades and good behavior have no correlation to esteem, a Google search for "Elementary School Mission Statements for Self-Esteem" got almost 25 million hits.

The movement even reached across the Pacific to Japan, creating a generation of what the Japanese popular press has dubbed "monster parents." These moms and dads put their children's self-esteem ahead of all else, as evidenced by this report from Fox News:

The stage was set, the lights went down and in a

suburban Japanese primary school everyone prepared to enjoy a performance of Snow White and the Seven Dwarfs. The only snag was that the entire cast was playing the part of Snow White.

For the audience of menacing mothers and feisty fathers, though, the sight of 25 Snow Whites, no dwarfs and no wicked witch was a triumph: a clear victory for Japan's emerging new class of "Monster Parents."

For they had taken on the system and won. After a relentless campaign of bullying, hectoring and nuisance phone calls, the monster parents had cowed the teachers into submission, forcing the school to admit to the injustice of selecting just one girl to play the title role.[19]

Self-esteem, like many California fads from primal scream therapy (born in Arthur Janov's Primal Center in Santa Monica) to, like, Valleyspeak, has faded considerably since it enjoyed gushy trendiness 25 years ago. At Loren Miller Elementary, after self-esteem training failed to improve truly awful test scores, the students returned to homework, drills and regular testing, leading to substantially better test scores. At Bessemer School in Pueblo, Colorado, a self-esteem-rich curricula led to only 12 percent of fourth graders reading at grade level. So in 1999, out went the California phenomenon and in came the basics - and 64 percent of the fourth graders quickly began reading at grade level. Said teacher Rhonda Holcomb, "Because the scores are better, kids feel better about themselves."[20] Funny how that works, isn't it?

These results haven't stopped John Vasconcellos, however. He still finds himself "longing to leave a lasting legacy that will preserve and sustain for future generations my radically new vision of government," and has created the Politics of Trust to create that legacy. He describes it on the Politics of Trust website:

What will best constitute this living legacy is the generation of a new movement in American politics, grounded in the belief that human beings are innately inclined toward becoming life-affirming, constructive, responsible and trustworthy. I believe that from this faithful view of our essential human nature, a whole new series of policies, programs, and political processes can emerge that truly serve to inspire and benefit the growth and healing potential of each and every citizen in our community.

Many of you know how hard I've fought to establish and implement a politics that more accurately reflects our emerging consciousness and desire for a healthier community. With your help I've successfully raised the banners of healthy self esteem, of diversity, inclusion and collaboration, and of the importance of searching out the deepest roots of our problems. I've defended the virtue of authentic leadership, elevated progressive ideals to the political and social mainstream, and developed strategic relationships with hundreds of cultural leaders like yourself who are committed to developing healthier communities and a higher standard of government.[21]

So, even after humankind's healing potential failed to clear his arteries; even after the self-esteem movement in education failed to create a case for human beings being naturally inclined toward becoming constructive and responsible, Vasconcellos soldiers on still. Maybe he will eventually succeed in creating a new American politics devoid of the cynicism and dysfunction of politics today. Or maybe he will just continually fall short of achieving the Progressive ideal, because like so many leftists, he is unswayed as the evidence stacks up, showing again and again that human nature tends to cause humans to produce results that are less than ideal.

TAG, YOU NEED PROTECTION

For all this, Vasconcellos' beloved self-esteem is hardly dead. As the Pacific Research Institute's Lance Izumi said of today's recently accredited teachers (see "The PEER Axis" in Chapter 1), "These teachers care primarily about not damaging the self-esteem of your child or anybody else's child. They think it's more important to preserve their mental state than whether they can actually work with their brains." So, the self-esteem movement lives on in classrooms, albeit in a less provocative form, and it is at the root of at least two other trends that were birthed in California schools and continue to grow nationally: First, the belief that individuals are so valuable the state must protect them from harm - the foundational principle of the political correctness and "nanny state" movements.

Second, the devil's corollary of self-esteem, that it's better for many to suffer in order to protect one person from suffering, as long as the one suffering is from a class Progressives believe has experienced social injustice.

Perhaps First Lady Michelle Obama would do better in her efforts to create a healthier generation of kids if she stopped touting carrots and celery for school lunches and started attacking the nanny-state mentality. A game of tag would get kids into shape quicker than veggies at lunch, after all. But California's fixations with self-esteem and protecting the individual from criticism or hurt has led educators to conclude that tag and similar sorts of physical activity are exactly the wrong thing to expose children to.

Pat Samarage, the principal of Franklin Elementary School in Santa Monica, was the first educator on record to put fretting over the game of tag into action. She explained it, saying, "We had some children who were not playing 'it' appropriately. Little kids were coming in and saying, 'I don't like being 'it.' They weren't feeling good about it." So, rather than trusting the kids to work it out and learn something about striving to achieve and dealing with defeat in the process, the whining of a couple kids led Samarage to take tag away from all the students.[22] Many other tag bans followed, including ones in Attleboro, Massachusetts in 2006, and Colorado Springs in 2007. But once again California led the way.

Parenting also has become a no-contact sport, out of fear of harming the apparently very breakable members of American's biggest designated underclass, children. I recently heard a pastor tell his congregation about his daughter's experience as a nanny for a wealthy family in Santa Barbara. She was one of a nanny brigade, since the couple hired a separate nanny for each of their children in order to minimize the risk of conflict and judging. All the nannies were told that if a child was acting badly, she was only allowed to try to turn the child's attention to something else, but was never, ever to say "no" to the child or discipline the little monster.

This fixation on protection soon morphed into the elevation of the interests of special classes at the expense of individual freedoms for less popular groups. Leading this charge was state senator Sheila Kuehl, who played Zelda Gilroy in the early television sitcom "The Many Loves of Dobie Gillis," and went on to become the first openly gay person to be elected to the California Legislature. In 2006, as a Democratic state senator from Liberal West Los Angeles, she spearheaded an effort to rewrite the state's textbooks so they would include materials related to famous gays, for no other reason than that they were gay. Gays, she posited, need more self-esteem and certainly represent a special class deserving of special protection. Of course, the addition of new materials in textbooks necessitates the removal of old materials, but the old materials dealt too much with the white, straight privileged class. So, Kuehl's bill envisioned a California where kids might learn all about a marginally famous gay actor from the 1920s at the expense of, oh, Ronald Reagan, who, although once an actor, was not gay. Gov. Schwarzenegger, no girlie-man, signaled that he didn't like the bill, so it was amended to say school textbooks in California should not include material that is discriminatory towards gays. He then signed it.

The resulting bill dodged directly promoting a gay curriculum in schools by creating instead a "Safe Schools" curriculum that focused on bullying. Since gay students frequently are bullied, "Safe Schools" gave Kuehl exactly what she wanted in the first place, an excuse to teach a gay curriculum without involving parents in the process, or giving them the opportunity to "opt out" their children from the classes. Parental frustration over this flared up in 2009 in Alameda Unified School District, across the bay from San Francisco, when a new curriculum was proposed that would include a 45-minute LGBT session each year, from kindergarten through fifth grade. (Thanks to the success the gay movement has enjoyed in bringing its issues to the fore, you probably don't need to be told that LGBT stands for lesbian, gay, bisexual and transgender.)

Alameda Unified's teachers and administrators embraced the curricula - after all, Coming Out Week was already a staple in the area. Under the district's "Safe Schools" curricula, the sexual content of the Safe Schools curriculum would escalate each year until the fifth graders would be learning about sexual orientation and sexual stereotypes. Justifying the curricula, district superintendent Kirsten Vital said, "Students were feeling bullied. This work is in response to teachers asking for tools to combat name-calling and bullying at school."[23] Reportedly, some kindergarteners were calling each other "fag." It apparently never occurred to anyone at Alameda Unified that the kindergarteners likely had no idea what "fag" means.

When the matter came before the school board for consideration, 500 angry parents showed up at a five-hour public hearing. Certainly, there were voices in support of the curriculum, like Michele Neill, whose views, captured in a letter she sent to the Alameda Journal, were not dissimilar from what the school board heard from some during the public hearing:

> Come on [anti-curriculum spokespeople] Adam Wooten and Rev. Dion Evans of the Chosen Vessels Christian Church, admit it! You are homophobic, and you want to continue to be allowed to spread your vile ideas and brainwash your flock without the school board members pointing out to young people that you are not teaching Christ's views, but your own. ... Just admit it, you don't like us, you don't think we should have equal rights (i.e. marriage equality) and you don't want your children to learn to accept us.[24]

Voices like Neill's were outnumbered by parents who felt the teaching of sexuality, straight or gay, had no place in elementary school curricula. Others pointed out there are five categories of protected classes of which sexual orientation is but one, and asked why discrimination against other classes - like the religious - was not included in the courses.

After taking in the public testimony, the school board voted 3-2 to impose the curriculum, and the district's superintendent denied parents' requests to pull their children from the classes, leading 20 parents to file suit to earn the right to remove their children from the curriculum. The parents' attorney, Kevin Snider of the Pacific Justice Institute, filed a Public Records Act request for the school district's discipline records and found that in the previous 10 years, only 10 of the 171 cases of bullying and harassment at the district were due to sexual orientation, and none of those cases was at the elementary school level.[25] When the actual nature of bullying in the schools became public, the school district realized it would not be able to successfully defend the creation of an exclusively gay-oriented curriculum while ignoring the bullying targeted at kids because of their gender, race, physical appearance, religion, nationality or disability. So it dropped the curriculum. After the decision, the Pacific Justice Institute issued a statement saying, "We are remaining vigilant and will continue to keep an eye on the district."[26] Good call.

California Progressives are nothing if not dogged in their dedication to the cause. Following the successful legal challenges to Kuehl's "Safe Schools" approach, the man who assumed her mantle as the Legislature's premier gay rights crusader, Democratic San Francisco state Sen. Mark Leno, offered up a bill that would require school districts in the state to include the contributions of LGBT people in their social studies curricula. (At publication, Leno was running for Congress.) Gov. Schwarzenegger vetoed Leno's bill when it passed the Legislature during the governor's last term, but it was passed on a party line vote after Jerry Brown was ensconced in the governor's office. Brown hurried to sign it, saying at the signing ceremony, "History should be honest."

That statement has been picked apart by conservative pundits, who said an honest history was one based on a person's historical significance, not a person's acting out of non-traditional gender roles. Tchaikovsky, after all, is rightfully included in music history texts because of his music, not his preference for men as sexual partners. A proposed proposition to overturn Leno's bill floundered during signature-gathering, so employers now can be sure that when they hire a California high school grad, their new employee will be able to rattle off a list of LGBTs who helped to shape the world - even if they can't punctuate a sentence or run some percentages.

THE WORST OF THE WORST

The valedictorian of California's failure at running an education system is the Oakland Unified School District, which gained national prominence in 1996 when its board declared "Ebonics," black ghetto English, to be "genetically based," not an English dialect, and therefore just fine for use in its schools. With the pounding of a gavel, "Yo, I ain't got no hope, Homes" became just as good as, "I don't have a chance, Sir" in Oakland's schools. Oakland's Ebonics move-ment might have been a manifestation of black pride, or it might have just been a way to cover up the sad fact that Oakland's teachers were incapable of lifting most of the district's black students above "barely proficient" in the state's English competency exam.

The OUSD school board's attention should have been focused elsewhere, since when it passed the Ebonics resolution it was midway between its first incident with a state receiver, who was assigned in September 1989, and its full-blown bankruptcy and take-over by the state in 2003. In 1989, when the Legislature put the 48,000-student district under the control of a state auditor in return for approving a $100 million bond sale that was supposed to bail out the district, the Oakland Police Department had an 11-member squad assigned full-time to trying to get to the bottom of all the fraud, embezzlement, theft and other crimes being carried out by OUSD administrators.

After the first round of state oversight proved futile, the district filed for bankruptcy in June 2003 and was once again bailed out by the Legislature and taken over by the state. In the years that followed, progress toward normalcy has been slow. It took a full three years for the first of OUSD's operational functions to be deemed fit for return to local control after scoring seven on a 10-point scale - basically, the equivalent of a C. That function, community relations and govern-ance, has nothing to do with actually educating students, which OUSD still can't seem to do.

In 2010, OUSD emerged from state control - $89 million in debt and facing an $18 million budget gap for the 2010-2011 school year. Said school board member David Kakishiba of the district's emergence from state receivership, "On the one hand, the district is out of a crisis, near-bankruptcy environment. On another level, we're creeping back to a very dangerous financial situation. We are going to be right up against the edge of the cliff."[27]

The best that can be said of the state's fiscal oversight is that at least the district appears to know how deep in the red it is. When it went into receivership, estimates of its deficit ranged from $35 million to $100 million. No one could figure out its byzantine accounting system well enough to nail down an exact figure. Meanwhile, two years of negotiations with its teachers union left a deadlock on almost every major issue, with the parties unable to reach a settlement primarily because of OUSD's financial condition, which an independent fact-finder declared to be "woeful."[28]

With Los Angeles' school district struggling with 2010-2011 school year deficits of $640 million (up from $140 million just one year earlier), San Francisco's looking down a $113 million hole, San Diego's trying to fill a $48 million gap and districts from Dublin to Visalia in the red as property tax revenues plummet, one can only wonder how many more Oaklands are in store for California.

CHAPTER EIGHT:

ENVIRONMENTALISM: BEING - AND BURNING - GREEN

Even in the depths of the recession, California enthusiastically passes costly environmental regulations that choke economic recovery.

WHENEVER CALIFORNIA'S CHRONIC BUDGET shortfalls lead to the closure state parks, which has been a frequent threat in recent years, there's never any worry that the Hearst Castle on California's isolated Central Coast will fall victim to the cuts. After all, it's the rarest of state resources: It's popular and it makes money, with nearly 700,000 visitors a year paying up to $30 for a tour.

Media magnate William Randolph Hearst started the castle on the family's 250,000-acre ranch in 1919, when he told architect Julia Morgan, "Miss Morgan, we are tired of camping out in the open at the ranch in San Simeon and I would like to build a little something."[1] Build it they did - perched 1,600 feet above the Pacific midway between Los Angeles and

San Francisco, Hearst's "little something" grew to become a 90,080-square-foot retreat with 56 bedrooms, 61 bathrooms and 41 fireplaces, surrounded by 127 acres of gardens, pools and terraces.[2]

Magnificent and popular as it is, Hearst Castle probably couldn't be built under California's current hyper-green regulations. While it was a real job generator - more than 100 workers at any one time toiled on the site from 1919 to 1947 - they were accompanied by exhaust-belching machinery and greenhouse gas-farting draft animals. They moved millions of tons of dirt and poured at least as many tons of greenhouse gas-generating concrete for the building's reinforced concrete construction - quarrying rock near the site, and digging up sand from the beach. They planted 70,000 trees and uncounted flowers and shrubs not native to the chaparral-covered hills of the Santa Lucia Mountains. And all the comings and goings, all the hauling of loads up some five and a half miles from San Simeon Cove to the top of the hill, came via a road built across streambeds and through chaparral.

So as I toured the castle with my family, I couldn't help but ask the tour guide how many environmental permits Hearst needed before he could start work on the project. The tour guide conferred with another guide for a moment before delivering the answer: None.

Today, San Luis Obispo County would have to review and approve an environmental impact report covering everything from aesthetics to water supply, outlining hundreds of mandates Hearst would have to fund to offset or reduce the anticipated impacts of his project. The California Coastal Commission would have to approve an amendment to the county's Local Coastal Plan, along with an Implementing Agreement and a Coastal Development Permit. The commission would likely seek the death penalty for anyone mining sand from one of California's beaches and it frowns on big, showy homes in the Coastal Zone so Hearst might have had to scale back a bit, from 90,000 square feet to maybe 5,000 square feet. The Department of Fish and Game would make sure Hearst's "little something" didn't harm any endangered little something crawling or growing on the property. The Central Coast Regional Water Quality Control Board would scrupulously review the project's runoff, going into bureaucratic conniptions if a drop of muddy water flowed off the site. County and state fire officials would have to sign off on a fuel modification plan to protect the property from wildfires - fighting a battle of wills with Fish & Game and the Coastal Commission, which wouldn't want native habitat to be "modified" at all, even if it meant significantly greater fire risk.

Of course the California Air Resources Board would get into the mix, reviewing all the plans and demanding changes to reduce air pollution during and after construction - including making sure none of those 41 wood-burning fireplaces ever did anything so silly as actually burn wood. That's if the plan would be allowed to move forward at all, since under California's Sustainable Communities and Climate Protection Act, the climate crusaders at CARB would see the castle as smog-generating leapfrog development. They would encourage Hearst to move his castle to a loft near a bus stop in San Luis Obispo instead.

If construction ever did start, inspectors would cover the site, looking for the ounce of sediment in the stream, the non-regulation ladder or the crushed sprig of chaparral. Biologists with citation books would make sure no grading occurred for much of the year so nesting birds wouldn't be disturbed, and air quality experts with sensitive sensors would make sure no dust rose up as the earth was re-contoured. Representatives of local Native American tribes would monitor all grading, lest the tiniest Native American artifact be disturbed. Whenever some bit of broken bowl - or, heaven forbid, piece of human bone - was unearthed, all construction would grind to a halt until the tribes and a slew of archaeological peer reviewers opined on the artifact's significance. If it were deemed important enough, it might have to be left in place, and the project would have to be redesigned to accommodate it undisturbed.

Hearst would have had to hire dozens of consultants and attorneys to push the project through these obstacles, and each of the agencies would demand fees for filing and processing the plans, and would assess penalties for the least infraction. The penalities would fire up the attorneys and consultants once again to fight the fines. Going by current figures for the premium environmental regulation adds to construction costs in California, all this would have added 33 percent to the bottom line of the castle's construction cost, much to the consternation of a tough old capitalist like Hearst. But no such thing happened because the California Hearst knew was the old California, the California that actually worked, not the new Golden State tarnished green, with all its strangling environmental over-regulation.

IT'S NOT INEXPENSIVE BEING GREEN

In that new California, in cubicles at dozens of agencies, thousands of state functionaries routinely fill their staff reports with thin justifications for questionable environmental regulations and suspect proof that the regulations will be cost-effective. But they never can explain how it makes any sense at all for the state that is already the nation's greenest to continue spending ever more money to enact and enforce ever more costly environmental regulations in a declining economy.

The eco-crats continue to do just that in part because they are true believers and in part because the state Legislature has become very adept at not making any decisions that would actually cost anyone a job or force a business out of state. They leave such unpleasantness to willing and zealous technocrats at the state's environmental agencies and the unelected boards of directors of those agencies. The perfect example is AB 32, the California Global Warming Solutions Act of 2006. When signed into law with much fanfare by Gov. Schwarzenegger, the bill merely laid out broad directions, not specific actions. For example, it told CARB to "prepare a scoping plan for achieving the maximum technologically feasible and cost-effective reductions in greenhouse gas emissions ... by 2020." CARB decided one really good way to do that would be to autocratically impose on California the nation's first state-run cap-and-trade program, which imposes an energy tax on companies that produce greenhouse gases as a byproduct of their manufacturing processes. Another good way to act on that mandate, CARB determined, was to impose frightfully complex and costly regulations on business, some of which will be discussed in this chapter.

It all happened without one state senator or Assembly member actually having to vote "aye" on cap-and-trade, or CARB's initiative to force truckers to replace perfectly good engines with less reliable, more expensive ones, or the California Energy Commission's crusade against big-screen TVs. Votes like those could prove unpopular, causing campaign contributions to dry up and re-election bids to be lost. Fearing that, the Legislature has simply stopped casting such votes, because they've shifted responsibility and blame for costly consequences to the most powerful force in the state, California's technocratic regulatory agencies.

In her unsuccessful 2010 run for governor, Meg Whitman campaigned hard on regulatory reform, making the point that if California just moved up four notches in the rankings of the states that have the most onerous environmental regulations, it would add 500,000 jobs to the state's workforce, and significantly reduce the $13,000 the average Californian pays annually because of the state's penchant for over-regulation. Another study, prepared for the California Small Business Administration, put the total cost of regulation in California at just shy of $500 billion a year, or five times the state's general fund budget. That's almost a third of California's gross product and amounts to $134,122.48 for each small business in the state. The half-billion-dollar hit also translates to 3.8 million jobs lost, equal to one-tenth of the state's population.[3]

Should California's environmental regulatory agencies ever threaten the status quo by thinking sensibly about nursing an ailing economy back to health by rolling back environmental regulations, their colleagues in academia and the environmental movement (which in many ways are one and the same) stand ready to shore up their courage. Two such academics, Sean Hecht and Rhead Enion of UCLA, did just that as business groups were asking legislators to draft a fiscal 2011-12 state budget that provided relief from environmental over-regulation. "Brown must establish stable, robust funding for core environmental regulatory activities," they argued. "Environmental monitoring, permit-writing and enforcement are at risk, despite the clear successes from our state's four decades of environmental protection: cleaner air, water and energy."[4] Among their recommendations: Raising $1 billion from California's businesses through new regulatory fees and fines. Not mentioned were any of the dirtier tales of the economic and personal price paid for the state's quest to be the nation's greenest - tales so numerous I can share only a few here.

CALIFORNIA-CORRECT OIL

When Curtis Henderson's office phone in the City of Long Beach Gas & Oil Department rang recently, the caller had an unusual request: "Could you turn the waterfalls on early tonight? We're having a party." Henderson, the manager of the department, said he'd do what he could, then called Bill McFarlane at

Occidental Petroleum Corporation, which operates four man-made oil production islands just offshore of the Southern California city of 460,000. Sure enough, that evening when the caller, a resident of a high-rise condo overlooking Long Beach harbor, invited his guests to step out on the balcony and take in the view, the 45-foot-tall, pastel-lit waterfall on the nearest oil island was in full action.

Welcome to politically acceptable oil production in green-crazed California.

This story starts in the 1930s with the discovery of the Wilmington oil field, the nation's fifth largest. Oil wells promptly appeared like a swarm of mechanical locusts in Long Beach and other coastal L.A. communities to exploit the find. But as residents of Long Beach began having to deal with oil derricks in their neighborhoods, they turned against oil production, voting overwhelming in 1956 to deprive Long Beach of hundreds of millions of dollars in future oil revenues, so residents wouldn't have to be bothered with petroleum's unpleasantness.

Eventually the draw of all that money got the better of city leaders, and they came up with a proposal: Move the oil production out of the city proper and onto new man-made islands just offshore, and disguise the islands as artsy outcroppings, pleasing to the sensitivities of coastal Californians. That was something Long Beach voters could live with, and in 1962 they voted to let the city and its oil company partners haul in 640,000 tons of boulders and 3.2 million cubic yards of sand to create the islands, at a cost of $8 million. Then, in an expenditure totally in tune with coastal Californians' phobia of having any contact with things industrial, they spent almost twice that amount to landscape and camouflage the islands to hide what they'd done. Now the islands sport derricks disguised as condo towers, along with waterfalls, palm trees and abstract sculptures designed by a Disney artist and made from massive, arching slabs of colored concrete, all to shield residents from any noises or views that might hint that oil is actually being drilled in their city.

Such a plan wouldn't have a ghost of a chance of getting by California's regulators today (and it's certainly not how they do it in Texas!), but it's good for 11 million barrels of crude and 15 billion cubic feet of natural gas a year. The islands have been a windfall in a cash-starved state, generating more than $450 million annually for Long Beach and more than $4.25 billion for California with the recent surge in oil prices. Yet, when a proposal was floated in the 2009 state budget talks to reduce the state's budget deficit through the sale of some additional oil drilling rights off the Santa Barbara coast, the Legislature's Democrats showed their green colors and rallied and railed in opposition.

Santa Barbara Democrat Pedro Nava led the rhetorical charge, saying "Oil drilling off our coast would have minimal effect on supply, would have no effect on prices at the pump, but could have a potentially devastating effect on our environment and our economy. It is a risk that California is unwilling to take."[5] Many Californians were more than willing to take the risk, believing Nava lacked a fundamental understanding of supply and demand, but with strong support from the state's environmental lobby the off-shore drilling measure was defeated on a 43 to 28 party-line vote. Then, in an almost unprecedented act of cowardice, Democratic floor leader Alberto Torrico, whose Bay Area district is more than three hundreds miles away from the proposed leasing area, made a motion to expunge the vote from the public record, fearful it would anger voters concerned about rising gas prices and the state's ballooning budget crisis. The Democratic majority approved Torrico's subterfuge on a voice vote, so those who voted to deprive California of oil revenue successfully hid their vote from the budget-strapped folks back in their districts.

"George Orwell would be proud," said the lead supporter of expanding off-shore drilling to help balance the budget, then-GOP Assemblyman and failed 2010 senatorial candidate Chuck DeVore of Irvine - who recently gave up on California and moved to Texas.

Shipping Jobs Out of State

Just a couple miles north of the oil islands are the bustling ports of Long Beach and Los Angeles, the busiest in the nation. True to form, California isn't working to build on its ports' success; rather, it's making shippers and land transportation companies pay the high cost of being green, forcing uncompetitiveness onto otherwise well-managed operations. Decreasing competitiveness is making port administrators fearful that thousands of California jobs will disappear when an expansion program for the Panama Canal is completed in 2014. At that point, the canal will be big enough to handle huge trans-Pacific cargo ships, making it possible for them to bypass increasingly costly California ports and head directly to friendlier, less expensive Gulf Coast and East Coast ports. When that happens, the usual culprits will be there to blame: environmental radicals, their cohorts in the state's regulatory agencies, the unions and Californians' incessant compulsion to be a world leader in the environmental movement, no matter what the cost.

Environmental evangelism forced the Los Angeles and Long Beach ports to be the first in the nation to make environmental sensitivity a core operating principal, with their 1995 Green Ports initiative. The plan didn't grow from the ports' desire to strangle themselves, rather, it was driven by litigation filed by the Los Angeles Alliance for a New Economy. LAANE is a George Soros-funded environmental justice group that is a front for unions. Its board includes representatives from the Los Angeles County Federation of Labor, the California Teachers Association, the Service Employees International Union, the International Brotherhood of Electrical Workers, the International Brotherhood of Teamsters and Unite Here!, a union representing minority workers, legal and illegal. LAANE convinced primarily non-English-speaking minority residents near the ports that exhaust fumes from ships, trucks and trains were killing their babies (even though babies there were dying at the same rate as elsewhere in the region). As local politicians dutifully jumped on the bandwagon, port managers saw the writing on the wall and acquiesced, announcing the Green Ports initiative and promising air pollution from the ports would be cut an astounding 45 percent over five years.

The environmental initiatives that followed consume almost $71 million a year, 10 percent of the Port of Long Beach's budget, and a similar amount of its capital improvement budget. The Port of Los Angeles spends a proportional amount. The ports recover the green programs' exorbitant cost through higher fees to everyone who uses the ports, from Chinese shipping conglomerates to independent truckers. Ships are required to power down while in-port and plug into electrical power, a change that required $21 million in dock improvements at the Port of Los Angeles alone. The cost was passed on to shipping companies, who are also billed for the high-cost California electricity their ships use while tethered to the docks.

Operators of the 10,000 or more trucks that serve the ports have been required to sell perfectly functional trucks and replace them with new, cleaner-burning models that cost as much as $200,000 each to buy - a $2 billion environmental mandate. Plus, the trucks cost about 50 percent more to operate than older models and are not expected to last as long, according to drivers. Those costs get added to the bills paid by companies receiving goods from the port, and are passed on to consumers. California is currently the only state with such requirements. It's not surprising, then, that the ports of Southern California's share of Asian shipments to the United States have fallen from 85 percent in 2000 to about 55 percent now.[6]

The Southern California ports are no longer pushing back against the regulatory onslaught, even though they are rightfully scared ship-less of the consequences of a larger Panama Canal that is capable of handling the ships L.A. and Long Beach are unloading today for continental cross-shipment. Instead of knocking their heads into the green wall of California environmentalism, they want the federal government to force ports in other states to adopt the very programs that made them uncompetitive. And the anti-port activists at LAANE - which no longer says what the "LA" in its name stands for - are pushing their agenda forward in Oakland, New York, New Jersey, Seattle and Florida. California's ports may shrink, but the state ultimately may succeed in shipping record amounts of costly environmental regulations to ports throughout America.

REGULATED TO DEATH

As described in Chapter Six, *Business: Roll Up the Red Carpet and Call the Moving Van*, much of California's current heavy-handed environmental regulation stems from AB 32. At the forefront of its implementation is a gargantuan agency that consumes $650 million annually, the California Air Resources Board. (It tries stubbornly to use "ARB" as its acronym, but most call it "CARB," like the carbon it hunts down with a dedication reminiscent of Simon Wiesenthal tracking Nazis.) The agency's war on carbon led to a frequently reported story that CARB bureaucrats tried to ban black cars from the state, in the name of fighting global warming. Google "CARB black car ban" and you'll find numerous articles on the subject - all sufficiently outraged that government could take away the second most popular car color with nothing more than a wave of the regulatory wand. But these articles aren't accurate. In fact, CARB merely tried to force auto manufacturers, against their will and better sense, to use paint that would reflect sunlight to keep the car's interior cooler, to reduce the amount of energy burned by automotive air conditioning. The effort stopped when it became apparent current paint technology wasn't up to the job. It would have led to no black cars in California not because black was banned, but because the closest the paint companies could come to black with their reflective paint formulas was an appropriately earthy shade of muddy brown. CARB dropped the idea, but the black car ban went on to become a California urban myth - a myth with a high degree of believability because CARB routinely suggests and imposes outrageous new regulations.

Just a few months after the black paint debacle, CARB announced its next scheme - forcing Californians to buy cars that have a metallic window glazing on all glass surfaces, low-drag tires on their wheels and low-viscosity oil in their engines. The regulators had found that a reflective glass did in fact exist, even if a suitable reflective paint did not, so they could continue to mandate automobiles only an eco-freak could love. The climate-crusading regulators liked the window tint for the same reason they liked reflective paint - cooler cars, less air conditioning - and low-drag tires and low viscosity oil were a hit with them because both improve gas mileage ever so slightly. They estimate requiring these changes will add a mere $1,500 to the price of a new car. But regulatory agencies are famously adept at under-estimating the cost of their regulations.

All those mandates are fine if your only concerns

in automotive design are carbon reduction and planet salvation, and you're not particularly worried about saving the carbon life forms that occupy the vehicles. Reflective glass is heavier than regular glass, so cars meeting the new regulations would be more top-heavy and more prone to roll-overs - and that extra weight would reduce fuel efficiency. Low-drag tires may make up for the loss in mileage caused by heavy reflective glass, but they do not perform as well as wider, stickier tires. All this was confirmed recently when the instructor at my daughter's teen defensive driving class said the Toyota Prius, with its eco-friendly skinny tires and considerable weight, is the worst-handling car the school's instructors have experienced. It handles so badly, the instructor said, that the school recommends parents do not allow their teen drivers to drive it.

With mandates like these, whether they realize it or not, the bureaucrats have put CARB into the auto accident fatality business. And if a car owner thinks he'll just strip those skinny tires off his new car and replace them with a meatier set, consider Assembly Bill 844, one of the last new laws signed by Gov. Gray Davis before his recall. The bill requires "that replacement tires sold in the state be at least as energy efficient, on average, as the tires sold in the state as original equipment on these vehicles."[7]

As for that low-viscosity oil, it doesn't hold up as well at high temperatures, so engines won't last as long on it as they will on higher viscosity oils. That means the California car of the future will not only be less safe, it will wear out sooner, with profound carbon footprint consequences CARB is choosing to ignore.

In their drive to justify their jobs and save the planet, CARB overlooked another drawback of reflective glass - it jams, distorts and otherwise befuddles all manner of in-car electronics, including GPS devices, cell phones, satellite radio systems and garage-door openers.[8]   Convicted criminals may like it, though, since the glass also blocks signals from the ankle bracelets worn by paroled armed robbers and sex offenders. A garage door that won't open on a stormy night or a convicted pedophile driving full-bore towards the nearest elementary school - who cares? Certainly not CARB.

PLANET-SAVING FICTIONS

CARB is also leading the way on tough regulations on diesel emissions under its proposed truck and bus regulations, an effort masterminded by one of the agency's top researchers and statisticians, Hein Tran. He posited that emissions from diesel-powered off-road equipment cause 18,000 premature deaths a year in the state. That led to proposed new regulations for all heavy diesel trucks, buses and off-road equipment in the state, which force them to be the same sort of clean - but costly - trucks required by the Los Angeles ports. CARB's statisticians claimed the move will save 9,400 lives annually and reduce health care costs by $68 billion.

The regulation was fought by operators of diesel-powered equipment, who are concerned about the $12 billion it would cost trucking and grading companies already battered by the recession to switch over to CARB-approved engines. The California Dump Truck

Owners Association (CDTOA) was one of many industry associations that tried to work with CARB on the regulation but gave up, claiming "a lack of cooperation and empathy" which led them ultimately to sue to stop the regulation, claiming it would bring an end to their entire industry. "Because the rule requires replacement of otherwise perfectly useful trucks much earlier than would otherwise be required, most CDTOA members will be unable to continue their business," the lawsuit claims. "Not only will CDTOA members be prohibited from purchasing replacement trucks due to a lack of financial resources, they will be prohibited from earning any income at all because the rule prohibits them from operating their current trucks." Plus, like the Green Port trucks, trucks and grading equipment with CARB-approved engines are less efficient, are more prone to break-downs and will not last as long as current engines. Since the out-of-state market for perfectly good but non-CARB-compliant trucks will be swamped, many operators likely won't be able to sell their trucks for enough to cover the loans they took out to buy them. (Out-of-state truckers must meet CARB standards if they enter the state, so many wouldn't be interested in purchasing non-compliant trucks.)

Industry arguments against the truck and bus regulations were bolstered when the conclusions of CARB statistician Tran were challenged by Dr. James Enstrom, an epidemiologist and UCLA faculty member for more than 30 years. In the course of his analysis, Enstrom questioned Tran's methodology, conclusions and credentials, a challenge that was repeated by Dr. S. Stanley Young of the National Institute of Statistical

Sciences. As the regulation marched toward finalization, Young complained in a letter to Gov. Schwarzenegger that CARB's study was "too flawed to be done by a capable statistician," and charged that the study's authors were not statisticians. That led Tran to respond - on state letterhead - that his team was up to the job and he was, in fact, not just a statistician, but a U.C. Davis-educated Ph.D. statistician.

Tran's ruse crumbled one day before CARB was scheduled to vote on the rule, when it was disclosed that his Ph.D. was from Thornhill University, whose campus is located in a UPS store post office box in New York City, and that Tran had fabricated his resume with the nonexistent University of California doctorate. Unflustered by the revelation, CARB dismissed any concerns that so impactful a regulation could be so suspect. CARB chair Mary Nichols called Tran's deceit "an annoying distraction" and its executive officer, James Goldstene, convinced the board to approve the regulations anyway, saying, "What Tran did was bad, but the science was sound."[9] Unknown to the Board, Nichols and Goldstene, among other top officials at the agency, had worked hard to cover up Tran's lie as the hearing approached, as laid out in a scathing letter by CARB board member John Telles, which said in part:

> On December 8, 2008, the Chief of the Research Division asked [Tran] if he had a Ph.D. in Statistics from UC Davis. ... [Tran] on the evening of December 10, 2008, confessed to the Chief of the Research Division that he did not have such a credential. The following morning, the day [CARB] had convened to deliberate on the Truck

Rule, this chief informed the Executive Officer, the Chief Deputy Executive Officer, the Deputy Executive Officer, the Chief of the Heavy Duty Diesel In-Use Strategies, the Chief of the Mobil [sic] Source Control Division, the Chief of the Health and Exposure Assessment Branch [What a fantastic illustration of "too many chiefs!"] and at least one Board Member of [Tran's] confession. ... This information was not, however, relayed to the full Board. ...

Last week, on November 11, 2009 [nearly one year later], I learned that the Chair of CARB [Mary Nichols] was also aware of this information prior to the Vote .... Thus, neither the Staff nor the Board Chair informed the full board of this discovery prior the Vote. The Public, of course, was also not informed.[10]

Thanks to this subterfuge, the rule was passed, although its implementation has been delayed because an analysis found Tran's crackerjack statistical analysis had overestimated pollution from diesel equipment by 340 percent and overstated the number of projected diesel-caused premature deaths by 8,800 annually (about half the original projection of 18,000). Tran was suspended for 60 days and demoted, but still works at CARB. Dr. Enstrom, on the other hand, was fired by UCLA because his faculty colleagues charged that his research "is not aligned" with the academic mission of the department. He continues to teach while appealing the action. California's attorney general, Kamala Harris, a Democrat from San Francisco and supporter of CARB, has refused to investigate Tran's fraud and the ensuing cover-up.

Shortly after this embarrassment, CARB followed up with another, when it brassily proposed to require that no one submitting information to the agency could knowingly and willingly "falsify, conceal or cover up by any trick, scheme, or devise a material fact." The draft rule was met with howls of protest and the resurrection of the entire Tran controversy, creating a storm of embarrassing media coverage (except in the deep green Los Angeles Times, which has ignored the Tran scandal in its entirety). Asked if the regulations might also call into question other scientific studies prepared by the air board staff, CARB chair and Tran co-conspirator Nichols told the San Francisco Chronicle, "No, no, no, no, no, no, no and no." That may be easy for her to say, but evidence points to the real answer: CARB can't be trusted to follow its own proposed regulation - or issue new ones - because its staff has been caught red-handed presenting data that is false, false, false, false, false, false, false and false.

CARBON TITHES

Still, Nichols, like the broken clock that has the right time twice a day, sometimes gets things right. She did that in 2011 when she said of proposed cap-and-trade rules that would tax carbon expellers in order to reduce greenhouse gas emissions, "I had my doubts. It is a form of California [green] leadership that involves some risk."[11] Those words didn't stop her, however, from joining the rest of the CARB board to impose the nation's first state-run cap-and-trade program.

California's cap-and-trade program, which imposes iron-fisted emission restrictions on 85 percent of California's economy, should go into effect in 2013, missing its target start-up by a year due to a lawsuit challenging the proposed rules. No, it wasn't truckers, manufacturers or electrical utilities that filed the litigation; it was a gaggle of environmental justice groups that sued because the initial rules weren't devastating enough to satisfy them. Among the arguments these groups made was that the regulations mandated the minimum amount of reductions required to roll back California's greenhouse gas emissions to 1990 levels, not the maximum. Of course the maximum reductions can only be met by shuttering factories and putting trucks up on blocks.

When CARB moved ahead with cap and trade, David Hochschild, the vice president of a government-subsidized solar energy company with operations in California, praised the move and made it quite clear why the green job sector wanted it so badly. "Cap and trade levels the playing field," he said. In other words, it drives up the cost of conventional energy and technology that's cheap and efficient in order to subsidize energy and technology that's too expensive to compete in the free market, all at taxpayer expense. And it's not just the field-leveling fees that will drive up the costs of conventional energy. I recently sat through a PowerPoint presentation by a Pacific Gas & Electric executive who presented a series of numbingly complex slides showing all the steps involved in documenting, reporting and verifying the mechanics of California's carbon tithe. As she went on and on ... and on ... about how her utility would work to meet the new reporting requirements imposed on it, it became increasingly evident that a lot of new staff and new equipment would be required. An interesting exchange followed her presentation.

"How much will PG&E have to pay to comply with these regulations?" the moderator asked.

"That is a very difficult number to calculate. There are a lot of variables," she demurred.

"Well, then, how will it affect your profitability?"

"It won't," she said. When she heard the noticeable buzz coming from a rather incredulous audience, she added, "It will be a consumer impact." In other words, the costs will be passed through to the ratepayers dollar-for-dollar, another reason why AB 32 and cap-and-trade are expected to add between $20 billion and $40 billion to the cost of power and gasoline in California over the next eight years.

Despite all this, California's Progressives are wildly enthusiastic about the program. Brian Leubitz, publisher of the leading California Progressive blog, Calitics, greeted cap and trade by brushing away any nagging fears of negative economic side effects:

> In Washington, Congress is twiddling its thumbs as they debate what science stopped debating years ago. Rather than aggresively [sic] taking on the environmental challenges of our lifetime and building a new sustainable economy, we are pretending the problems don't exist. Sure, we apparently care about the budget deficit that we are handing future generations, but a livable planet is apparently a luxury that we don't care to pass on.

But California, as they say, is different. We passed AB32, with a Republican Governor, yet. And today, we have a real system to put in place.[12]

Others saw another subsidy in the regulations - a big subsidy to Democrats who don't want to cut back on state spending. Warren Duffy, longtime Southern California talk radio host, does more than "apparently care" about the state's budget deficit. He is now running the anti-cap-and-trade group CFACT SoCal, and upon passage of cap and trade wrote:

When all of this money starts pouring into Sacramento, what's the state going to do with it? This scheme is a multi-billion-dollar windfall for our state government. I mean, nobody knows for sure how much money the state government is going to grab from this scheme, but I can tell you, it's going to be a ton of money. And officials at the California Air Resources Board have refused to say how they're going to spend all that money.[13]

Governor Brown hasn't refused to say how he'd spend the money, though. He has said he will use it to fund another unpopular environmentalist fantasy: California's proposed high-speed rail system. (See "High Speed Fail" in Chapter Five.)

PLASMA WARS

The California Energy Commission (CEC), yet another regulatory creation of Jerry Brown during his first round as governor, has grown just as notorious as CARB, thanks to its campaign against big-screen televisions. Until recently, Californians who wanted to watch a big flat-screen TV that uses more electricity than the dinky, boxy television their less-cool neighbors squint at could simply accept a higher electric bill and enjoy the bigger picture. Not surprisingly, that freedom has come to an end in California as eco-regulators have used global warming as a justification for stripping Californians of their right to watch the TV of their choice.

The move by the CEC to save the planet from the ravages of big-screen gluttony mandated that televisions sold in the state in 2011 must use 33 percent less electricity than those in use when the regulation was approved by the CEC in 2009, and 49 percent less electricity by 2013. The result is a practical ban of about one quarter of LCD and plasma televisions that found interested buyers in California in 2009.

After wending its way through the drafting and public hearing process for over a year, the matter came before the CEC on November 18, 2009. Of course, the commission heard testimony from environmentalists who praised the move but urged even greater cuts. But they got quite an earful from those who would be impacted by the proposal - television manufacturers and retailers, industry groups, and most poignantly, the owners of small businesses that install home theater systems with large-screen televisions.

Television manufacturers explained how the CEC was ignoring a record of free-market achievement in the reduction of electrical consumption by television sets. New LCD televisions, they said, are as much as

70 percent more energy efficient than the models that were sold just a few years earlier.[14]   Retailers and home theater installers argued that the ban would bring with it a significant economic cost - 4,600 jobs tied to TV sales, distribution and installation, and $50 million in lost sales tax revenues, according to consumer electronics industry advocates.[15]   Gerry Demple, vice president of a Santa Clarita supplier to home theater installers, described how the ban would affect his business:

> *The CEC's regulation is expected to cause my business to lose between $25 million and $30 million within the first few years of implementation. This will force us to consider business reduction strategies including site reduction and layoffs. We believe this regulation will put undue pressure on small retailers and servicers and companies who support them like [ours], where the loss of a few more sales or fewer service calls will push us over the edge - especially in today's challenging economic climate.*[16]

The CEC paid no attention to the opposition testimony and voted 5-0 to impose the ban, which took effect in January 2011.   Commission chair Karen Douglas said after the vote, "The real winners of these new TV energy efficiencies are California consumers who will be saving billions of dollars and conserving energy while preserving their choice to buy any size or type of TV."[17]   Sound bite aside, in fact Douglas and her colleagues had destroyed TV choice in California, stripping from the shelves hundreds of television models that had found marketplace acceptance prior to the ban. Douglas' ability to misrepresent the board's action might be explained by the fact that she fills the CEC seat reserved for an attorney, or, more specifically, a deep-green attorney. Prior to her appointment, she was director of the California Climate Initiative at the Environmental Defense Fund and general counsel of the leftist environmental group, the Planning and Conservation League. She is not a hold-over appointment of Democrat Gray Davis; she was appointed to the commission by Schwarzenegger.

In fact, Schwarzenegger appointed four of the five commissioners who voted for the ban, with Douglas joined by James Boyd, who previously served for 15 years on the CARB board; Jeffery Byron, a Silicon Valley energy efficiency consultant, and Julia Levin, who previously headed up Audubon's anti-global warming initiatives and even fought wind power - something the CEC broadly supports - at the American Wind & Wildlife Institute. Arthur Rosenfeld, a Berkeley physicist, was the only commissioner voting for the ban who was appointed by Grey Davis, not Schwarzenegger (although Arnold re-appointed Rosenfeld in 2005). Not a single representative of companies that make energy-using products or industries that use energy in their processes is on the panel. So it is little wonder that the commission didn't listen to arguments from businesses, and voted unanimously to set California farther down its course toward becoming the Don Quixote of environmentalism.

While the proposed ban rolled through the regulatory process, employees at CEC did their best to misrepresent its effects on the public's future ability to purchase the television of their choice, using a communications technique that is known to professionals as "lying." Here is how CEC addressed the proposed ban on an agency website FAQ:

> *Q: Is California considering banning plasma, large screen or HD televisions?*
>
> *A: No, the state is not banning any type of TV. Consumers have the freedom to choose any type and size of television that meets the efficiency standard.* [18]

Never mind that TVs that fry one electron more than the efficiency standard allows would be, you know, banned. If a private-sector company attempted to excuse its actions with language as transparently false, there would be justifiable howls of protest, but this language remained on the CEC's website without an edit throughout the many months the regulation was being considered. The website also explained that 850 models of televisions met the 2011 standard, but failed to mention that California consumers had about 1,200 models to choose from in 2010. So right out of the gate, 350 TV models that previously found willing buyers in California became unsellable. Next, the website said 231 current models meet the 2013 standard, without mentioning that nearly 1,000 currently available televisions would be summarily put off limits to California consumers when the next phase of the regulation goes into effect.

"Today's decision is little more than a stimulus

package for neighboring states," said San Diego home theater company owner Shawn Worst after the vote. "These regulations will effectively remove hundreds of big screen television models from California store shelves - leaving consumers with higher prices and fewer choices and forcing many to shop across state lines. Many local retailers, installers and distributors are already hanging onto their businesses by a thread. This decision makes clear just how tone deaf the state is to the economic woes of its small businesses."[19]

Seven months after the big TVs were supposedly regulated out of existence in California, I called Worst to check out whether his dire predictions had come true. He said the regulations haven't had as bad an effect as he thought they would because the free market trumped the regulators. Manufacturers quickly introduced the more energy-efficient big-screen TVs that were already in their pipeline. "But now the CEC is poised to regulate a lot more," Worst said. "They can't just say they did what they set out to do and back off. They feel they're not doing their job unless they're adding even more to the list of regulations that hurt small business people like me."

I also drove over to the showroom of one of South Orange County's most successful home theater installers, which had fared worse than Worst's business. The showroom, filled until recently with displays of enticingly gargantuan screens with booming sound systems and comfortable theater chairs, was gone, replaced by a Fisker Automotive dealership. Unlike the home theater business, which was on the losing end of regulatory fickleness, Fisker received $529 million in federal loan guarantees to build its plug-in hybrid sports car - in Finland.[20] Buyers of the car are eligible for a $7,500 credit from the feds and another $5,000 credit from California. The state incentive makes about as much sense as the CEC's crusade against home theater-sized televisions. It's designed to motivate Californians to buy a car that will lead to the state running out of electricity much more quickly than it would if the sale of inefficient big screen televisions had been subsidized instead of banned.

That's the conclusion of a recent analysis by the Department of Energy on the increased electrical demand imposed by plug-in hybrid electric vehicles (PHEVs) like those sold by Fisker. The study found that by 2030 California's total electrical generating capacity "may be insufficient to cover summer demand ... which is expected to soar by almost 95 [gigawatts] due to the PHEVs."[21] So, the question must be asked: Was California's war on big-screen TVs unwittingly outflanked by its war on the internal combustion engine?

POWERING DOWN THE PEOPLE

The dire Department of Energy prediction is actually rosy because it likely overestimated the amount of new electrical generation that will come online by 2030. After all, California is exceptionally good at being mindlessly, dangerously, expensively green. Environmental groups that argue for the absolute necessity to switch to subsidized green power use the California Environmental Quality Act (CEQA), their legions of lawyers and grassroots organizing to fight wind farms because wind generators kill birds, attack desert solar energy farms because they make tortoises unhappy and litigate to delay the power lines that would carry energy from these remote energy farms to cities because they promote growth.

Government itself also gets in the way even as it promotes alternative power, as evidenced by Los Angeles' $10,000 permitting fee for home wind generators. Even more threatening to the fulfillment of California's renewable energy dreams are its unions, which are adept at greenmailing companies proposing to build alternative-energy facilities. As soon as a company announces plans for an alternative energy plant, it's visited by union representatives who ask the companies to commit to using union labor for the construction and operation of the plants. If they don't, the union representatives make clear, their lawyers will make their approval processes a hellish ordeal, filing challenges and litigation at every step of California's already complex, costly and time-consuming environmental review process.

Companies that ignored the threat have experienced union wrath - like FPL Group, which was hit with 144 data requests from California Unions for Reliable Energy (CURE), over its planned 250-megawatt desert solar farm. Another solar company trying to avoid unionization, Stirling Energy Systems, must be doing something right because it received just 143 data requests from CURE for its desert solar farm. Meanwhile, the union group testified glowingly in favor of BrightSource Energy's very similar solar plant proposal - which will be built with union labor.[22]

CURE's chairman, Bob Balgenorth, sees all this as a noble venture, not blatant greenmailing:

> *[N]o one is more interested in creating jobs for Californians than I am. But I'm not interested in creating just any jobs. I want the kind of safe, sustainable and skilled jobs that will support workers and their communities over the long-term [sic], and that are critical to the State's future. ...*

> *This is environmental democracy, giving those affected by development a voice in its design, and it is exactly what the authors of CEQA intended to guarantee. ...* [23]

Even in progressive California, it's unlikely the authors of CEQA thought greenmailing solar energy companies into unionizing their facilities was exactly the sort of thing they wanted to see happen under the law.

Despite the mess California is making of its energy future, its programs have big fans, including one who sits in an oval office 3,000 miles away. In October 2009, President Obama signed an executive order mandating that the federal government begin reducing its greenhouse gas output, much like AB 32 is forcing California to do, with a series of likely unachievable and certainly expensive goals. At least a dozen states are taking a similar path. So thanks to California, citizens across the country may soon watch enviously from their tiny CARB-designed eco-car, devoid of crumple zones, prone to roll-overs, and painted a dazzling shade of pond scum green, as the president's motorcade passes - a fleet of heat-sucking, gas-guzzling, greenhouse gas-spewing black Secret Service SUVs flanking the President's behemoth Cadillac One limousine.

THE NANOMANAGERS OF THE COAST

In San Clemente, just a few miles from President Nixon's Western White House, the work of California's greenest environmental agency - greener by far than either CARB or the CEC - was on display where once a humble asphalt sidewalk ran alongside the town's coastal bluffs. Over the years, a portion of the beachside sidewalk had been covered by a veneer of mud eroded off the bluffs, and a couple hardy plants, saltgrass and pickleweed, had taken root. Wanting to clean up the mess, the city's public works department filed a Coastal Development Permit application with the California Coastal Commission - and $200,000 or so later, the problem with the mud and weeds was resolved in true Coastal Commission fashion.

The 12 appointed coastal commissioners reviewed a 22-page report on the matter - virtually tweet-length, compared to most Coastal Commission reports, which often stretch to hundreds of pages - and saw their staff's conclusion that the presence of saltgrass and pickleweed made the project area "a wetland area overlying a partially buried pre-existing asphalt side-walk ... that ... however degraded, still meets the commission's definition of a wetland." The agency's wetland definition is the greenest in the land: If any one of the three generally accepted wetland parameters - vegetation type, soil type and hydrology - is present, it's a wetland. Just about every other regulatory agency in the nation, even in California, requires all three indicators to be present.

The Coastal Commission doesn't allow wetlands to be destroyed, so San Clemente's plan was summarily rejected. Instead, the city had to leave the sidewalk intact and build a wood-and-steel footbridge that arches over it, complete with full-color interpretive signs and a transparent bottom so sunlight can reach the saltgrass and pickleweed. Getting through the Coastal process required the city to use lawyers and a wetland biologist who argued gamely that an asphalt sidewalk shouldn't be confused with a wetland. After their arguments failed to make the commission embrace logic, the city had to pay for the design, engineering and construction of the bridge and the accompanying interpretive signage. Altogether, trying to get some mud off a sidewalk cost the city about $200,000 - an amount that could have been used to make up almost one-quarter of the drop in general-fund revenues San Clemente had experienced in the preceding year.

The San Clemente wetland designation followed in the tradition of a successful effort a few years earlier to have a gravel parking lot in Huntington Beach declared a wetland. That decision in turn vindicated the commission's staff, which had failed in an earlier effort to get a Los Angeles shopping center's asphalt parking lot declared an Environmentally Sensitive Habitat Area. Such is the regulatory climate in the area the Coastal Commission reigns over. From Border Fields State Park just north of Tijuana to the secluded Pelican State Beach hugging the Oregon border, the commission controls whatever happens on 1,100 miles of beaches, rocky crags and fog-swept coastal mountains - as well as all the homes, businesses, sidewalks, power plants, roads and whatever else happens to lie within the 1.5 million-acre Coastal Zone. Authorized to protect coastal resources and assure public access, it uses environmental protection as a reason to challenge property rights and micromanage everything that happens along California's shore. In fact, "micromanaging" understates the Coastal Commission's power and authority; "nanomanaging" would be the better word, as San Clemente found out.

George and Sharlee McNamee of Corona del Mar found out about nanomanaging as well, as the commission forced them to remove lawn furniture from their private property because it created "a perception of privatization." Sharlee, who has a complete set of Ayn Rand first editions in the couple's bedroom, refers to the commission as nihilists.

Dennis Schneider discovered it when the commission decided his proposed 10,000-square-foot home in Cayucos would be an affront to kayakers, and told him to limit the house to 5,000 square feet - and move it inland, away from the breathtaking ocean view.

Dan and Denise Sterling felt it when the commission told them they could build a home on their 143 coastal acres, but only if they started farming all the land except for a 10,000-square-foot building site for their home. The land had never been farmed before.

The U.S. government experienced it when the commission nixed a water pipeline to the Space Launch Center at Vandenberg Air Force Base - and in the process forced the mightiest military the world has ever seen to open several miles of beach to the public and not fire missiles when seals are birthing new seal pups.

And the residents of the North Coast hamlet of Gualala experienced nanomanagement when the commission defined "development" - any sort of which it has the power to regulate - to include shooting off some fireworks, thereby taking control of the town's Fourth of July celebration. This campaign by the San Francisco-based commission against a red-blooded American holiday was so emblematic of over-regulation in California I decided to visit with the leaders of the Gualala Festivals Committee, the targets of the commission's attack. Shortly after I arrived in town, one of the committee members, Marshall Sayegh, spotted me and stopped his vintage first-generation Toyota Prius in the middle of Pacific Coast Highway, rolled down the window and shouted out my name. I walked over and, standing in the road, had a nice chat with the Internet entrepreneur and property-rights patriot. After a few minutes, even though no cars had passed by, he acknowledged that it was an odd place to be chatting and pulled over to the side of the road. I was relieved, since in my home of Orange County, I would have been lucky to survive for three seconds in the middle of Pacific Coast Highway before being run over in quick sequence by a tanned Viagra-hound in a Lamborghini, a Toyota pickup full of landscapers without green cards and a 17-year-old beach girl in a new BMW 3-series convertible.

Life in Gualala, population 2,000, a picturesque wide spot in the road along the Mendocino County coast 50 miles north of San Francisco, definitely moves at a relaxed pace most of the time. The fireworks controversy, though, had made emotions there every bit as intense as the latest episode of "The Real Housewives of Orange County," as the town's abundant left-wingers took on the members of the town's much smaller conservative community.

"All we want to do is have a fireworks show, honor America, celebrate freedom, and bring some visitors to town who will spend money at our businesses," Sayegh told me over dinner in one of the town's handful of restaurants. "The Coastal Commission wants to stop all that, presumably because the fireworks disturb some birds that aren't even endangered. But it's really a fight for our rights against an unaccountable and out of control state agency - and that's a fight we're eager to take on."

A year and a half later, he would email me, "I am moving from California - the Coastal Commission and other things about California are too much!" So it goes when mere citizens take on the Star Chamber of the Coast.

Fourth of July fireworks shows occur in coastal towns along the length of the California coast, with many of the displays exploding over wildlife refuges and preserves, such as the show in Monterey, which takes place near the Monterey Bay Marine Sanctuary. But the commission's longtime (and recently deceased) executive director Peter Douglas was no fan of these patriotic celebrations over his coastline. He and his staff set their sights on Gualala after failing a protracted court battle to stop nightly fireworks shows in San Diego's Sea World. On July 4, 2008, Gualala's dark skies, devoid of the rocket's red glare and bombs bursting in air, showed that the commission had prevailed at depriving people of their pursuit of patriotic happiness.

The Festivals Committee created the fireworks show in 2006 to attract more summertime visitors to the remote town, which sits on the low bluffs between the Gualala Lagoon and the redwood-covered coastal hills above. Pacific Coast Highway runs through the town and a smattering of woodsy motels, restaurants, boutiques and sports equipment rentals vie for the trickle of passing tourists. The Festivals Committee thought fireworks could be great for business, and the 2006 and 2007 shows were just that, attracting thousands of money-spending visitors to the town. That was hardly good news to local no-growthers, who didn't own businesses in the town and didn't appreciate the crowds of visitors. This coalition of the unwilling had clashed with the Festivals Committee once before, when the committee hoisted up a 40-foot-tall community Christmas tree and, lacking a star to put on top, put on an American flag. The next Wednesday, the local newspaper published a series of letters demanding that "Bush's flag," "the symbol of death" and "the Republican flag" be removed from the tree.

Imagine what these letter-writers felt about a patriotic fireworks show. Wanting a bully on their side, they called in the Coastal Commission, and the 2007 show became an opportunity to document the fireworks' supposed impacts on some birds nesting on a rock over a mile south of the fireworks site. On the days before and after the 2007 display, federal agents from the Bureau of Land Management (BLM) crawled around the rocky shoreline south of Gualala, shoving infrared and digiscoped cameras into the birds' nests to document the number of eggs and nestlings. They hovered over the seabirds' nests in helicopters, rotors roaring and engines spewing exhaust fumes into the pristine coastal air, so they could shoot photographs to document the supposed devastation caused by a 15-minute fireworks show. If they were cognizant of their own activities' impact on the birds, they didn't let anyone know, reporting instead only what they witnessed as the fireworks lit the summer sky:

> *Brandt's Cormorants quickly changed from resting to erect postures at the first fireworks, followed by birds moving about or departing the island. Western Gulls also flushed, circled and called during the fireworks display.*[24]

The BLM report said of 90 cormorant nests, seven were abandoned between July 5 and 7, with some additional abandonments following, all "likely" resulting from "fireworks disturbances." The biologists don't explain how they determined fireworks were the cause, or how they were able to discount the impact on nesting of their own intrusive actions. Biologists familiar with the species say that the number of nests abandoned is not unusually high for early July;[25] and besides, neither Brandt's cormorants nor western gulls are listed under the state or federal endangered species acts, so the commission has no authority to protect them from harm.

Nevertheless, with the BLM report in hand, Douglas and his staff were ready to pounce on the Festivals Committee. The fate of the show was debated in nearby Santa Rosa on June 13, three weeks before the scheduled show, when the Commission considered a cease-and-desist order against the Festivals Committee, should it "undertake or threaten to undertake development" without a coastal development permit. "Development" may seem to be a strange way to refer to something as fleeting as a fireworks show, but not in California - or at least not along its coast, where the Coastal Act defines development very broadly, as "the placement or movement of any solid material, discharge of any material, or change in density or intensity of land or water use."[26]

The staff report delineated the many reasons why the fireworks show should be regulated, including that "the launching of fireworks will temporarily disrupt public access to and along the Gualala Bluff Trail prior to and during the fireworks display by closing a portion of the Gualala Bluff Trail to the public." Not said was that the trail would only be closed during the show - at night, when it's not really safe to walk on a trail that hugs the edge of 50-foot-high coastal bluffs. But the crux of the staff's argument against the show was the 47-page report from the BLM. Using the report, staff argued:

> As discussed more fully herein, a similar fireworks display occurred in approximately the same location last year and had a demonstrated adverse effect on the nesting birds, including **most likely** causing actual nest abandonment and consumption of abandoned eggs and/or juvenile chicks by predators, a permanent impact. ... [Emphasis added]

The hearing was on a weekday, when it was hard for business owners to close their businesses and make the 40-mile trek down the coast, across the coastal range and to Santa Rosa. Not so with the mostly retired opponents of the fireworks show, who lined up to share with the commission their sense of horror that something as awful as fireworks would be allowed in Gualala, one even going so far as to say the impact of the 15-minute fireworks show would be "permanent and unmitigatable." Ultimately, the commission went along with its staff and the crowd, swiftly and unanimously approving the cease-and-desist order against the Festivals Committee's show.

Most of the anti-fireworks speakers gave their residence as The Sea Ranch, a sprawling Sonoma County planned community of 1,211 homes just across the county line from Gualala. Many of them addressed the issue of restricted public access along Gualala Bluff Trail during the show, which was more than a little ironic, given The Sea Ranch's own sordid history with the Coastal Act. The Sea Ranch stretches for 10 miles along the northern Sonoma coast, and for years in the 1960s its residents refused to allow any non-resident to cross their land, effectively blocking access to beaches that belonged to the people of California. This led to the formation of Californians Organized to Acquire Access to State Tidelands (COAST), which placed an initiative on the Sonoma County ballot to force The Sea Ranch to include public trails to the beach. The initiative failed but became the *cause célèbre* of supporters of what followed, Proposition 20, which sought passage of the California Coastal Act and the creation of the California Coastal Commission.

Ultimately, a deal was struck between The Sea Ranch and California's coastal protectors: In return for eight public access points that were none too convenient and required long treks from parking lots to the shore, the Sea Ranch would be forever exempted from the Coastal Act's authority. So without a wisp of oversight by the subsequently formed Coastal Commission, over a thousand homes have been built there - some of them approaching the size of the home Dennis Schneider had wanted to build in Cayucos, many quite ugly and some both. In one of these homes, a rambling mass of salt-bleached wood and expanses of glass directly above the Pacific, lives retired gynecologist and bird watcher Richard Kuehn, one of the leaders of the campaign against the Gualala Festivals Committee's fireworks show. The wave-splashed rock outcropping just offshore of his home is the very spot studied by the BLM in the report the Coastal Commission staff used to justify the cease-and-desist order. While the Coastal Commission's staff aligned itself with Kuehn against the Gualala fireworks show, it had no say whatsoever when the workers who built his house used power saws and noisy hammers right next door to the seabirds' home, disturbing them for much longer than Gualala's fleeting fireworks show did.

The pro-property rights Pacific Legal Foundation tried its best to secure for Gualalans their fireworks show, filing a lawsuit that focused on the Coastal Act's definition of development. From a property rights point of view, limiting the definition of development in the Coastal Act was far more important than any single fireworks display. The lawyers therefore argued that such "literal construction" of the Coastal Act's definition of development "is fatally flawed," and that absurd results would follow unless limitations were placed on the definition of the word under the Act. In March 2010, a three-judge appeals panel disagreed, ruling that the gases emitted by the fireworks and the scraps of cardboard that drifted into the ocean and onto the beach from the exploded shells were enough to constitute "development" under the Act. They did not rule as to whether so broad a definition was sheer lunacy.

"This loss is terrible," PLF attorney Paul Beard told me. "First, it's a published decision, so it's binding on the trial courts and persuasive in the courts of appeal. But worse is the power it gives to the Coastal Commission because it basically says any human activity - breathing, driving, etc. - is a 'development,' and it's up to the commission to decide what it wants to exempt and what it doesn't." He paused for a moment, exhaled deeply, and added, "You know, with the recent claims by the EPA that CO_2 is a pollutant, is it a stretch to think that the Commission will soon require people to get permits to breathe in the Coastal Zone? I mean, breathing does fit their definition of 'development.'"

Sayegh was more to the point when he shared with me after the loss that he was planning to leave California: "This means that every fireworks show on the coast is now subject to the whims of the Coastal Commission." He's right - the Commission is now considering similar bans in Santa Barbara and La Jolla. Lest you think this is something that could only happen in California, consider this: People for the Ethical Treatment of Animals awarded the Coastal Commission its "Compassion in Action" award just four days after Gualala went dark on July 4, 2008.

BURNING GREEN

Maybe California isn't going down the tubes after all. Maybe it's going up in smoke.

As the long summer's dry heat bakes moisture out of the scrubby California landscape, and dry winds blow off the hot desert inlands towards the ocean, a strike of lightning or an arsonist's torch can easily turn the Golden State all red and orange. In 2007, one of the worst fire years in California history, 8,881 wildfires broke out in the state, scorching 1.6 million acres - an area nearly twice the size of Rhode Island - reducing 3,830 homes to ashes and killing at least eight people.[27]

Horrifying as all this seems, Californians have gotten used to the annual wildlfire season, which generally runs from August through October. Unless your neighborhood is under a forced evacuation - as ours was once, with all the expected drama - the big smoke clouds on the horizon are other people's problems and rarely result in large-scale human tragedies. Even the biggest fires, like 2009's Station Fire, which burned more than 160,000 acres in the mountains near Los Angeles, killed only two people - both firefighters - and left most Angelenos going about their lives unbothered, except for periodic slowdowns on the freeway as drivers gawked at the fire's towering pyrocumulous clouds.

California has fires because much of it is covered by an ignition-hungry plant palette of black sage, Manzanita, scrub oak and about two dozen other low-growing plants. This plant palette is pretty for a couple months of the year, fragrant with sage, resplendent in purple and yellow flowers. But in most years it has browned out by May or June and looks dead for the rest of the year - unless it burns. The oily leaves of these plants may make for intense fires, but they're not all that's to blame for the devastation wildfires cause in the state. State regulators' fanatical embrace of regulation also plays a part.

The members of the Coastal Property Owners Association of Big Sur blamed the Coastal Commission for the incineration of 20 homes in their neighborhood in 2008. They alleged the commission's stringent protections of coastal chaparral made it illegal to take basic precautions to protect their properties from wildfires. Were it not for the regulations, they said, bushes could have been trimmed to create a protective buffer around their homes. The commission routinely requires buffers around wetlands and stands of trees to protect animals, but it makes it very hard to get permission to create buffers around homes to protect humans.

"Even when everybody could see the fire was raging," said homeowner Lisa Kleissner, "[the commission] said we had to get permits to cut. People didn't have a choice. They had to get permits. Finally, the firefighters jumped right in, and of course they helped the property owners remove trees. It shouldn't take a disaster like this to put some sense into the process."[28]

When the fire was finally out and homes lay

smoldering in ruins, the Coastal Commission refused to accept any blame for what had happened. "Those fires were caused by natural forces," commission Legislative Director Sarah Christie told a reporter, adding haughtily, "The Coastal Commission can't control lightning."[29]

The Coastal Commission is not alone in putting plants ahead of people in California. In fact, it could learn lessons from the Tahoe Regional Planning Agency (TRPA), which Richard Carlson often thinks about as he looks out his cabin window at the beautiful view of Lake Tahoe. Because of TRPA, he says, his enjoyment of the scenery is tempered by the understanding that if he sees forest-fire smoke below him, he has at best 10 minutes to clear out before the fire will block his only exit route.

"Behind my home, it's nearly impossible to hike off trail because you have to wade through knee-deep piles of dead branches. The forest is ready to explode. We have too many trees, but no one dares do anything about it," he wrote in the San Francisco Chronicle[30] after a wildfire incinerated the homes of 242 of his neighbors in July 2007. Carlson joined other Lake Tahoe area homeowners in blaming TRPA for their loss, not the unattended campfire that actually started the blaze. The agency, a California-Nevada joint land czar bureaucracy dedicated to protecting the renown clarity of Lake Tahoe at all cost, is led by a board of directors stuffed with representatives of environmental groups, making it a foot soldier in the environmental movement's effort to deify forests.

TRPA earned the nickname the Tree Nazis because of its near-maniacal obsession with prohibitions on tree cutting and trimming, which, they say, leads to more exposed soil and therefore more sediment running into the lake. TRPA mandates that anyone who cuts a tree in Tahoe first go through a permitting process that's stacked against tree cutting. Ignore the permit, and the homeowner will be looking at fines of $1,000 for each tree removed. The agency then uses fine revenues to find more people to fine, in an endless run of fine-assessing, or tree-saving, depending on whether you're a homeowner or a regulator.

Before the 2007 fire, TRPA's four-page application for a tree-trimming permit explained that trees with a diameter of under six inches - smaller around than the circle you make with your thumb and forefinger when signaling "OK" - could be trimmed without a permit, but any growing thing even slightly larger was untouchable. The problem with this is that a fir tree that's six-and-a-quarter inches in diameter is basically a Roman candle awaiting ignition. Unlike pines, which are fire-adapted and drop their lower branches, fir branches reach all the way to the ground, so they're called "ladder trees," serving as a fire's stairway to the heavenly, flammable larger branches above. TRPA also kept homeowners from removing any old-growth dead trees, and forbade "substantial trimming" unless the trimming occurred within 10 feet of a building to reduce fire risk - as if a tree incinerating just 10 feet and an inch from a home isn't a risk.

Of course, TRPA's rigidness led to one minor negative side-effect: 242 homeowners who watched in horror as those trees burst into flame and ignited their houses. Following the fire, the charred trees and burned homes exposed vast expanses of bare, denuded acres to the winter's rains and snows, and Lake Tahoe was pummeled with the silt, ash and algae-spawning organic material TRPA's regulations were meant to limit.

After the fire, TRPA's then-director, John Singlaub, stood up to the criticism heaped by those who lost their homes and spoke boldly in defense of his organization's apparent preference of trees over homes. When he tried at a town hall meeting to explain that TRPA wasn't responsible for the tragedy because it allowed tree-trimming, albeit very limited tree-trimming, a crowd of more than 1,200 angry citizens defiantly shouted him down. The homeowners were all too familiar with the limited and nonsensical trimming the agency allowed. Two days later, Singlaub resurfaced at the side of Gov. Schwarzenegger, who was touring the fire damage. Locals ignored the governor and shouted questions at Singlaub, demanding that he address TRPA's culpability for the fire. Again, he said the agency wasn't to blame for the fire.

"TRPA was terrified, terrified after the fire," Carlson, the San Francisco Chronicle op-ed writer, told me. "They were truly hated by people within the basin." There was substantial political power behind that hatred, and the Nevada Legislature, recognizing it had a disaster on its hands and a window of opportunity to do something about it, moved swiftly to control TRPA's policies, even if California didn't. The agency, seeing the handwriting on the wall, changed its policies quickly, releasing its authority on trees up to 14 inches, easing up on its trimming and clearance regulations and transferring some permitting authority to local fire departments, which are more interested in fire control than lake clarity. But of course, all this only happened after a catastrophe, and none of it helped the 242 families who lost their homes.

The "new, more radical urban environmentalists who value money and ideology above science, homes and human life" that Carlson referenced in his op-ed were furious about the slightly kinder, gentler TRPA. They sued TRPA under the federal Clean Water Act to halt any efforts to speed up trimming programs, demanding instead a return to the agency's pre-fire draconian regulatory fervor. The litigation likely will succeed, at least in part, proving once again that history teaches no lessons to California's environmentalists inside and outside government.

SOLVING THE ECO-CRAT DILEMMA

Ask Democrat legislators how the economy-crushing burden of regulation can be eliminated, given that they've ceded power to eco-crats, and you'll get a blank stare or an equally uninformative babble of words in response. Ask a Republican and you'll hear, "Elect more Republicans so we can appoint the directors and boards." That's much like saying Cleveland can solve the problem of having a chronically underperforming professional football team by hiring better coaches and players - it's an obvious, but for all intents and purposes undoable, answer. California's demographics and politics are not favorable for Republicans, as we saw in the 2010 midterms when, in defiance of national trends, every Democratic incumbent in the state was re-elected.

Whenever the business or agriculture industries

start another push to reform CEQA, the state's powerful environmental lobby pushes back forcefully and effectively. Recently, some Democrats have gotten behind making CEQA less oppressive - if it's to speed the approval of a job-generating new development - as long as its an NFL stadium, not a factory or subdivision. The greens, however, are convinced that no recession, no deep depression, will ever loosen their hold on the state for something as silly as creating jobs. Here's one frequent leftist commentator on California environmental issues, who blogs under the pseudonym CaliCon:

> I've see articles (obviously from the right) claiming that Calirfornia [sic] is dominated by "Green Jihadis" and its [sic] destroying the economy. Usually these articles call for the reform (mostly removal) of California's environmental laws and link the 12% unemployment as justification. But based on what's happening [with CEQA exemptions for NFL stadiums] are the Democrats coming around to that line? Do they see a link between enivornment [sic] and unemployment here? Or are they desperate enough for votes in 2012 since California's economy has barely nudged and the Democrats have a full sweep of state government?

He needn't worry. California's leftist politics will survive the 2012 election with all its job-killing proclivities undiluted. Even if Sacramento were to change, the environmental organizations will continue to hone their already considerable ability to slow jobs and growth by exploiting California's environmental laws - as long as pro-growth factions allow them to. Mario Santoyo, the assistant general manager of the Friant Water Authority, one of the major water providers to California's Central Valley farms, thinks it's time to take that power away from the environmentalists. Santoyo is a co-founder and leader of the California Latino Water Coalition, the group that organized the 2009 march on Sacramento by farm laborers and owners that turned the tide in California's water wars.

Speaking recently to a water forum in Southern California, he said, "Whenever we sit down at the negotiating table with the environmentalists across from us, we lose. But when we bring our constituents with us - like we did when our constituents marched on Sacramento - we win. If we start inviting the people we represent - the workers, the laborers, the guys and ladies who bring home the paycheck - along with us to the negotiating table and committee hearing room, then we can start rolling back the grip the environmental groups have on California."

Another solution may be 3,000 miles to the east. There, in a Capitol hearing room, Rep. Darrell Issa, R-Vista, chairman of the House Committee on Oversight and Government Reform, recently opened an investigation into CARB chair Mary Nichols' role in secret negotiations that led to the establishment of new federal fuel economy standards. These standards mimic the higher 35.5-mpg standards California was allowed to impose when President Obama gave the state a waiver from the federal fuel economy standard in 2009. Issa's investigation is predicated on the federal Energy Policy and Conservation Act, which says that "a State or a political subdivision of a State may not adopt or enforce a law or regulation related to fuel economy standards or average fuel economy standards for an automobile." He contends California did just that under the guise of regulating greenhouse gas emissions, and that CARB and the Obama White House then used the threat of a patchwork of different fuel economy standards around the nation - a costly-to-comply-with nightmare for auto manufacturers - to force the automakers to accept a new, higher federal mileage standard during possibly illegal secret negotiations.

A series of investigations like Issa's could diminish the California Legislature's unwillingness to undo the liberal, green technocracy it has carefully created over many years. The disregard California's technocrats show for due process could lead to many more congressional investigations. A Republican state attorney general could do the same - and keep in mind that, in the 2010 election, Republican Steve Cooley lost the AG race by less than 75,000 votes out of 10 million votes cast. California's Little Hoover Commission, which functions as something of a statewide grand jury, is free to open similar investigations. Its investigations can't lead directly to criminal charges, but charges could come if California's attorney general followed up on the commission's investigations. A few high-profile scandals culminating in several of California's heretofore immune regulatory agency directors being hauled before a court could lead to a successful ballot initiative curtailing the power of the state's agencies to establish regulations without the consent of the governed.

One can only hope that the governed of California would agree that getting rid of crazy, job-crushing green over-regulation would be a good thing.

CHAPTER NINE:

PENSIONS AND BUDGET: THE HIGH PRICE OF PROGRESSIVISM

The light at the end of the tunnel is a black hole.

EVERYTHING THAT'S GONE BEFORE in this book costs money, which comes as no surprise because the big-government Progressive movement is probably the most expensive and fiscally irresponsible form of government ever conceived by the human mind. That explains why California's payroll tax rate of 7.5%, top state marginal income tax rate of 10.3%, corporate tax rate of 8.84% and sales tax rate of 8.25% are all the highest or among the highest in the nation.[1]

The Progressives' compulsion to exert government control leads inevitably to over-regulation, which in turn leads to an abundance of well-paid regulators. That, in turn, leads to the increasing inability of those who are regulated to support those who regulate. Under Progressivism, those who govern and educate are the truly deserving class, not those who produce, so goverment workers and educators are given high salaries. California's public workers are the second-highest paid in the nation[2] and as noted in Chapter Seven, its teachers are the highest paid. In the Progressive ideal, they also deserve comfortable retirements - and California has the largest public-employee pension funding deficit in the nation. All this must be paid for by the harder-working producers who, shame on them, were not selfless enough to go into public service. Progressives also hold that success has eluded the poor because they are the victims of the free market's inherent unfairness and the greed of the successful, not because they're lazy schleps or high school drop-outs. So, Progressives think, the system owes them a living, at the expense of those, as President Obama puts it, who have been "luckier."

After 100 years of largely uninterrupted rule by those who hold to these beliefs, California has become the Greece of the West - and that's not good news for the rest of America. Speaking at the annual meeting of JPMorgan Chase & Co. in 2010, the company's CEO, Jamie Dimon, told investors that if California's budget woes cause it to miss its debt payments, "there could be a contagion." Dimon categorized the threat posed by California's budget deficit as more threatening to the U.S. banking system than what would occur if the entire European Union came apart.[3]

A large part of California's deficit comes from its coddling of its loafing class, which has become so costly that the state spends $26 billion a year on social services for them - about the same as Delaware, Hawaii, Iowa, Michigan and Nebraska *combined* spend on their *entire* budgets, not just social services.

California's government employees and teachers have built up an unfunded liability for their retirement pensions and health-care benefits estimated by Stanford University to be $500 billion - that's a half-trillion dollars - about six times more than every buck California collects in general-fund revenues each year. Public employee unions discredit the Stanford study and peg the pension shortfall at about half that - $240 billion, still a frightening sum. But the Stanford study uses a believable projection for investment returns instead of the pension plans' 7.75 or 7.5 percent return assumption. Who would bet on California's pension managers achieving a return more than 20 percent greater than the return assumption investment maestro Warren Buffet uses?

William Voegeli of Claremont University crunched some numbers and found just how more expensive it is to run progressive California than it is to run most other states. Looking at a 15-year period from the early 1990s to the mid-2000s, Voegeli found California's per-capita outlays grew by 21.7 percent, compared to just an 18.2 percent average for the other 49 states and the District of Columbia. That may not seem like a huge difference, but Voegeli pointed out that if California's spending increases had matched the other states', its annual expenses would have dropped by $10.6 billion. If that had been the case, Gov. Brown would have been able to crow about a $1.4 billion surplus in his initial 2012-2013 budget, instead of having to struggle to balance a deficit he estimated - under-estimated, actually - to be $9.2 billion. In May 2012, at the annual gubernatorial shucks-and-shuffle over the budget, Brown declared the actual deficit to be $15.7 billion -

$6.3 billion more than he called it in January. The nonpartisan Legislative Analyst's Office called him on that, pegging the deficit at closer to $17 billion.

The higher deficit was classic Crazifornia. Brown over-estimated tax revenue by $4.3 billion - assuming more businesses would stay in the state than did, and that the ones that didn't pick up their roots would expand more quickly than they did. Most of the balance of the bump comes from litigation filed by unions and others that successfully challenged the budget cuts he proposed earlier. The remainder came from a boost in the funds California schools will get under Proposition 98 - money that history has shown does nothing discernible to improve the performance of the state's elementary, junior and senior high schools.

Brown threatened more cuts to social service budgets. Good. Voegeli points out that California is now outspending "states not famous for the parsimony or integrity of their public sectors," including New York and New Jersey, both of which had slower growth in state spending during the period. And if California's spending had grown only enough to keep up with population growth and inflation, instead of growing to meeting increasingly preposterous Progressive programs, then "[the] resulting levels of per-capita government outlays ... would have equaled neither Somalia's nor Mississippi's, but ... Oregon's, which is rarely considered a hellish paradigm of Social Darwinism," Voegeli wrote.[4]

Like any overspending shopaholic, California is shuffling various credit cards to finance its many costly sprees. In addition to its bond debt - California issued more than $50 billion in new bonds in 2011 alone - the state routinely pays for its many progressive social programs by shorting its payments to other state entities. For example, thanks to the ballot-box budgeting that comes with its proposition system, the state is required to spend 43 percent of general fund revenues on schools. If the Legislature spends so much on its beloved social welfare and environmental programs that there's not enough money left to give the schools their due, in later years it must pay the shortfall back to the schools with interest. The bill for those broken promises to schools and community colleges is now $10.4 billion. The state owes another $4.5 billion to other California governmental entities, and $2.6 billion for shorted pension and health care payments. The bill for these many borrowings reached $33 billion[5] in early 2012 - almost as much as Virginia's entire state budget for that year.

Meanwhile, Sacramento's liberal lords of the budget behave as if any cut to social programs, even one that falls far short of bringing California into parity with other states, would be tantamount to sending the state non-stop back to the Dark Ages. And always, if revenues fall short and taxes aren't raised, Californians are told school children, parks rangers and public safety heroes will have their heads on the chopping block. Never cut are the environmental over-regulators or the armies of state bureaucrats who are content to sit in meetings, fill out expense reports and write memos to file until their retirement programs become fully vested.

It's little wonder 71 percent of California voters believe the Legislature is doing a lousy job. More difficult to explain is the 12 percent who can't make up their minds.[6] What more evidence do they need?

HOOTING AND HOLLERING OVER THE BUDGET

Californians witness the challenges of running a Progressive state every year as the Legislature struggles to develop a balanced budget in the face of fundamental fiscal imbalance. The resulting budget is always a work of fiction, projecting more income than will come in and promising more savings than will ever occur. The mid-year shucks-and-shuffle correction in May is always needed to account for this, but the charade goes on in all seriousness year after year. It's a tragedy; it's a comedy; it's Crazifornia.

Almost 50 state budgets ago, in 1966, the Legislature's top budget leaders and Gov. Pat Brown fled Sacramento for Palm Springs to try to sort out yet another horrific California budget mess. Nothing was getting done in soggy, cold Sacramento to fix the chronic problem of revenues not covering ever-increasing government expenses, and since Brown would face the voters in November hoping to win a third term, the Democrat was adamant that the budget would be balanced without raising taxes.

Joining the senior legislators in Palm Springs was a young legislative staffer, David Doerr, who felt lucky to get the chance to travel with the delegation, not so much because it involved a boondoggle trip to the desert, but because he actually hungered to see how California's budget sausage was made. And see it he did. Ultimately, the budget was balanced on a number of gimmicks, including one that was unusually elegant:

a switch to accrual accounting from cash. With the change, all the money due the state could be applied against expenses, no matter how far back the money due was in the pipeline. With this trick and a few others on the books, Brown was able to face Ronald Reagan in November armed with a balanced budget and no tax increase.

There were plenty of other gimmicks that came out of the Palm Springs session, but one really stuck in Doerr's mind. Showing his uncanny ability to remember financial matters from the distant past in exquisite detail, Doerr told the tale in a small conference room at the California Taxpayers Association's offices, the wall behind him lined with shelves displaying his 811-page tome, *California's Tax Machine, A History of Taxing and Spending in the Golden State*. His voice is light and wispy, the voice of a man who had heard far too many politicians argue far too loudly, and his hair is as white as snow - an expected side effect of being the single Californian who knows the most about the state's budget-making process.

"After not really getting much of anywhere in the negotiations," he said, "one of the suggestions that came up, casually, just sort of a throw-away, was, 'Why don't we just delay paying the state employees so one payday will go over into the next year?' At first everyone was quiet and I wondered if they would really do something like that, but then they began to hoot and holler, laughing like this was the craziest thing they ever heard of."

Doerr, who ultimately spent three decades as chief consultant for the Assembly Revenue and Taxation Committee before becoming the chief tax consultant of the California Taxpayers Association, continued the story: "Jumping forward over 50 years, no one in the Legislature hooted or hollered one bit when the idea of shifting one pay period into the next fiscal year came back, this time as a way to balance the 2008-2009 fiscal year budget. The Legislature just did it, knowing full well their action would come back to haunt them a year later, when they would have to balance a budget that had one extra payroll period in it."[7] The subterfuge saved $1.2 billion for the moment. That's what it cost per pay period in 2009 to pay the state's bloated payroll.

The 1966 junket to the desert ended up not doing Brown any good, as Ronald Reagan drubbed him by 16 points that November, sweeping all but three counties in the state. And the 2008 roll-over of one payday didn't help Gov. Schwarzenegger either, and he declared upon announcing the inevitable budget revise that May, "We've run out of Band-Aids."

"Gimmicks and Band-Aids aren't new," Doerr said. "There have always been battles over the budget and crazy balancing tricks as long as I've been here, and that's been 50 years, more than one-quarter of the time California's been a state."

BROWN IN THE RED

As Gov. Schwarzenegger came to the end of his celebrity governorship, he not only had fallen short of his promise to balance the budget, he had made things appreciably worse. His term wrapped up a decade in which state and local government spending increased by well over 30 percent as programs for the indigent grew and regulatory bureaucracies expanded. During the same period, the state's population had grown by just six percent - just one-fifth the increase seen in government spending.

Schwarzenegger tried to make back $1 billion by selling the State Compensation Insurance Fund, but lawsuits tied up the sale. Other lawsuits halted his attempts to cut Medi-Cal and social programs, and still other cuts - like those to prisons staffed by some of the most generous campaign contributors to California Democrats - never even made it out of legislative committees. He pumped up revenues by $7 billion he hoped to get from Washington, only to be met by a suddenly fiscally conservative Nancy Pelosi, who sniffed, "The idea that any state can say, 'This is my shortfall, pick up the tab,' is not one that would work well in Washington." So, in the end, Schwarzenegger and the Legislature cobbled together the surviving gimmicks and unreasonably rosy projections and kicked the can down the road.

In California, the first year of a governor's term is almost always something of a budgetary can-kicker since the governor barely has time to put the family photos on his desk before the budget is due. Brown's second budget, announced in January 2012, more clearly bore his administration's imprimatur, and it was true to his Progressive roots. It called for higher taxes, assuming there will be about $7 billion coming in from new taxes on the wealthy (defined as having an annual income of $250,000 or more) and a new sales tax hike. Instead of using the new revenues generated from the taxes to pay off some of the state's debt obligations, Brown's initial 2012-2013 budget burned through nearly all of it, with a $6 billion increase in state spending.

Even so, the state's Progressives howled. Senate majority leader Darrell Steinberg, D-Sacramento, immediately vowed to fight Brown on cuts to social programs, which included booting people off welfare after two years, instead of the current four. The Los Angeles Times referred to that as "cutting a swath through California's renowned assistance programs,"[8] even if those who lost their welfare benefits would still get other benefits, including medical coverage for their children. The other major paper in Los Angeles, the Daily News, headlined its budget story, "Gov. Brown's budget plan sparks fear, outrage in Southland."[9] Along with social service advocates and school district officials, it quoted Democratic county supervisor Zev Yaroslavsky, who did what another prominent Democrat, the president, has done: He blamed the prior Republican administration for the problem.

All of California's major newspapers dutifully reported Brown's proposed cuts and quoted numerous sources about the pain they would cause if the cuts were actually enacted. But nowhere did they point out that California has a lot of room to cut, since it spends so much more on social programs than other states. Nor did they consider the possibility that, if the programs were cut, unproductive people who choose to live in California because of its abundant and generous welfare programs might actually take their neediness elsewhere. Wouldn't it be better to lose unproductive welfare recipients than job-creating businesses?

Brown's initial 2012-2013 budget also showed he is

not willing to let fiscal reality get in the way of California's Progressive agenda, even as California continues to trail the rest of the nation's lackluster recovery. He has left in place the implementation of California's job-crushing crusades against greenhouse gases, including the state's first-in-the-nation carbon cap-and-trade program. That might be because cap and trade will yank at least $1 billion in carbon taxes out of the pockets of business during the fiscal year. He also kept the state's expensive high-speed rail program on track, despite reports from the rail commission's own peer review panel and the state Legislative Analyst's Office that the whole idea was a fiscal train wreck. And even more illuminating, Brown's budget provides funding for his new anti-business mega-agency, the Business and Consumer Services Agency. As described in detail in Chapter Six, the agency will blend together bureaucrats from several business regulatory agencies and add an entirely new Department of Business Oversight, whose job will be, unbelievably, finding even more ways to assure business owners they are not welcome in the Golden State.

Brown's first real budget took some swipes at remedying past ills, with promises to start working through the debts the state owes to other agencies, nibble at pension reform and make government more efficient. But more than solving California's fiscal maladies, Brown's budget made three of his beliefs abundantly clear: government is good, more government is even better, and there's no reason for Sacramento to consider that it might be good for California to support its businesses. With the May revise, he took some timid swipes at the government workforce in an effort to control spiraling costs, but litigation is sure to follow - and state employee unions usually win these court battles.

TWO ARISTOCRATS NAMED JOHNSON

When Brown came into office, a few commentators hoped he would turn his back on the public employee unions that funded his election and tackle the state's runaway public employee pension costs. Anyone watching his earliest appointments quickly learned otherwise, as Brown named labor activist Marty Morgenstern secretary of the Labor and Workforce Development Agency. Longtime labor union lawyer Ronald Yank was named the state's personnel director, responsible for negotiating contracts with the public employee unions. Consequently, when Brown announced his public pension reform package, it was evident the package did not do enough to bring public employee pensions under control. The 12-point program was far-reaching, but Brown offered it knowing that by the time it wends its way through the Legislature, most of his original proposal will be whittled away. Dan Pellissier, president of California Pension Reform, dismissed any hope of immediate resolution of the state's pension crisis, telling the Sacramento Bee, "We have little faith the Legislature will adopt anything of substance."[10]

The cost of runaway public-employee retirement and health benefits is not a problem that can wait. It is so big - so many public employees, so many benefits, so many years money will be paid out - that it's hard to encapsulate it into a chapter of a book, let alone a sound bite for the majority who get their news from television, or worse, Facebook. Ed Ring, a research fellow at the National Tax Limitation Foundation, came pretty close, though:

> *California has 1.85 million state and local government employees. Using an average career of 30 years and an average retirement of 20 years, the Golden State is on track to see 1.25 million retired state and local workers collecting, on average, $60,000 per year in retirement pension payments. That's $75 billion per year and growing. Should taxpayers, the vast majority of whom can expect Social Security benefits of no more than $15,000 a year on average, really be expected to fund those retirements? Will they do so willingly? Not likely.*[11]

This disparity between the retirements of public and private employees has grown so huge that it's broken like a massive migraine on the consciousness of California. A few years ago, concern about public employee pensions barely raised a blip on public-opinion polls, but recent polls show nearly three-quarters of California residents think it's time to do something about the problem. A look at two public employees named Johnson reveals the sort of high-profile abuse that has raised the public's awareness of public pensions.

The first Johnson, Greg, had struck it rich. At 50, he had a job that paid him more than a quarter-million dollars a year and a boss who loved him, showering him with benefits: free car washes, free golf, fat and automatic cost-of-living increases, an annual expense account of $15,000, a retirement plan that would pay him $200,000 a year and the one gold-plated benefit that gave him the most comfort of all - lifetime Cadillac medical benefits. When all was said and done, he had managed to get himself a salary, benefits, medical and retirement package estimated to be worth a cool $8 million.

Looking at Johnson's job, most would be surprised he'd have it so good. After all, he only managed 23 people and oversaw an annual budget of just $11.8 million. They'd be even more surprised to learn that Johnson was raking in so much dough while his employer was suffering in the economic downturn, and that Johnson had made no offer to cut back on his pay or benefits. After all, his boss didn't ask him to.

What made all this possible, of course, is that Johnson had a public sector job. He was the city manager of Indian Wells, a town near Palm Springs with a population of 5,000 that boasted a median age of 63.4 years and a median annual income of $128,127. With plenty of golf courses to play and upscale stores and restaurants to frequent while working a job that made few demands but paid remarkably well, Johnson thought he had it made. And he did ... until a do-gooder citizen, Haddon Libby, stood up at a city council meeting and questioned - actually questioned! - Johnson's pay and benefits package. Not only that, but Libby followed up with a Public Records Act request for all the city's records on Johnson's contract, salary and benefits.

Johnson, who had been employed by Indian Wells for 15 years, reacted swiftly. He fired off an angry email to Libby's boss, Scott Kavanaugh, CEO of First Foundation Bank. He lectured Kavanaugh, saying Libby needed to learn that "such public discourse comes at a price,"[12] and demanded Libby be fired. After Kavanaugh dilly-dallied, Johnson stepped up the email campaign, becoming increasingly aggressive and copying his emails to members of the city council. Presumably worried that bad relations with city hall could hurt the new bank's expansion plans, Kavanaugh fired Libby, claiming poor job performance. Libby, of course, thought otherwise, saying in the wrongful termination lawsuit he subsequently filed that he was let go so the bank could "curry favor with the powerful local officials."[13]

Less than one month after Libby's firing, Johnson was also gone, resigning as news of his benefits package and his campaign against Libby broke in the local paper. Instead of slinking off in shame, however, Johnson nailed down a $427,593 severance package with the city council, which approved his golden parachute on a 5-0 vote.

Of course, Greg Johnson is not the average government employee. Neither is the other Johnson, Glynn, recently retired from the Los Angeles County Fire Department as an assistant chief. No relation to Greg Johnson, Glynn Johnson retired at 55, locking in his pension at 90 percent of his final year's salary for as long as he lived, guaranteed. But his retirement wasn't worry-free because he was facing charges that he slugged a puppy several times in the face, then bashed it with a 12-pound rock. The puppy, Karley, was so severely injured she had to be put to death.[14]

Fortunately for Johnson, he retired fully vested

from the fire department before the case came to court. Since he wasn't found to be guilty of a felony until after he was no longer a county employee, his pension was protected. He spent his final days on the force ducking Riverside County Police Department detectives while on paid administrative leave, with the emphasis on "paid," since it meant his final year's income of $180,000 wasn't affected for benefit-calculation purposes.[15] Ultimately, he was found guilty, and on the day after April Fool's Day in 2010, he was sentenced in a court room brimming with animal-rights activists. The puppy's owner, Jeff Toole, told Johnson in court, "If Karley did this to you, her punishment would be death and if I were a judge that would be the punishment for you, too, but I'm not a judge. You're a danger to society and you need to be locked up before you hurt someone else."[16] He was locked up - for 90 days (to be served only on weekends), not the four years he potentially faced. His attorney said he will appeal.

So is Johnson a public safety officer or danger to society? As far as his generous pension is concerned, it makes no difference, despite pleas from Toole and others that the taxpayers not be obliged to pay for the puppy-beater's comfortable retirement. Johnson's well-timed retirement kept his entire pension intact, protected by a fortress of legislation and court victories that have given public employee unions a stranglehold on state and municipal treasuries in California.

With the wide dissemination of stories like those of the two Johnsons - and worse, that of Robert Rizzo, who used the city of Bell as his personal ATM - it's little wonder that California has become one of the main battlefields in the war over public employee salaries and pensions. California's Little Hoover Commission issued a report in early 2011 that concluded, "California's pension plans are dangerously underfunded, the result of overly generous benefit promises, wishful thinking and an unwillingness to plan prudently."[17] The report goes on to take the state out to the woodshed for a well-deserved whipping:

> One need look no further than the actions of some 200 public agencies in the months since the steep decline in the stock market and housing values in 2008: Rather than foreswear risky behaviors, these public agencies in California instead have improved pension benefits for their employees. Up and down the state, cities, counties, and fire and water districts rewarded employees with "golden handshake" agreements that provide extra service credit to retire early; introduced favorable methods to calculate pension benefits based on the single highest year of compensation; and lowered retirement ages that extend the government's obligation to pay lifetime retirement benefits. These actions further burden pension plans that already are unsustainable.
>
> In its study of public pensions, the Commission found that the state's 10 largest pension funds - encompassing 90 percent of all public employees - are overextended in their promises to current workers and retirees. The ability and willingness of leaders to contain growing pension obligations

> *should concern not only taxpayers who are seeing*
> *vital services and programs cut to balance budgets,*
> *but the public employees who have the most to*
> *lose. A pension is worthless without a job to back*
> *it.*

It is the last point - the loss of jobs due to pension costs - that is finally giving some elected officials in California's cities and counties some fire in their bellies over the need to reform pensions. They are seeing their ability to fund services that were formerly seen as essential hampered by the rising bite their pension programs are taking out of their budgets. Similarly, Democratic legislators are seeing pension expenses eat into funding for their cherished social welfare and environmental programs. This would be more upsetting to them if they didn't have the power to propose tax increases, which they fight for in order to keep the public employee unions that funded their campaigns, and the welfare recipients who vote Democratic, happy.

THE CRUSADING SUPERVISOR

Public employee union leadership - and much of the rank and file - stand behind their right to drive cities, counties and ultimately the state into insolvency in order to protect their benefits. Their fervor in the face of rising public anger often leads them to vilify any elected official who stands up to them. That would explain why the two Santa Ana police officers were both grinning like Cheshire Cats one day in 2006 - they had just pulled over John Moorlach! This would give them bragging rights in the duty room for months.

Indeed, sitting in the car in front of them, stopped for a violation a judge would later mostly dismiss, was Moorlach, Orange County's Treasurer-Tax Collector who at the time was running for a seat on the Board of Supervisors. He was not well-liked by the police - in fact, one police magazine described him as the Great Satan. Ever since the Orange County Board of Supervisors rushed through a retroactive increase in public safety pensions in the wake of the 9/11 attacks, he had taken every opportunity to speak out against over-rich public employee retirement plans. "People would ask me to speak about something else," he told me, "But there really isn't anything else to speak about."

In September 2001, few understood how the public-employee unions were mining a rich vein of taxpayer gold, nor did they know the calamitous consequences that would surely follow. When the increase was passed, revenue was plentiful, flags were waving, and everyone, elected officials especially, wanted to show their support for the heroes who wore police and fire uniforms. Moorlach's voice was nearly alone as he warned anyone who would listen that a fiscal melt-down was ahead because for years, pension plan contributions had been set at a level to fund the pre-9/11 benefits, not the new, richer package. The retroactive increase had no provision for filling this funding gap.

The traffic stop on the shoulder of the Newport Freeway was professional, all "Sir" and "Thank you" from the policemen, but their iciness would have been more appropriate had they pulled over Osama bin Laden, rather than the County Treasurer. Moorlach just grinned back in response. After all, the police officers' reaction was nothing if not confirmation that he was on the right track.

Over a breakfast at Denny's - he is a fiscal conservative to his bones - Moorlach spelled out the fundamentals of the problem to me. "What's dysfunctional is the budget process and the entitlement mentality," he said. "In an up-cycle we hire all kinds of employees and give them better benefits, and in a down-cycle, they don't go away. They're still there, and they demand the taxpayers to pay more taxes to take care of them. With that philosophy in mind, you're headed for disaster - it's just a matter of time. There is literally no light at the end of the tunnel."

When the county supervisors passed another pension increase over his protests in 2004, Moorlach decided to run for supervisor himself in 2006. The public employee unions spent hundreds of thousands of dollars smearing Moorlach, but he kept his focus on his single issue, public-employee pensions. All the union money did no good; he smashed his union-sponsored opponent, then goaded the unions in his victory speech, saying to thunderous applause, "There is a country where the bureaucrats are served by the taxpayers. They call it France. We are not France. This is Orange County!"[18]

Once elected, Moorlach tried to turn the situation around by convincing the other supervisors to challenge the earlier pension increases. He had studied the California Constitution and found no provision in it allowing such retroactive increases. In fact, the opposite was true. The state constitution specifically forbade municipalities taking on new debt without a two-thirds vote. This amendment to the much-amended constitution came as a result of many California cities and counties having to declare bankruptcy in the late 1800s because their elected leaders had bet big - and lost - on railroads. Landing railroad stations, switching yards and other support infrastructure was the green job promise of that earlier day. City councils and county boards of supervisors consequently approved massive bond measures - often on a bare majority vote - to build the infrastructure the railroads demanded. If they landed railroad facilities all was good, but if the railroad picked the next town or county over, the municipalities were faced with huge debt and no way to pay it off. From that earlier failed government venture into commerce, California came to require that all tax measures require a two-thirds vote.

He hired as his chief of staff a law professor and tasked him with researching the constitutionality of the retroactive increase. The law professor's conclusion: "I think we have a lawsuit here." The board, intimidated by the thought of suing public safety officers, hired an independent attorney to review the issue. His conclusion: "The retroactive increase is unconstitutional." A third attorney advised them that the lawsuit could lose on a technicality because "judges get state retirement benefits too."

In a closed meeting, Moorlach told the other supervisors, "We took an oath to uphold the Constitution of the State of California. We're stuck. We know what we know, we took an oath, so we have to act." They voted to sue, and issued a Request for

Proposals to law firms. "We got responses from a half dozen of the best law firms in the country and all of them said, 'You have a case and we want to be a part of it.'" Ultimately, the law firm of Kirkland and Ellis was hired to bring the lawsuit, and the eyes of the public sector were glued to Orange County. How Orange County v. Sheriff's Deputies turned out would decide whether the gravy train was still on the tracks or had derailed.

Ultimately, it remained on the tracks - because judges get retirement benefits too, it turns out. Judges on the California Court of Appeals and the California Supreme Court simply decided votes on pension increases were exempt for the two-thirds vote rule, and dismissed the lawsuit. With that arrow gone from the quiver, it may fall to California's fickle propositions system to solve the problem. Many propositions addressing pensions have been, and are being, proposed, but all face withering assaults from the well-funded and powerful public-employee unions.

Their power was displayed when California Pension Reform qualified a reform measure for the ballot in 2012, leading to the next step in the process: the Attorney General's drafting of a ballot title and summary.

California's attorney general is Kamala Harris, a San Francisco liberal and great friend of the unions, who were primary funders of her tough campaign for her seat. The ballot statement she drafted for the pension reform initiative said the measure reduced pension benefits for current employees, but it didn't. It said the measure prohibited death and disability benefits, while it specifically allowed them. And, showing the deliberateness of her effort to paint the proposition in a bad light, Harris' ballot statement singled out teachers, nurses and police officers as those whose benefits would be cut. She could have used any of hundreds of state job categories to illustrate her point, but chose only the ones polls show voters respond most favorably to. Faced with an understandable drop in campaign contributions after Harris published her ballot summary, California Pension Reform was forced to end its signature-gathering efforts.

As reform propositions are picked off one-by-one, the state's pension problem continues to grow. Under a worst-case scenario of California counties' pension liabilities developed by the Northwestern University Kellogg School of Management, by 2015 six counties would be paying 75 percent or more of their operating budgets for pension costs.[19] Salaries for teachers, nurses and police officers - not to mention clerks, janitors and functionaries - would be squeezed down to 25 percent of current levels or less, as would the budgets for providing care to the indigent, keeping parks and libraries open, paving roads and picking up trash. Worst off is Fresno County, whose pension expenses would take up 142 percent of its operating budget under the worst-case scenario. Despite the dismal future darkening the horizon, the Fresno Bee recently reported:

> *Fresno County managers have begun making plans for dealing with a labor strike since negotiations with the county's biggest employee union have stalled.*

Representatives of Service Employees International Union and county negotiators, after four months of talks, have been unable to reach agreement on a new contract for some 4,100 workers, from lower-paid receptionists to higher-paid health clinicians.

This month, the county put forth what it calls a final contract offer for the employees, proposing an across-the-board 9% pay cut. Labor leaders scoffed at the deal. ...

The union, which plans to vote on the contract over the next month, represents about two-thirds of county employees.[20]

DOES THE BLACK HOLE HAVE A SILVER LINING?

Maybe things really aren't so bad. After all, three prominent California Progressives recently wrote in the state's leading liberal blog, "We believe in our state. We believe in our country. We are patriots of the first order who know that true love of state or county manifests not in slogans" - good thing; we can do without much more chanting of "We are the 99%!" - "but in deeds that offer a brighter future to the next generation than to ours."[21]

The three, California Federation of Teachers president Joshua Penchthalt, Anthony Thigpenn, president of California Calls, which claims 328,000 Progressive supporters, and Rick Jacobs, chair of the online Progressive activist group Courage Campaign, which claims 750,000 members, go on to recognize that

"California is in a chronic, grinding decline," and they recognize that "the answer will not come from Sacramento. ... It needs to come from all of us." Are they finally recognizing the obvious? Are they conceding that a trillion dollars in unfunded public employee pension and healthcare obligations will not mean a brighter future for the next generation? Have they acknowledged that government as a "milk the rich" scheme won't work because the rich are simply moving away? Not hardly. They have a different way to express their patriotism:

> *The first step is admitting that we need more money to pay for our present, much less our future. That's why it's time for the 1%, those who benefited the most from our state's past investments, to invest in our state's future. Our state needs perhaps $20 billion a year in new revenue to assure that kids grow up to lead. That will take time, but for now, we see a clear path to $6 billion or so a year that would at the very least restore a large portion of the most recent cuts to education, healthcare, safety and transportation. All it takes is the 1% chipping in and paying more income tax. ...*

> *Should every child in California have access to an excellent, rigorous, free education through college and beyond? Should they have healthcare to assure that their minds are sharp and their bodies fit? Should they know that at any point after high school, whether they choose college or another path, they can find a good job? Should they be the*

sail that lifts our economy to new heights in energy and technology solutions of tomorrow?

Yes.

The leaders of the state's public employee unions and the activators of its Progressive activists aren't really paying attention to the warning signs. They are content to employ their considerable power to protect the status quo, so their promises to tomorrow's Californians are empty. By ignoring the fact that their policies are proving fiscally unsustainable, they are ensuring the next generation will inherit little beyond the debt of the preceding generation's greedy indulgences.

I asked Bill Hauck, who recently retired as executive director of the California Business Roundtable after coming to Sacramento with Ronald Reagan in 1967, if there was a solution to this kind of thinking, and for the state's chronic budget problems.

"There might be, but it's pretty ugly," he responded. "What if 20 or 25 creditors of the state of California who were owed maybe $50,000 to $100,000 apiece filed suit in federal court, seeking to put the state in some form of receivership? The court system has already done that with the healthcare system in the state prisons, where the federal court has the jurisdiction to direct the state to pay the prison system's creditors.

"If that occurred more broadly, you'd have a functional bankruptcy. I had a conversation with Jerry Brown about it today and he said, 'Boy, that's an interesting question. I'm going to have some of my people look into it.'" They should. If the state fails to make a bond payment, expect the bondholders to go to court to force just such an action.

On the pension front, one potential saving grace may be found in younger public employees who see their older peers lying on feather beds, being fed grapes by beleaguered taxpayers, while the younger employees work under different contracts that have fewer benefits and require larger employee contributions. They could rise up, joined by those older employees who truly believe in good governance and public safety, and elect a new class of union leaders who are willing to sacrifice the aging fat cats - if indeed they can be sacrificed at all.

The major problem is that most current public employees are guaranteed defined-*benefit* plans, under which their *benefits* are guaranteed no matter how well, or badly, the underlying pension investments perform. Reforms include, at a minimum, a shift to defined contribution plans for new hires, under which employees *contribute* a certain amount, usually with matching *contributions* from the taxpayers. The final pension payout then is not guaranteed, but depends on how well the investments perform. The taxpayers are not on the hook for poor investment performance.

Jack Dean, proprietor of Pension Tsunami, a website that has succeeded in raising journalists' awareness of the public-employee pension crisis, explained to me over lunch why the public employee fat cats will continue to present a problem no matter what the younger employees do, or what sort of lesser pension plan they are forced to accept.

"I do talk radio shows," he said between bites of

his sandwich, "and people will call in and ask, 'What can we do to stop this right away?' and my answer is, 'You can't stop it.'

"We're stuck with what's in the pipeline right now - all the current employees with contracts that spell out their pensions, and judges who rule those contracts cannot be breeched. So, all we're left with is switching to a defined-contribution plan for new hires, instead of the defined-benefit plan the earlier employees have."

I said that would help in 30 or 40 years when the new-hires retire with fully vested benefits, and wondered if the state could survive the long and well-paid retirements of the current generation of workers.

"You're right," he said. "We're going to have to live through something that's like the Deepwater Horizon oil leak in the Gulf. You can cap it off so there's no more oil coming out - but then you have to deal with everything that's floating around in the Gulf, and you say, 'What in the Hell do we do with all this stuff now?' What do we do with all the liabilities from the current employees' defined benefit plans, which we'll have to pay on from when they retire until they die?"

What do we do indeed? The answer might be found in another run at the courts - this time using RICO, the federal Racketeer Influenced and Corrupt Organizations Act. Here's how it could work. Most public-sector contracts are negotiated by public employees for public employees. A city manager sits across the table from a city union representative and they hammer out a contract that forces under duress a third party, taxpayers, to cough up the necessary dough. The city manager knows that every time employee pay is hiked and benefits are padded, his boat will rise as well, so the next time his contract comes up for review, he will have an easier time getting similar or even greater increases for himself. What is that if not racketeering?

Of course it doesn't always work that way. Sometimes consultants represent the city, and city managers often drive hard bargains. But there are municipalities enough in California where self-interested negotiations occur, and any of them would be outstanding candidates for the first public employee pension challenge brought under RICO. Berkeley is one of them. Its former city manager, Phil Kamlarz, retired at the end of 2011 with a starting pension of $266,000, even though his ending salary was "only" $250,000. Daniel Borenstein, who covers pensions aggressively for the Contra Costa Times, estimates that about 25 percent of the public agencies in the CalPERS public employee retirement system have uncapped benefit packages like Berkeley's.[22] Then there's the Santa Clara Housing Authority, which used $16 million it received from the federal government to sweeten employee retirement benefits, instead of improving housing for the poor.[23]

One of the more interesting pension abusers in California is Ventura County, because it illustrates how supposedly fair-minded government can exploit some and shower riches on others. Rank-and-file employees hired since 1979 by Ventura County have one of the lowest pensions in the state - $18,000 a year on average, plus Social Security. But its firefighters and sheriffs get pensions that are $10,000 to $15,000 a year more than sworn officers in comparable counties. And then there's the ruling class - the management aristocracy who draw pensions exceeding $200,000 a year. Ventura County counts 24 high-ranking retired public-safety and county-agency administrators in its $200,000-plus pension club, three times more than in Santa Barbara, Kern, Sacramento, Fresno and San Mateo counties - combined.[24] In an opinion column in the Ventura County Star, two members of the Ventura County Taxpayers Association explained just how out of control the Ventura benefits are:

> It is not surprising a majority on the Board of Supervisors and upper management [has] resisted meaningful pension reform; they all benefit from inaction. Former County Executive Officer Marty Robinson used this lucrative mechanism to increase her compensation by $24,537 to spike her lifetime pension at taxpayer expense.[25]

How can Ventura County hope to exact meaningful cuts from its rank-and-file employees if it allows its senior managers - including those ultimately responsible for negotiating labor contracts - to milk the system? It can't, obviously.

The benefit of a successful RICO challenge is that it would make all the untouchable pension deals defined in current public employee contracts potentially illegal. If those contracts could be thrown out as the products of racketeering, then existing employees could be forced into more affordable, less aristocratic, pension plans. Cities, counties and the state, finally worried about the devastation pension expenses are wreaking on their general funds, would immediately begin working to void the more unconscionable salary and benefit packages, limiting the taxpayers' long-term liability for this self-anointed privileged class.

I asked Orange County Supervisor John Moorlach if a RICO challenge could be successful. His answer was one I've grown accustomed to hearing in response to many potential solutions for the state's dilemmas.

"It's an idea that has merit," he said. "The problem is, the case would be heard before judges who are public employees, and who have pension and benefit packages they want to protect."

CONCLUSION:

A CENTURY OF PROGRESSIVE POLITICS COMES HOME TO ROOST

N THE INTRODUCTION OF CRAZIFORNIA, I outlined a pathway toward California's recovery from its many ills. In the parlance of recovery, it was "hitting bottom." In California's case, I saw the most obvious pathway to the state's recovery was not fixing itself proactively, but rather, having to dig itself out from a number of catastrophes - a number of bottom-hitting events. In this scenario, after the state's education system collapses, the state will fix its education system. After its budget collapses, the state will fix its fiscal system. After its economy collapses, the state will stop beating up on businesses and hiking taxes on job creators. Unfortunately, "and so on" needs to be added to these three examples, since they are hardly the complete list of California's dysfunctions.

There's an obvious flaw to this reasoning. The state's education and fiscal systems and its economy all have collapsed, yet in the face of these serial calamities, the state hasn't fixed anything. In fact, California's legislators, courts, and legions of technocrats, eco-crats and bureaucrats continue to do more to worsen the state's condition than they do to better it.

Perhaps, as many drunks say to excuse their ongoing self-destruction, California hasn't really hit bottom yet. It's just skipping like a stone over the surface of true bottom-hood, they say, and things aren't quite bad enough to merit true behavioral change. If that's the case - and in a moment I'll say why I think there's growing evidence that it's not - the future for California may be something like this:

IF A STATE FALLS IN THE FOREST AND NO ONE IS THERE TO HEAR IT ...

The October 26, 2022 earthquake wasn't really the Big One, the long-awaited temblor with Hollywood-scale devastation that has been predicted for years. Big One buffs refused to grant it Big One status, for starters because it didn't even occur on the famed San Andreas fault. Instead, it hit along the much smaller Hayward Fault, a tyke of a tear in the earth's mantle, just 74 miles long and not nearly as feared or well known as the San Andreas. And even more telling, the quake didn't come close to measuring 7.9 or 8.5, like the Big One would. Instead, it measured a respectable but hardly major league 6.9.

It was centered just west of Vallejo, under San Pablo Bay, the northern reach of the San Francisco Bay, at the northern end of the Hayward fault. The temblor was the biggest thing to happen in Vallejo since the city filed for bankruptcy in 2008. When all the city's collapsed buildings and homes were picked through, 12 bodies were found - a tragedy for sure, except that many more would have died but for the fact that

Vallejo in 2022 was a shadow of what it had been ten years earlier. Petrochem, the city's largest industrial employer in 2012, shuttered its plant and moved to North Carolina in 2015, unable to remain competitive under the state's Green Chemistry Initiative and other burdensome regulations. The Six Flags Discovery Kingdom amusement park, Vallejo's second-largest private employer (Kaiser's hospital was first), had closed a year later. From the company's headquarters in Grand Prairie, Texas, CEO Charles Willington blamed California's commitment to alternative energy for the closure. "There are no solar-powered or wind-powered roller coasters," Willington said. "We use a lot of electricity on our rides, and California's commitment to unreliable solar and wind power has led to too many brownouts and blackouts, and has driven up electricity costs. That drove down our customers' theme park experience and drove up ticket costs, so we had to give up on California."

As other Vallejo-based businesses also closed or fled California's hostile business environment, the number of unoccupied homes climbed as well. Thirty-two unoccupied homes and one shuttered apartment building were heavily damaged in the quake, as were several shuttered stores and Petrochem's empty facility. No one died in any of these empty structures, although one firefighter broke his ankle while climbing over debris of the collapsed apartment complex.

In nearby Richmond, California's war on oil finally paid big benefits. Chevron's sprawling Richmond refinery suffered moderate damage, but it had been abandoned five years earlier, a victim of the high carbon tax imposed by the California Air Quality

Board. As a result, no tanks of freshly refined diesel or gasoline had breached and exploded. Although once there were 1,700 employees at the refinery, when the earthquake hit, there were no highly paid production workers on the site to become casualties. The California economy suffered no economic effect from what a few years earlier could well have been a billion-dollar impact.

There were only 23 fatalities in the cities along the northern reaches of San Francisco Bay - terrible, but not enough to earn it a "Big One" designation. But it came to be known as the Big Little One because of the damage it caused 50 miles to the east, in the sparsely populated farmland of the Sacramento-San Joaquin Delta. The unstable, peat-rich soil of the Delta amplifies ground movement ten-fold compared to the more stable soil around Vallejo, and the shaking had devastating effects.

The 1,600-square mile delta is made up of miles of channels and sloughs that surround over 70 landforms that are euphemistically called islands. We know islands as things that rise above the surrounding water, but continued plowing and watering has caused these islands to sink as much as 30 feet below the channels and sloughs. The levees protecting 18 islands liquefied and failed in the shaking, sending walls of water cascading over fields and farm houses. Fatalities were numerous, but that was just the start of the problem.

The islands' combined size was 402 square miles, and as they filled with water, the level of the Delta fell by several inches. Since water will always flow to lower areas, salty ocean water surged in to fill the void. Within four days, saltwater reached the massive pumping plants in the south Delta. The pumps, and the aqueducts they fed, shut down, stopping the flow of life-sustaining water to 25 million Californians from San Jose to San Diego, as well as the farms of the San Joaquin Valley, America's biggest source of food crops.

Fresh water could have continued to flow undisturbed by the earthquake if the long-planned tunnel that was supposed to carry Sacramento River water under the Delta to the pumping stations had been completed - but it hadn't. A blitzkreig of litigation from environmental groups, Delta farmers and Northern California water agencies had delayed it for years. While the lawsuits were slowly wending their way through the process, Democrats in the Legislature pushed through a new law restricting the use of concrete because of the greenhouse gases produced in its manufacturing. It took two years to get an amendment through that exempted the water tunnel. As a result of these delays, workers and drilling machines were just beginning their work deep beneath the Delta when the earthquake waves rolled through. Hearts pounded, foreheads broke out in sweat and prayers were raised to heaven, but the tunnel held fast, just like the engineers promised it would.

It would take several more years for the tunnels to be operational, but an interim solution to this catastrophe should have reduced the quake's economic impact. As early as the 1990s, plans were outlined for the strategic stockpiling of gravel, rocks and heavy plastic sheeting around the Delta, so the materials could be used to build a temporary salt-free channel through the Delta to the pumps. But the state had chosen to spend more money on social programs, so enough supplies never were purchased. It wouldn't really have helped much, since Delta fishermen and farmers, backed by some of the nation's largest and most powerful environmental groups, froze the project in the courts for two and a half years because they wanted that fresh water to flow into the Delta and out to sea, not to the pumping stations.

So, as months stretched into years, two-thirds of California's residents suffered from severe water shortages. America's most productive farm fields turned to dust, water-dependent industries left the state, long baths and showers were outlawed, pools evaporated and were not re-filled, and local breweries disappeared. It takes 30 gallons of water to make a bottle of beer, after all. Experts had predicted in 2009 that the financial impact of a disaster like this would be $40 billion. But that was in 2009. The 23 years between the estimate and the earthquake had not been good to California. The same thing that kept Vallejo's death toll down - departed businesses and shuttered houses and factories - was repeated throughout the state, and in the end, the bean-counters tallied the impact of the collapse of the Sacramento San Joaquin Delta to be "just" an inflation-adjusted $27 billion.

THE RUST COAST

Could that scenario actually happen? Certainly. The U.S. Geological Survey ranks the Hayward Fault as the Bay Area's most likely fault to generate a serious earthquake in the next 30 years - a probability of .32, compared to the San Andreas' .21.[1] The potentially catastrophic economic impact of a well-positioned strong quake on California's water supply also is well documented.

Another source of potential California catastrophe that fascinates me is a slow-rolling one: the state's relentless pursuit of more regulation. Sacramento can't balance a budget, can't dig schools out of the scholastic pit they've fallen into and can't control politically active unionized employees - but, boy, can California's entrenched power base regulate. Take energy efficiency as an example. The state has the most stringent requirements in the country, and consequently, it has the most energy-efficient homes and offices. Apparently being number one in the nation in costly and demanding energy efficiency regulations is an honor Sacramento's eco-crats aren't ready to risk. So, in May 2012 the California Energy Commission voted unanimously to adopt a new set of energy efficiency standards that ratchet up California's green game even more.

When the regulations go into effect, new homes will have to be built with roofs equipped to accept solar power systems, and must fulfill new requirements covering whole-house fans, insulation-wrapped pipes, three-pane windows and sensor-controlled lights that turn off if no one is in the room. Of course, they also turn off if someone is merely sitting still reading a book or watching TV. Never being particularly sensitive to economic realities, the CEC also deigned that new homes in hotter regions, where the economy is in much worse shape than the cooler coastal regions, will have to be built to even stricter, and costlier, standards because residents there tend to use air conditioning more.

In hyping the new regulations, the CEC touted that Californians have saved $66 billion in electricity and natural gas costs since the state started requiring tighter energy efficiency standards in 1978.[2] But that's Crazifornia accounting. The multiple reports and news releases on the CEC website that refer to the number - which was dutifully picked up by the L.A. Times and other newspapers - provide no documentation showing how the $66 billion in savings was computed. If anyone has verified the number by looking at actual energy bills, they're not telling us. More likely, the eco-crats merely applied manufacturers' stated efficiency gains against a baseline, assuming the claims are correct and the products are operating at optimum efficiency. Plus, it appears they're only figuring the energy savings while ignoring the rising costs the regulations bring. The new round of regulations alone is expected to add $1,500 to the cost of the average California home - and even more in the recession-wracked inland areas. And it will lead to higher office leasing rates (office buildings also must pay for equipment that meets the new standards) and food costs (supermarkets will have to install more energy-efficient equipment), and scare off the state's few remaining computer data farms, since they will face big expenses to meet the new standards.

"The only thing good about these new regula-tions," said Building Industry Association of San Diego executive director Borre Winckel, "is that they don't go into effect until 2014."

With financially tone-deaf actions like this continuously coming out of Sacramento, is it any wonder the state remains stuck, like a mastodon in the

La Brea tar pits, in a deep and long-running recession? Did the Sacramento technocrats think that perhaps they should wait until the state's reeling economy regains its strength before delivering another regulatory body blow? Did they think that since California already is the king of energy efficiency, perhaps the CEC could rest on its laurels for a few years? No. California is; therefore it regulates.

All these regulations and statist planning directives, coupled with California's high taxes and crumbling municipal finances, will encourage the continuing mass exodus of people from the state. In the 2000s, nearly four million more people left California than moved here.[3] That's more people than live in the entire state of Oregon. All the signs indicate the number of people departing will rise considerably in this decade. The Green Chemistry Initiative, cap and trade, rising electricity costs and falling electricity reliability, high taxes and onerous regulations will continue to force businesses to close or move to more business-friendly states, leading more people and more capital - monetary and intellectual - to leave the state. When I started writing this book, California was the world's eighth-largest economy; as I finish, it's fallen to ninth. There's plenty of reason to believe that the current holder of the number 10 spot, India, will pass it soon.

If California continues down its current path - and until the June 2012 primary election, laymen and pundits alike saw no indication it's changing direction - then the Golden State could soon come to be called the Rust Coast, more like Detroit and Cleveland than the Silicon Valley.

Taking the "Crazy" out of Crazifornia

But something interesting happened in that June primary that might just keep the Rust Coast moniker at bay. Sixty-six percent of the voters in San Diego and 70 percent of them in San Jose voted like adults ready to take responsibility, for a change. In both cities - the eigth and tenth largest in America - Democrats strongly outnumber Republicans, yet even so, both passed ballot measures that sought to contain the death grip their public employee unions hold on city finances. The cities are both looking bankruptcy in the eye because many of the employees they staffed up with in earlier good times are now retiring the instant they reach maximum retirement plan vesting, happy to trade their paycheck for generous pension and health care benefits. And they keep drawing those benefits for two or three decades until their deaths finally remove them from the red-inked pension ledger book.

Consequently, voters in both cities have watched city services deteriorate as payments into the city employees' retirement kitty rocketed into the stratosphere. In San Diego, pension fund payments increased from $43 million in 1999 to $231.2 million in 2012. In San Jose, the jump between 2001 and 2012 was from $73 million to $245 million.[4] The specifics of the two voter-approved plans are different, but the direction is the same: Employees will be forced to take more personal responsibility for their retirement, and the cushiness they've enjoyed is coming to an end.

The voters of San Jose and San Diego built on a basic change in municipal thinking that began in the Orange County city of Costa Mesa in 2011. The city of

116,000 made national headlines when its city council sent layoff notices to 210 of its 472 employees. Mayor Jim Righeimer, who was swept into office on a pension reform platform despite a concerted $100,000-plus effort by the unions to stop him, said at the time: "Just do the math - this is unsustainable. Under these kinds of burdens, we can't do everything the city needs to do." I love how the progressive enviromentalist buzz word of unsustainability, which has been used to justify all sorts of costly and ill-conceived programs, is so perfectly resonate with the issue of public employee pension costs.

In cities across the country, leaders are discovering that Righeimer spoke the truth: They can't meet their pension obligations, maintain city services and balance their budgets. The June 2012 election showed that more and more voters - an attention-commanding 70 percent of them in San Jose - are not the least bit interested in racking up more debt and cutting back more city services in order to pay for municipal employee retirement benefits that are much more generous than their own. In the cynical, self-preserving world of elected life, this election will be read as resounding evidence that voters will support officials that push back against the public employee unions to support a balance sheet unburdened by soaring public employee benefit costs.

In the response of these three cities to the pension crisis is evidence that there exists a will in California to do what needs to be done to save the state. In all three cities, a few politicians have made politically tough decisions and thrived - something politicians else-where should find very interesting. Voters have spoken forcefully, so supporters of reform will be emboldened to put forward similar measures in their own cities and counties. And perhaps most importantly, the forces of the status quo have spent massive sums and excerted exceptional efforts to protect their members' benefits and have failed. Of course, the Progressives are not giving up. On the day after the election, San Jose public employee unions filed a lawsuit challenging the will of 70 percent of the people they serve. That case will be heard by a judge who will retire with a state pension, so it's obvious that one election in two cities doesn't mean California is out of the woods; not hardly.

Still, there are likely to be many more examples of this sort of positive behavior, not less, and it could finally bring about what California needs most - a pendulum swing. The possibility has opened that in cities throughout the state, a chorus of personal responsibilty will rise and public employees will ultimately have to bow to it and start taking more responsibilty for their own retirements. But the public employee pension crisis is but one of the issues that has driven California to the edge of craziness and beyond. Even if the people rise up and force change in pensions, will social program budgets be cut to levels aligned with the social welfare programs of neighboring states? Will new laws more responsive to business replace existing laws that drag down profits? Will the school system be purged of ridiculous mandates from Sacramento and demands from the teachers unions, so they can return to excellence? Or even improve to mere mediocrity? Will the state's swooning fascination with environmentalism mellow into a more pragmatic relationship with Mother Earth?

All these 180-degree changes are needed to take the "crazy" out of Crazifornia and turn California back into the Golden State. All still seem a long way off, but at least in the June 2012 primary we got a look at who it is that can drive these changes: individual citizens. As their quality of life is negatively impacted by how truly awful and unsustainable things have become in California, in increasing numbers they will start to take personal responsibilty for the state. They have begun to vote as if it were their responsibility to turn things around, and - even though this may strike some as Pollyannaish - they just might continue to vote intelligently, and in the broader public interest, like this:

- *They can start to evaluate each proposition that appears on the ballot based on the measure's impact on the state's future, not on how good passage might make them feel, and they can share these insights with their family members and neighbors.*

- *They can stop joining frivolous class action lawsuits and instead support measures that take power away from a small group of business-killing, super-rich lawyers. And they can talk to their Facebook friends about the need for this to become a movement, not just the action of a few individuals.*

- *They can turn against costly government boondoggles like high speed rail or California's quixotic battle against greenhouse gases. Such costly endeavors shouldn't be measured by their "feel good" quotient, but rather by how they drag down the economy and further burden the state with debt. And, again, they can talk to others about their newfound wisdom.*

- *They can express voter revulsion when Gov. Brown and other politicians try to force them to measure any act of fiscal responsibility against the jobs of fire fighters, police officers and teachers, and the health of poor orphans and forgotten widows. Instead, they should tweet, post, text and talk to everyone they know, telling them that fiscal irresponsibility protects the jobs of the technocrats, eco-crats and bureaucrats who use their power in ways that harm those who work for a living. They can speak forcefully to how the state can and should continue to protect the orphan and widow without also supporting the millions of ne'er do wells who are happy to exploit the nation's most generous and loose social welfare system.*

- *And most powerfully, they can support and vote for candidates who share their newly emerging point of view, and vote against and work against those who cling to the old way. This goes for judges, too. Voters need to remember those judges who have dismissed the majority's will and overturned a law or proposition designed to help bring California back from the brink. In California, the people*

> *have the right to recall a judge, and every 12 years appellate judges, all the way up to the state Supreme Court, must be reinstated by a vote of the people. It was a reinstatement vote that cost California Supreme Court Chief Justice Rose Bird and two of her associate justices their jobs in 1986.*

Californians can make the changes that are needed - and they will have to if there's any hope for the state. California's Assembly and Senate and the governor are getting better at pretending to care about these issues, but a look at the legislation they pass shows that they remain content to steer towards the icebergs instead of away from them. And the armies of California bureaucrats aren't even pretending to address these issues yet.

It was obvious in the San Jose and San Diego votes that a great many Democrats didn't vote like Democrats, and a great many Independents voted like conservative Republicans. That should not come as a surprise to anyone other than Democrat party leaders, because the ills foisted on California by generation after generation of Progressive leaders do transcend party lines. Increasingly, I hear California liberals complain that the social programs they support can't be maintained in the face of the budget squeeze caused by pension contributions and the costs of less justifiable social welfare programs. I hear more Democrats who sound more like the blue collar industrial union Democrats of a generation ago than the latte-sipping urbanites who dominate the party today. They are fed up with environmental regulations that cost them jobs with no discernible benefit to the environment, and they'd rather pursue more personal wealth themselves than support efforts to take it away from others.

The Progressives won't let go easily, if they let go at all. Remember: They faced down even the Conservative icon Ronald Reagan, and when he left the governorship, they were poised to launch a massive increase in government's grip on the state. They succeeded splendidly. Now all they have to do is defend what they've done with all that power.

The Progressives' defense of their programs will become increasingly difficult, as California's accelerating fall from greatness provides ever more evidence that their agenda for the state is too expensive and too unsuccessful. The very future of the state rests on whether 51 percent or more of California's voters in future elections decide they're no longer buying the Progressives' defense of their policies and practices. If by some transformational political miracle that does happen, California can avoid becoming the Rust Coast. It can return to civic and fiscal sanity, and no longer be Crazifornia.

ENDNOTES

INTRODUCTION

[1] Brooks, Jon, "San Bruno Stories: 'He still had smoke coming off his entire body,'" News Fix blog, KQED News, Aug. 30, 2011. http://blogs.kqed.org/newsfix/2011/08/30/san-bruno-stories-he-still-had-smoke-coming-off-his-entire-body/

[2] "Friend: Woman, 20, at boyfriend's house when killed by fire," Bay City News, Sept. 11, 2010. http://www.sfgate.com/cgi-bin/article.cgi?f=/baycitynews/archive/2010/09/11/firevictim11.DTL

[3] "Pipeline Accident Report: San Bruno, CA, Natural Gas Pipeline Explosion and Fire, September 9, 2010," National Transportation Safety Board, http://www.ntsb.gov/news/events/2011/san_bruno_ca/index.html

Chapter 1

[1]   Balzar, John, "Anti-Toxics measure: Prop. 65 gets
top billing in stars' caravan," Los Angeles Times,
Sept. 29, 1986.
http://articles.latimes.com/1986-09-
29/news/mn-10553_1_drinking-water

[2]   "California's Prop. 37 Will Open Litigation
Floodgates," Western Farm Press, Aug. 3, 2012.
http://www.westernfarmpress.com/government
/californias-prop-37-will-open-litigation-
floodgates

[3]   Reed, Chris, "California has more recipients in key
welfare category than next eight states combined,"
San Diego Union Tribune, July 2, 2009.
http://www.utsandiego.com/weblogs/americas-
finest/2009/jul/02/california-has-more-
recipients-in-key-welfare-cate/

[4]   Fueling California, "Issue Brief: California
compared - fuel taxes and fees."
http://www.fuelingcalifornia.org/docs/Fueling%
20California%20HQP%203%200.pdf

[5]   Glenn Beck Show, Feb. 5, 2010

[6]   Will, George, "Candidate in a state of Dystopia,"
Washington Post, September 10, 2009.
http://www.washingtonpost.com/wp-
dyn/content/article/2009/09/09/AR20090909022
07.html?nav=rss_opinion/columns

[7]   "Editorial: Californians incredible shrinking
      incomes," the Orange County Register, Sept. 18,
      2011.
      http://www.ocregister.com/opinion/california-
      317494-percent-income.html

[8]   Leibovich, Mark; New York Times Magazine, July
      1, 2009. Who Can Possibly Govern California, p. 1.
      http://www.nytimes.com/2009/07/05/magazine
      /05California-t.html?_r=2&th&emc=th

[9]   "Californians & their government," Public Policy
      Institute, May 2011.
      http://www.ppic.org/content/pubs/survey/s_5
      11mbs.pdf

[10] Masters, Kim, "Steve Bing takes a hit," The Daily
      Beast, March 30, 2010.
      http://www.thedailybeast.com/articles/2010/03
      /30/steve-bing-takes-a-hit.html

[11] "David Brower Biography," ActistCash.com.
      http://activistcash.com/biography.cfm/b/3507-
      david-brower

[12] Ibid.

[13] "Obama file 58: Hilda Solis - Obama labor
      secretary's socialist connections," New Zeal Blog,
      Dec. 20, 2008.
      http://www.oregonspectator.com/images/THE_
      OBAMA_FILE_w-o_Endnotes.pdf

[14] Pai, "Union leaders welcome Solis choice as labor
      secretary," People's World, December 19, 2008.
      http://www.peoplesworld.org/union-leaders-
      welcome-solis-choice-as-labor-secretary/

[15]   Malcolm, Andrew, "Dramatic tapes of Hilda Solis-White House emergency radio chatter," Top of the Ticket, Los Angeles Times, Feb. 6, 2009. Dramatic tapes of Hilda Solis-White House emergency radio chatter

[16]   Engler, Mark, "Hilda Solis: Protecting workers, not corporations," Talking Union, Democratic Socialists of America, March 4, 2010. http://talkingunion.wordpress.com/2010/03/04/hilda-solis/

[17]   Drier, Peter et al., "Movement Mayor: Can Antonio Villaraigosa change Los Angeles?" Dissident, Summer 2006. www.dissentmagazine.org/article/?article=656

[18]   "Professor profiles: Juan Gomez-Quinones," UCLA Profs.com. http://www.uclaprofs.com/profs/gomez.html

[19]   "About Us, Historical Foundation," MEChA Official National Website. http://www.nationalmecha.org/about.html

[20]   McGrath, Roger D., "Race to the top: Antonio Villaraigosa's radical past," The American Conservative, Feb. 23, 2009. http://www.thefreelibrary.com/Race+to+the+top%3A+Antonio+Villaraigosa%27s+radical+past-a0194428831

[21]   Drier, loc cit.

[22] Mitchell, Dan, "Texas thumps California,"
      International Liberty, The Cato Institute, March 10,
      2010.
      http://danieljmitchell.wordpress.com/2010/03/1
      0/texas-thumps-california/

[23] Murphy, Robert P. and Clemens, Jason, "Labor
      Day fix: cut taxes, spending, regulation," San
      Diego Union Tribune, September 6, 2009.
      http://www3.signonsandiego.com/stories/2009/
      sep/06/labor-day-fix-cut-taxes-spending-
      regulation/?uniontrib

[24] Glenn Beck Show, Feb. 5, 2010.

[25] Schultz, Max, "Obama may not realize it, but
      California is a dependent neighbor," Human
      Events, January 12, 2009.
      http://www.manhattan-
      institute.org/html/miarticle.htm?id=3670

[26] Organizing for America, "Barack Obama unveils
      initiative to combat global warming,"
      April 20, 2007.
      http://www.presidency.ucsb.edu/ws/index.php
      ?pid=93194#axzz1pRDln64O

[27] Mufson, Steven, "Vehicle emission rules to
      tighten," Washington Post, May 19, 2009.
      http://www.washingtonpost.com/wp-
      dyn/content/article/2009/05/18/AR20090518018
      48.html

[28] Walters, Dan, "Two data sets neatly frame state's
      budget crisis," Sacramento Bee, July 14, 2009.
      http://www.allvoices.com/news/3671980-dan-
      walters

[29]   "Highway Statistics," California Highways.
       http://www.cahighways.org/stats.html"
       target="_blank">

[30]   "Vehicle Registrations (Estimated Fee-Paid), Los
       Angeles County as of December 31," Los Angeles
       Almanac.
       http://www.laalmanac.com/transport/tr02.htm

[31]   "Teen pregnancy and parenting in California,"
       California Department of Education.
       http://www.cde.ca.gov/ls/cg/pp/teenpregnanc
       y.asp

[32]   Robert Langley, "Illegal immigration costs
       California over ten billion annually," About.com,
       December 2004.
       http://usgovinfo.about.com/od/immigrationnat
       uralizatio/a/caillegals.htm

[33]   Yes, Prop. 98 started at 40 percent, but the
       percentage has crept up to 43 percent according to
       the Department of Finance.
       http://www.dof.ca.gov/budgeting/budget_faqs/
       #7

[34]   Glen Beck show, Feb. 5, 2010

[35]   Cruickshank, Robert, "It's OK that the California
       Republican Party is irrelevant," Calitics.com,
       March 19, 2012.
       http://www.calitics.com/diary/14254/its-ok-
       that-the-california-republican-party-is-irrelevant

CHAPTER 2

[1] "John Randolph Haynes," West Adams Heritage Association, July 18, 2007.
http://www.westadamsheritage.org/index.php?option=com_content&task=view&id=90&Itemid=1

[2] Sinclair, Upton and Coodley, Lauren, "Upton Sinclair's California," Heyday Books, 2004, Google Books Edition, pg. 82.
http://books.google.com/books?id=EN7nQVa6E0wC&printsec=frontcover&dq=The+land+of+orange+groves+and+jails:+Upton+Sinclair%27s+California&hl=en&ei=nKCKTOSzIYmosAOalYDjBA&sa=X&oi=book_result&ct=result&resnum=1&ved=0CC8Q6AEwAA

[3] "Report on the causes of municipal corruption in San Francisco, as disclosed by the investigations of the Oliver Grand Jury, and the prosecution of certain persons for bribery and other offenses against the state," 1907, The Virtual Museum of the City of San Francisco (scroll about half way down),
http://www.sfmuseum.org/hist5/graft1.html

[4] "Report on the causes of municipal corruption in San Francisco," loc. cit.

[5] Starr, Kevin, "California: A History," Kindle location 2, 205-16. Anyone who writes about California - myself very much included - is indebted to Kevin Starr for his outstanding chronicling of California history. I asked him once if he was related to David Starr Jordan, the Stanford University president who wrote the influential early 20th century essay in The Atlantic Magazine on the state. "No, but I wish I was," he

replied. And *vice versa*, probably.

[6]   Wheeler, Benjamin Ide, "Inaugural Address as the President of the University of California," October 25, 1899.
http://bancroft.berkeley.edu/CalHistory/inaugural.wheeler.html

[7]   Jordan, David Starr, "California and the Californians," 1898, Houghton, Mifflin & Company, reprinted from The Atlantic Monthly.
http://www.books-about-california.com/Pages/CA_and_the_Californians/CA_and_Californians_text.html

[8]   Ibid.

[9]   Cooper, John S., "Hiram Johnson: The Bull Moose Running Mate," American Presidents, reprinted in Suite101.com, June 9, 2000. Regrettably, the link to Cooper's article is now as dead as the senior Johnson's political career after the invisible ink ballot debacle. I decided to leave the story in because it is such an amusing piece of "Californiacana," and because I hope a reader will provide a link to a verifying source.

[10] Starr, ibid., 2, 132-43.

[11] West Adams Heritage Association, ibid.

[12] Weatherson, Michael A. and Bochin, Hal, "Hiram Johnson, Political Revivalist," University Press of America, 1995.
http://books.google.com/books/about/Hiram_Johnson.html?id=VU_Puy36oGgC

[13] Ibid.

[14] Weatherson, loc cit

[15] Pat Brown, Wikipedia.
http://en.wikipedia.org/wiki/Pat_Brown

CHAPTER 3

[1] Varshney, Sanjay B. and Tootelian, Dennis H.,
"Cost of AB 32 on California Small Businesses -
Summary Report of Findings," Varshney &
Associates, June, 2009.
http://www.sbaction.org/get_resource.php?table
=resource_kmqap4_18z4ys&id=kmqaq1_1ed1wo

[2] Bacher, Dan, "Schwarzenegger statues should
celebrate his green legacy as governor," Calitics,
Sept. 28, 2011.
http://www.calitics.com/diary/13890/schwarze
negger-statues-should-celebrate-his-green-legacy-
as-governor

[3] Jacobson, Dan, "Governor Brown sets off green
fireworks with Laird appointment," YubaNet.com,
Jan. 1, 2011.
http://yubanet.com/california/Governor-Brown-
Sets-Off-Green-Fireworks-with-Laird-
Appointment.php

[4] Henwood, Doug, "He's Back! Jerry Brown, on a
white horse," Left Business Observer, Feb. 1992.
http://www.leftbusinessobserver.com/Jerry-
Brown.html

[5]   Landsbaum, Mark, "Improvement in 2011 would be California dreamin'," Orange County Register, Dec. 30, 2011.
http://www.ocregister.com/opinion/spending-282212-taxes-california.html

[6]   Ibid.

[7]   Borenstein, Daniel, "Brown's pension plan provides some hope, but falls short," Oakland Tribune, Oct. 28, 2011.
http://www.insidebayarea.com/news/ci_19217868

[8]   Greenhut, Steven, "Jerry Brown's Game of Chicken," CalWatchdog, Dec. 20, 2010.
http://www.calwatchdog.com/2010/12/20/jerry-browns-game-of-chicken/

[9]   Calle, Brian, "Election makes Laffer less gloomy," Orange County Register, Nov. 14, 2010.
http://www.ocregister.com/opinion/laffer-275814-tax-money.html

CHAPTER 4

[1]   "Project MKULTRA," Wikipedia,
http://en.wikipedia.org/wiki/MKULTRA

[2]   Wolfe, Tom, "The Electric Kool-Aid Acid Test," Kindle edition location 456-62 through 468-74.

[3]   "Environmental Heresies," Conservation Magazine, April-June, 2006.
http://www.conservationmagazine.org/2008/07/environmental-heresies/

[4] Brand, Stewart, "We Owe In All to the Hippies," Time Magazine, April 1, 1995. http://www.time.com/time/printout/0,8816,982 602,00.html

[5] Magid, Larry, "FCC chairman outlines broadband plan for kids," CNET News, March 12, 2010. http://news.cnet.com/8301-19518_3-10468123-238.html

[6] Markoff, John, "Apple's visionary redefined digital age," New York Times, Oct. 5, 2011. http://www.nytimes.com/2011/10/06/business/steve-jobs-of-apple-dies-at-56.html?_r=2&pagewanted=all

[7] "A social history of America's most popular drugs, Amphetamine" "Drug Wars," Frontline, PBS, http://www.pbs.org/wgbh/pages/frontline/shows/drugs/buyers/socialhistory.html

[8] Thompson, Hunter S., "Fear and Loathing in Las Vegas: A Savage Journey to the Heart of the American Dream" Random House, 1971, pp. 66-68.

[9] Grinspoon, Lester and Bakalar, James B., "Psychedelic Drugs in the Twentieth Century," Psychedelic Drugs Reconsidered, Chapter 3, Basic Books, New York, 1978, quoting "Braden 1970, pg. 413."

[10] Johnson, Scott, "The return of 'Freeway' Ricky Ross, the man behind a crack empire," Oakland Tribune, Jan. 9, 2011. http://www.insidebayarea.com/top-stories/ci_17113312

[11]   Warth, Gary, "Kamikaze pilots, Beats and Hells
       Angels all part of meth crisis history," North
       County Times, Sept. 9, 2007.
       http://www.nctimes.com/news/local/sdcounty/
       article_6b86ea26-3264-5833-9e90-
       997b469ad7b0.html

[12]   Shafer, Jack, "The meth capitol of the world -
       where is it?" Slate, Aug. 4, 2005.
       http://www.slate.com/articles/news_and_politic
       s/press_box/2005/08/the_meth_capital_of_the_w
       orld.single.html

[13]   Pearce, Laer, "Keep your eyes on California," The
       Daily Caller, Dec. 7, 2010.
       http://dailycaller.com/2010/12/07/keep-your-
       eyes-on-california/

[14]   Gieringer, Dale, "State's war on drugs a 100-year-
       old bust," San Francisco Chronicle, March 4, 2007.
       http://articles.sfgate.com/2007-03-
       04/opinion/17234672_1_anti-drug-dens-harrison-
       act

[15]   Marti, Gerardo, "Hollywood faith: holiness,
       prosperity, and ambition in a Los Angeles
       Church," 2008, p. 51.

[16]   Ibid., p. 41.

[17]   "Film Censorship," Digital History.
       http://www.digitalhistory.uh.edu/historyonline/
       film_censorship.cfm

[18] Westen, John-Henry, "In new book actor Dan Aykroyd says he would support bestiality if animals were sentient," Lifesitenews.com, Sept. 16, 2008.
http://www.lifesitenews.com/news/archive/ldn/2008/sep/08091610

[19] Leung, Rebecca, "Porn in the USA," 60 Minutes, CBS News, December 5, 2007.
http://www.cbsnews.com/stories/2003/11/21/60minutes/main585049.shtml

[20] Hayford, Jack W. and Moore, S. David, "The Charismatic Century: The enduring impact of the Azusa Street revival," 2006, via Wikipedia.
http://en.wikipedia.org/wiki/Azusa_Street_Revival

CHAPTER 5

[1] California Online Voter Guide, 2002.
http://www.calvoter.org/voter/elections/archive/2002/general/Propositions/topten.html#50

[2] "Public interest energy research, 2009 annual report," California Energy Commission, March 2010.
http://www.energy.ca.gov/2010publications/CEC-500-2010-018/CEC-500-2010-018-CMF.PDF

[3] "Proposed AB 118 air quality improvement program funding plan for fiscal year 2010-1022," California Air Resources Board, May 24, 2010.
http://www.arb.ca.gov/msprog/aqip/fundplan/AQIP_FP_JUNE%202010-FINAL.pdf

[4]   Marois, Michael B., "Million-dollar nurses show
        California's struggle to cut payroll," Bloomberg,
        Dec. 16, 2011.
        http://mobile.bloomberg.com/news/2011-12-
        16/million-dollar-nurses-show-california-s-
        struggle-to-reduce-payroll-costs

[5]   Loeb, Susanna et al., "Getting Down to Facts:
        School Finance and Governance in California,"
        Stanford University, 2007, p. 10.
        http://irepp.stanford.edu/documents/GDF/GDF
        -Overview-Paper.pdf

[6]   "The statewide Case Management Project faces
        significant challenges due to poor project
        management," California State Auditor, Feb. 2011.
        http://www.bsa.ca.gov/pdfs/reports/2010-
        102.pdf

[7]   Walters, Dan, "California Judicial Council halts
        court case management system," Sacramento Bee,
        March 27, 2012.
        http://blogs.sacbee.com/capitolalertlatest/2012/
        03/california-udicial-council-halts-controversial-
        court-case-management-system.html

[8]   Dinzeo, Maria, "California court construction costs
        tower above national average," Courthouse News
        Service, October 14, 2011.
        http://www.courthousenews.com/2011/10/14/4
        0644.htm

[9]   Pignataro, Anthony, "Caltrans accused of waste
        and sloth," CalWatchdog, March 18, 2010.
        http://www.calwatchdog.com/2010/03/18/new-
        caltrans-accused-of-waste-sloth/

[10] Piller, Charles, "Questions raised on Bay Bridge structural tests," Sacramento Bee, Nov. 12, 2011. http://www.sacbee.com/2011/11/12/4050167/questions-raised-on-bay-bridge.html

[11] "Caltrans confirms number of new but idle vehicles," In the News, California Dump Truck Owners Association, Dec. 21, 2009. http://www.cdtoa.org/news/inthenews/951-december-2009/933-caltrans-confirms-number-of-new-but-idle-vehicles

[12] Miranda, Nanette, "Caltrans spends millions on idle vehicles," KABC Los Angeles, October 26, 2009. http://abclocal.go.com/kabc/story?section=news/state&id=7084083

[13] "Investigations of Improper Activities by State Employees: February 2007 through June 2007," California State Auditor, September 2007. http://www.bsa.ca.gov/pdfs/reports/I2007-2.pdf

[14] Dolan, Jack, "Caltrans-owned homes get costly new roofs," Los Angeles Times, June 18, 2011. http://articles.latimes.com/2011/jun/18/local/la-me-caltrans-roofs-20110619

[15] "Energy consumption in California homes," U.S. Department of Energy. http://apps1.eere.energy.gov/states/residential.cfm/state=CA%23elec%09

[16] "Subsequent events - California's energy crisis," Energy Information Administration, U.S. Department of Energy. http://www.eia.doe.gov/cneaf/electricity/california/subsequentevents.html

[17] "California's utopian renewable energy mandates already threatening power shortages and higher utility bills," Center for Individual Freedom, CFIF.Org - Energy, July 8, 2009. http://www.cfif.org/htdocs/legislative_issues/federal_issues/hot_issues_in_congress/energy/Californias-Utopian-Renewable-Energy-Mandates-Already-Threatening-Power-Shortages-and-Higher-Utility-Bills.htm

[18] California Online Voter Guide, The California Voter Foundation. http://www.calvoter.org/voter/elections/2008/general/Prop.s/Prop.1A.html

[19] Richards, Gary, "Alarming state report predicts $294 billion shortfall for transportation over next decade," Mercury News, Nov. 5, 2011. http://www.pwmag.com/industry-news.asp?sectionID=770&articleID=1758497

[20] Reisman, Will, "PR firm for high-speed rail quits before being fired," San Francisco Examiner, July 4, 2011. http://www.sfexaminer.com/local/2011/07/pr-firm-high-speed-rail-project-quits-getting-fired

CHAPTER 6

[1]   Donlon, J. P., "Best/Worst States for Business,"
      ChiefExecitve.net, May 3, 2011.
      http://chiefexecutive.net/best-worst-states-for-
      business

[2]   Gaines, Ted, "Company's departure a sign state's
      business climate is in the trash," Sacramento Bee,
      Dec. 17, 2011.
      http://www.sacbee.com/2011/12/17/4128644/c
      ompanys-departure-a-sign-states.html

[3]   Will, George, "Golden no longer," Town Hall, Jan.
      10, 2010.
      http://townhall.com/columnists/georgewill/201
      0/01/10/golden_no_longer/page/full/

[4]   Vranich, Joseph, "Record in 2010 for Calif.
      companies departing or diverting capital," Fox
      and Hounds blog, Jan. 28, 2011.
      http://www.foxandhoundsdaily.com/blog/josep
      h-vranich/8543-record-2010-calif-companies-
      departing-or-diverting-capital

[5]   Watson, John, "State needs to adopt common-
      sense business principles," Sacramento Bee, June
      1, 2011.
      http://www.sacbee.com/2011/06/01/3667327/st
      ate-needs-to-adopt-common-
      sense.html#storylink=misearch

[6]   Vranich, Joe, "The top ten reasons why California
      companies are calling the moving companies,"
      The Business Relocation Coach blog, April 2011.
      http://thebusinessrelocationcoach.blogspot.com/
      2011/04/why-do-companies-leave-california-
      here.html

[7] "California's tax climate is nation's second worst," CalTaxletter, Nov. 5, 2010.
http://www.caltax.org/caltaxletter/2010/110510 _california_tax_climate_second_worst.htm

[8] Finley, Allysia, "Joel Kotkin: The Great California Exodus," The Wall Street Journal, April 20,2012.
http://online.wsj.com/article/SB100014240527023 04444604577340531861056966.html

[9] "California Green Chemistry Initiative Final Report," December 2008, Foreword.
http://www.dtsc.ca.gov/PollutionPrevention/Gr eenChemistryInitiative/upload/GREEN_Chem.p df

[10] Hewitt, Hugh, "'Green chemistry' is California's new job-killer," The Washington Examiner, Jan. 31, 2011.
http://washingtonexaminer.com/opinion/colum nists/2011/01/green-chemistry-californias-new-job-killer

[11] "Briefing Report: What AB 32 Hath Wrought," Republic Caucus of the California State Senate," February 10, 2010.
http://cssrc.us/publications.aspx?id=7521&Aspx AutoDetectCookieSupport=1

[12] "California's cap-and-trade slush fund," Orange County Register editorial, Feb. 10, 2012.
http://www.ocregister.com/opinion/california-339832-warming-state.html

[13] Gardner, Michael, "State fees on greenhouse gas output could be near," San Diego Union Tribune, September 6, 2009.
http://www.utsandiego.com/news/2009/sep/06/state-fees-greenhouse-gas-output-could-be-near/?uniontrib

[14] Kotkin, Joel, "Green jobs can't save the economy," Forbes.com, Aug. 4, 2009.
http://www.forbes.com/2009/08/03/green-jobs-economic-growth-opinions-columnists-joel-kotkin.html

[15] Glantz, Aaron, "Number of green jobs fails to live up to promises," New York Times, Aug. 19, 2011.
http://mobile.nytimes.com/article?a=830556&f=19

[16] Puzder, Andrew F., "Karcher's success story tougher to write today," Orange County Register, July 15, 2011.
http://articles.ocregister.com/2011-07-15/news/29785191_1_margaret-karcher-carl-cart

[17] Carter, Lisa, "Carl's Jr. parent eyeing Texas as possible new headquarters," Austin American-Statesman, Feb. 1, 2011.
http://www.statesman.com/business/carls-jr-parent-eyeing-texas-as-possible-new-1226264.html

[18] "California's utopian renewable energy mandates already threaten power shortages and higher energy bills," Center for Individual Freedom, CFIF.Org - Energy, July 8, 2009.
http://www.cfif.org/htdocs/legislative_issues/federal_issues/hot_issues_in_congress/energy/Californias-Utopian-Renewable-Energy-Mandates-Already-Threatening-Power-Shortages-and-

Higher-Utility-Bills.htm

[19] "Energy Crisis Inhibits Intel, CEO Says," San Francisco Chronicle, Jan. 9, 2001.
http://articles.sfgate.com/2001-01-09/business/17579938_1_craig-barrett-intel-spokesman-chuck-mulloy-power-plants

[20] Dorinson, Patrick, "The great electricity disconnect," Fox & Hounds Daily, Sept. 3, 2010.
http://www.foxandhoundsdaily.com/blog/patrick-dorinson/7737-the-great-electricity-disconnect

[21] Woody, Todd, "A move to put the union label on solar power plants," New York Times, June 18, 2009.
http://www.nytimes.com/2009/06/19/business/energy-environment/19unions.html?pagewanted=all

[22] Steinberg, Darrell, "A bold plan for sustainable California communities," Wall Street Journal, May 1, 2012.
http://online.wsj.com/article/SB10001424052702304811304577367992120682890.html

[23] Eicher, Theo S., "Municipal and statewide land use regulations and housing prices across 250 major US cities," p. 17, University of Washington, Jan. 14, 2008.
http://depts.washington.edu/teclass/landuse/housing_020408.pdf

[24] "AHF to file Cal/OSHA complaints over porn industry's blacklist on condoms," AIDS Healthcare Foundation news release, Aug. 19, 2009.
http://www.aidshealth.org/news/press-releases/ahf-to-file-calosha.html

[25] Hennessy-Fiske, Molly, "Advisory panel would consider increasing regulation of California's porn industry," Los Angeles Times, March 19, 2010.
http://articles.latimes.com/2010/mar/19/local/la-me-porn-safety19-2010mar19

[26] Klowden, Kevin et al., "Film Flight: Lost production and its economic impact on California," The Milken Institute, July 2010.
http://www.milkeninstitute.org/pdf/FilmFlight.pdf

[27] Rogers, John, "Porn industry mulls leaving LA if condoms required," Associated Press, Jan. 18, 2012.
http://news.yahoo.com/porn-industry-mulls-leaving-la-condoms-required-095300909.html

[28] "Governor's Budget Summary, 2012-2013" pg. 24.
http://www.ebudget.ca.gov/pdf/BudgetSummary/FullBudgetSummary.pdf

[29] CaliCon, "Lessons from the Texas budget," Calitics, April 5, 2011.
http://www.calitics.com/diary/13358/lessons-from-the-texas-budget

CHAPTER 7

[1] Dillon, Erin, "Is our students earning?"
Washington Monthly, Sept./Oct. 2011.
http://www.washingtonmonthly.com/magazine
/septemberoctober_2011/special_report/is_our_st
udents_earning031647.php

[2] Bookworm, "San Francisco School Board cuts
academic programs to fund gay rights at school,"
Bookwormroom, February 10, 2010.
http://www.bookwormroom.com/2010/02/10/s
an-francisco-school-board-cuts-academic-
programs-to-fund-gay-rights-at-school/

[3] "RAND report shows California school lag behind
other states on almost every objective
measurement," January 3, 2005.
http://www.rand.org/news/press.05/01.03.html

[4] Izumi, Lance T. et al., "Still not as good as you
think: 2009 update on why the middle class needs
school choice," Pacific Research Institute,
December 2009.
http://liberty.pacificresearch.org/docLib/200912
09_Still_Not_As_Good_As_You_Think.pdf

[5] "We're #4 … and #39 … and #68!" Lowell Alumni
Association newsletter, summer 2009, p. 5.
http://www.lowellalumni.org/download/laa_su
mmer09.pdf

[6] Seiler, John, "Admin costs crowd out teachers,"
CalWatchdog, July 26, 2010.
http://www.calwatchdog.com/2010/07/26/new-
admin-costs-crowd-out-teaching/

[7]   "California Proposition 1, the 'Alien Land Law'
      Initiative (1920," Ballotpedia.org.
      http://ballotpedia.org/wiki/index.php/Californi
      a_Proposition_1,_the_%22Alien_Land_Law%22_I
      nitiative_(1920)

[8]   Nevius, C.W., "Dirty secret of black-on-Asian
      violence is out," San Francisco Chronicle, May 2,
      2010.
      http://www.sfgate.com/cgi-
      bin/article.cgi?f=/c/a/2010/05/02/BAT01D7H71
      .DTL

[9]   Abad, Terence, "SFUSD stiffs Lowell by $400K,"
      Lowell Alumni Association newsletter, summer
      2009, p. 1.
      http://www.lowellalumni.org/download/laa_su
      mmer09.pdf

[10] Will, George, "Can California be sold on E-Bay's
      former leader?" Town Hall, July 5, 2009.
      http://townhall.com/columnists/GeorgeWill/20
      09/07/05/can_california_be_sold_on_ebays_form
      er_leader

[11] Loeb, Susanna et al., "Getting Down to Facts:
      School Finance and Governance in California,"
      Stanford University, 2007, pg. 7.
      http://irepp.stanford.edu/documents/GDF/GDF
      -Overview-Paper.pdf

[12] Sections 44930 through 44988.
      http://www.leginfo.ca.gov/cgi-
      bin/displaycode?section=edc&group=44001-
      45000&file=44930-44988

[13] Loeb, loc. sit., pg. 15.

[14] Harrington, Theresa, "Bay Area girl suspended for videotaping unruly class," Contra Costa Times, June 23, 2009. Reproduced in California Political News & Views, June 24, 2009.
http://capoliticalnews.com/blog_post/show/2459

[15] Song, Jason, "Firing tenured teachers can be a costly and tortuous task," Los Angeles Times, May 3, 2009.
http://www.latimes.com/news/local/la-me-teachers3-2009may03,0,679507.story

[16] Colvin, Richard Lee, "Losing faith in the self-esteem movement," Los Angeles Times, January 25, 1999.
http://www.des.emory.edu/mfp/302/302losingfaith.PDF

[17] "Toward a state of esteem, the final report of the California Task Force to Promote Self-esteem and Personal and Social Responsibility," January 1990., pg. 62 in original.
http://eric.ed.gov/PDFS/ED321170.pdf

[18] Colvin, Richard Lee, loc. cit.

[19] "Japanese school caves to 'monster' parents, gives all kids lead in school play," Fox News republication of a Times of London story, June 7, 2008.
http://www.foxnews.com/story/0,2933,364265,00.html

[20] Colvin, loc. cit.

[21] Vasconcellos, John, "A message from John Vasconcellos," The Vasconcellos Project. http://www.politicsoftrust.net/vas_legacy.php

[22] "School says game of tag is out," FoxNews.com, June 20, 2002. http://www.foxnews.com/story/0,2933,55836,00.html

[23] "Landon, Katie, "Gay curriculum Proposal riles elementary school parents," FoxNews.com, May 22, 2009. http://www.foxnews.com/story/0,2933,521209,00.html

[24] Neill, Michele, "Vocal critics do not represent majority," Alameda Journal letter to the editor, August 20, 2009.

[25] Gleason, Keith, "Parents and lawyer say lawsuit against Alameda district is question of parental rights," The Oakland Tribune, August 20, 2009.

[26] "Alameda District discontinues K-5 LGBT ("Lesson 9") curriculum; parents dismiss opt-out lawsuit," Pacific Justice Institute website, May 19, 2010. http://www.pacificjustice.org/news/alameda-district-discontinues-k-5-lgbt-curriculum-parents-dismiss-opt-out-suit

[27] Murphy, Katy, "Oakland school district: Is it better off after the state takeover?" Oakland Tribune, March 26, 2010. http://www.insidebayarea.com/ci_12753927?source=most_emailed

[28] Oakland Unified School District website, For Our Community / Labor Negotiations. http://publicportal.ousd.k12.ca.us/199410331174 255857/blank/browse.asp?A=383&BMDRN=2000 &BCOB=0&C=57331

Chapter 8

[1] "Hearst Castle - La Cuesta Encantada," http://www.hearstcastle.org/history/the_castle.a sp

[2] "Facts and Stats," http://www.hearstcastle.org/history/facts_stats. asp

[3] Varshney, Sanjay B. and Tootelian, Dennis H., "Cost of State Regulations on California Small Business Study," September 2009. http://arc.asm.ca.gov/member/3/pdf/CostofReg ulationStudyFinal.pdf

[4] Hecht, Sean B. and Enion, M. Rhead, "It's no time to drop ball on environment," Sacramento Bee, Jan. 20, 2011. Copy of original: http://today.ucla.edu/portal/ut/it-s-no-time-to-drop-ball-on-environment-191389.aspx?link_page_rss=191389

[5] "Legislators oppose oil and gas drilling off California's coast," California Progress Report, April 15, 2009. http://www.californiaprogressreport.com/site/le gislators-oppose-oil-and-gas-drilling-california%E2%80%99s-coast

[6] Comments of Wendell Cox to Pacific Research Institute, March 20, 2010.

[7]   Assembly Bill No. 844, Chapter 645, Legislative
        Counsel's Digest.
        http://www.energy.ca.gov/transportation/tire_e
        fficiency/documents/2007-11-09_AB844.PDF

[8]   Webber, Kevin D., Toyoto Motor Engineering &
        Manufacturing, comment letter to Air Resources
        Board, June 24, 2009.

[9]   Walters, Dan, "Air board's cover-up casts pall on
        diesel rules," Sacrament Bee, Dec. 2, 2009. Copy of
        original:
        http://www.waltersreport.com/2009/12/dan-
        walters-air-boards-cover-up-casts.html

[10]   "Dr. John Telles' letter to CARB Chief Legal
        Counsel Ellen Peter regarding the Hien Tran
        fraud," Kill CARB.org.
        http://killcarb.org/JohnTelles2EllenPeter.html

[11]   Cart, Julie, "California panel reaffirms carbon
        trading program," Los Angeles Times, Aug. 25,
        2011.
        http://articles.latimes.com/2011/aug/25/local/l
        a-me-cap-trade-20110825

[12]   Leubitz, Brian, "CARB approves nation's most
        aggressive CO2 emissions regime," Calitics, Oct.
        20, 2011.
        http://www.calitics.com/diary/13959/carb-
        approves-nations-most-aggressive-co2-emissions-
        regime

[13]   Duffy, Warren, "CARB's unanimous vote to begin cap and trade," CFACT SOCAL, Podcast #027, Oct. 30, 2011,
http://www.cfactsocal.org/2011/10/30/podcast-027-carbs-unanimous-vote-for-cap-trade-1-1-12/

[14]   Californians for Smart Energy, "Common Sense Solutions."
http://dynamicvisionds.com/casmartenergy.com/solutions.php

[15]   Consumer Electronics Association, "New study shows Proposed California TV mandate would cost jobs, reduce state revenue and limit consumer choice," April 2, 2009.
http://www.ce.org/Press/CurrentNews/press_release_detail.asp?id=11712

[16]   Ibid.

[17]   "California approves new energy efficient TV regulations," California Energy Commission, Nov. 18, 2009.
http://www.energy.ca.gov/releases/2009_releases/2009-11-18_tv_regulations.html

[18]   California Energy Commission, "Frequently Asked Questions - FAQ. Energy efficiency standards for television."
http://www.energy.ca.gov/appliances/tv_faqs.html

[19]   "Smart Energy Coalition Outraged over CA Energy Commission's Unjustified Regulations to Ban Televisions Based on Energy Use," Californians for Smart Energy, Nov. 18, 2009.
http://web2.sys-con.com/node/1193342/mobile

[20] Mosk, Matthew et al., "Car company gets U.S. loan, builds car in Finland," ABC News, Oct. 22, 2011.
http://abcnews.go.com/Blotter/car-company-us-loan-builds-cars-finland/t/story?id=14770875

[21] Hadley, Stanton W. and Tsvetkova, Alexandra, "Potential impacts of plug-in hybrid electric vehicles on regional power generation," U.S. Department of Energy, Jan. 2008, pg. 61
http://www.ornl.gov/info/ornlreview/v41_1_08/regional_phev_analysis.pdf

[22] Woody, Todd, "A move to put the union label on solar plants," New York Times, June 18, 2008.
http://www.nytimes.com/2009/06/19/business/energy-environment/19unions.html

[23] Balgenorth, Bob, "The California Environmental Quality Act: A vital tool for economic and environmental progress," Calitics, June 1, 2011.
http://www.calitics.com/diary/13538/the-california-environmental-quality-act-a-vital-tool-for-economic-and-environmental-progress

[24] United States Department of Interior, Bureau of Land Management, California State Office and The Sea Ranch California Coastal National Monument Stewardship Task Force, "Seabird and Marine Mammal Monitoring on Offshore Rock Islands in Sonoma County and Mendocino Counties

[25] Interview with Tony Bomkamp, July 2007.

[26] California Coastal Act, §30106.
http://www.coastal.ca.gov/coastact.pdf

[27]   "Wildfire protection, California 2009," Bureau of
       Land Management.
       http://www.blm.gov/pgdata/etc/medialib/blm
       /ca/pdf/caso/publications.Par.31582.File.dat/Sin
       glePages.pdf

[28]   Ibid.

[29]   Ibid.

[30]   Carlson, Richard, "A preventable tragedy," San
       Francisco Chronicle, July 1, 2007.
       http://www.sfgate.com/cgi-
       bin/article.cgi?f=/c/a/2007/07/01/INGMVQNLI
       Q1.DTL

Chapter 9

[1]   "California: The facts on California's tax climate,"
       Tax Foundation fact sheet, 2012
       http://taxfoundation.org/research/topic/15.html

[2]   "Revised census data reports CA public workers
       are among highest-paid in the nation," California
       County News," Feb. 2012.
       http://www.californiacountynews.org/2012/02/
       revised-census-data-reports-ca-public-workers-
       are-among-highest-paid-in-the-nation.html

[3]   Quinn, James, "California is a greater risk than
       Greece, warns JP Morgan chief," The Telegraph,
       Feb. 26, 2010.
       http://www.telegraph.co.uk/finance/financetopi
       cs/financialcrisis/7326772/California-is-a-greater-
       risk-than-Greece-warns-JP-Morgan-chief.html

[4] Voegeli, William, "Failed State," Claremont
Review of Books, Dec. 17, 2009.
http://www.claremont.org/publications/crb/id.
1650/article_detail.asp

[5] "Fiscal Myopia," Riverside Press Enterprise
editorial, Jan. 16, 2012.
http://www.pe.com/opinion/editorials-
headlines/20120116-state-fiscal-myopia.ece

[6] Public Policy Institute Statewide Survey, January
2012.
http://www.ppic.org/content/pubs/other/APR_
CalLegislature0112.pdf

[7] Doerr, David, personal interview with the author,
Feb. 17, 2010

[8] Mishak, Michael J. and Megerian, Chris,
"California in retreat on social service spending,"
Los Angeles Times, Jan. 7, 2012.
http://www.latimes.com/news/local/la-me-
state-budget-20120107,0,746147.story

[9] Villacorte, Christina and Pamer, Melissa, "Gov.
Brown's budget plan sparks fear, outrage in
Southland," Daily News, Jan. 6, 2012.
http://www.dailynews.com/news/ci_19692731

[10] Ortiz, John, "California group moves to put
pension overhauld on 2012 ballot," Sacramento
Bee, Nov. 2, 2011.
http://blogs.sacbee.com/the_state_worker/2011/
11/california-group-moves-to-put-pension-
reform-group-submits-initiative-Proposals-for-
ballot.html

[11]   Ring, Ed, "Popping the public-pension bubble,"
       City Journal, July 26, 2011.
       http://www.city-journal.org/2011/cjc0726er.html

[12]   Peele, Thomas, "Unbelievable but true: Man fired
       for questioning city manager's salary," Contra
       Costa Times, October 29, 2011. Copy here:
       http://www.highbeam.com/doc/1P2-
       29978827.html

[13]   Brambila, Nicole C., "Indian Wells banker Haddon
       Libby protests firing in lawsuit," Desert Sun,
       October 21, 2011.

[14]   Wagner, James, "L.A. County fire official arrested
       in dog's beating," Los Angeles Times, November
       8, 2008.
       http://articles.latimes.com/2008/nov/08/local/
       me-dogkilling8

[15]   "Update: Animal cruelty charges - Glynn Johnson
       MIA," California Fire News, Nov. 11, 2008.
       http://calfire.blogspot.com/2008/11/update-
       animal-cruelty-charges-glynn.html

[16]   Asbury, John, "Probation, weekend jail for puppy
       beating," The Press-Enterprise, April 2, 2010. Copy
       here:
       http://www.riversidejailbailbond.com/tag/felon
       y/

[17]   Little Hoover Commission, "Public Pensions for
       Retirement Security," Report #204 transmittal
       letter, Feb. 2011.
       http://www.lhc.ca.gov/studies/204/Report204.p
       df

[18] Greenhut, Steve, "A message to the unions," The Orange County Register, Orange Punch blog, June 6, 2006.
http://orangepunch.ocregister.com/tag/election-2006-june/

[19] Lusvardi, Wayne, "Counties still ignore pension tsunami," CalWatchdog, Jan. 17, 2012.
http://www.calwatchdog.com/2011/04/22/counties-still-ignore-pension-tsunami/

[20] Alexander, Kurtis, "Fresno County braces for strike by biggest union," Fresno Bee, Nov. 24, 2011. Copy here:
http://dialog.newsedge.com/portal.asp?site=2007100814443105593225&searchfolderid=pg2007100814522209759333&block=default&portlet=ep&nzesm=on&syntax=advanced&display=SERVICE+EMPLOYEES+INTERNATIONAL+UNION&action=sitetopics&mode=realtime&nzenb=left&criteria=%5Bcompany%3D5661607%5D&searchID=731189&datetime=%5Bt-minus%3D7%5D&hdlaction=story&storyid=%5Bstoryid=TKPN_UFTUK7uvfeU6jLDWHZ6OZzkGB52dif5kdFlPo7gtzdCO5C9IZ7SAxA9lPPY%5D&rtcrdata=on&epname=NACEO&

[21] Jacobs, Rick et. al., "California has one option left to stop the bleeding," Calitics, Nov. 28, 2011.
http://www.calitics.com/diary/14032/california-has-one-option-left-to-stop-the-bleeding

[22] Borenstein, Daniel, "Berkeley city manager not unique retiring with bigger pension than salary," Contra Costa Times, Jan. 7, 2012.
http://www.contracostatimes.com/news/ci_19691120

[23] "Santa Clara County Housing Authority used $16 million for pension boosts instead of homes for the poor," California Taxpayers Association, Aug. 19, 2011.
http://www.caltax.org/homepage/081911_waste.html

[24] Wilson, Kathleen, "Ventura County pensions: Best or worst?" Ventura County Star, Feb. 18, 2012.
http://www.vcstar.com/news/2012/feb/18/ventura-county-pensions-best-or-worst/

[25] Thomson, Dick and Grau, David P., "County leaders whiff on meaningful pension reform," Ventura County Star, Jan. 7, 2012.
http://www.vcstar.com/news/2012/jan/07/thomsongrau-county-leaders-whiff-on-meaningful/?opinion=1

CONCLUSION

[1] Working Group on California Earthquake Probabilities, "Earthquake probabilities in the San Francisco Bay Region,2000 to 2030 - A summary of findings," U.S. Geological Survey, 1999.
http://geopubs.wr.usgs.gov/open-file/of99-517/#_Toc464419658

[2] "California approves new energy efficiency rules," San Francisco Chronicle, May 31, 2012.
http://www.sfgate.com/cgi-bin/article.cgi?f=/n/a/2012/05/31/state/n181253D68.DTL

[3] Finley, Allysia, "Joel Kotkin: The great California exodus," Wall Street Journal, April 20, 2012.
http://online.wsj.com/article/SB10001424052702304444604577340531861056966.html?KEYWORDS=kotkin+california+exodus

[4]   "San Diego and San Jose approve pension cuts in a landslide vote," Business Insider, June 5, 2012. http://www.businessinsider.com/san-diego-and-san-joe-approve-pension-cuts-2012-6

ACKNOWLEDGEMENTS

The encouragement of two people in particular must be acknowledged here, because Crazifornia wouldn't exist without them. The first is my long-time friend Hugh Hewitt, who I've known since he moved to Orange County in the late 1980s to oversee the creation of the Nixon Presidential Library. During the 2004 election campaign he encouraged me to start blogging, and that led to the creation of my blog Cheat-Seeking Missiles, where the Crazifornia concept first took flight. The second person earning extra acknowledgement is my wife of 30 years Beth, who in 2009 encouraged me to put my blogging time to better use. After my usual pouting, I decided she had a good idea and thought I could turn Cheat-Seeking Missiles' Crazifornia posts into a book. She then became the first person to tell me it was a good idea. As soon as I had an outline fleshed out, I showed it to Hugh, who told me he too thought it was a winner. And I was on my way.

Beth also helped greatly with her comments on the manuscript, as did my co-workers Scott Starkey and Ben Boyce, and my daughter, Lauren. CalWatchdog editor John Seiler helped with his editing of the manuscript.

Many who have written about California need to be thanked: Steven Greenhut, Joel Kotkin, Wayne

Lusardi, Debra Saunders, Kevin Starr, William Voegeli, Joe Vranich and Dan Walters in particular. Dan gets an extra thank you for sharing the story of Jerry Brown's oil holdings with me.

Jon Fleishman also was pivotal to the book, as his FlashReport.org website is a daily treasure chest of California news. Flash Report regularly linked to articles I've written for CalWatchdog.com, edited by Steven Greenhut and then John Seiler, the Washington Times and The Daily Caller. Portions of many of these columns make a showing in Crazifornia.

My old (as in years known) friend Shawn Bell did a fantastic job counseling me on print-on-demand and electronic book protocols and practices, and also sweated out the details of formatting the print and electronic versions.

Folks who helped me get my arms around new subjects included Matt Adams of the Building Industry Association of San Diego, on the cost regulation adds to housing; Paul Beard II of the Pacific Legal Center on the Coastal Commission; Bookworm, the anonymous Bay Area blogger, for recounting her experiences at Lowell High School in San Francisco (and for being a great supporter of Cheat-Seeking Missiles and this book); former senator Jim Brulte of California Strategies on the California energy crisis; Lake Tahoe resident Richard Carlson on the Tahoe Regional Planning Agency; Jack Dean of Pension Tsunami and the Fullerton Association of Concerned Taxpayers on California's pension crisis; Dave Doerr of the California Taxpayers Association on the fascinating history of California taxes; Lucy Dunn of the Orange County Business Council for her "Squirrel!" alerts on particularly bad legislation; Bill Hauk, former CEO of the California Business Roundtable on the shifting balance of power in Sacramento; Gary Hunt of California Strategies for his often-offered and always-welcomed helping hand; Lance Izumi of the Pacific

Research Institute on education; Joanne Kozberg of California Strategies on the UC system; Corona del Mar residents George and Sharlee McNamee on the Coastal Commission; Orange County Supervisor John Moorlach on Orange County v. Sheriff's Association and the larger pension crisis; Holly Schroeder and Dr. Mark Grey of the Building Industry Association on stormwater regulation; and Sacramento lobbyist John Mocker on education. Mocker, the author of Proposition 98 - the measure responsible for California's schools receiving over 40 percent of general fund revenues, no matter how poorly they perform - is the only person I interviewed for this book who didn't allow me to record the session.

Frank Breeden, my literary agent, worked hard trying to sell Crazifornia to every conservative publishing house in America. Every one of them told him the same thing: "Great concept, well-written, but we're only looking for books of national scope by authors with established media platforms." He then encouraged me to self-publish, which I greatly appreciate. Hugh Hewitt, Jon Fleishman and Lucy Dunn pitched in to help Frank, writing endorsements of me and the book's concept.

The many biblical scholars who worked together from 1965 through 1978 to create the New International Version of the Bible, and Zondervan, who published it, deserve thanks for creating the only version of the Bible I've found that translates Ecclesiastes 10:2 as it's presented at the beginning of Crazifornia, "The heart of the wise inclines to the right, but the heart of the fool to the left."

Finally, my faithful Twitter followers Jeanette (@jayher17) and daughter Lauren (@lapearce) were big helps, tweeting me links to stories on some new California craziness or another, some of which found their way into the book.

18224853R00208

Made in the USA
Lexington, KY
27 October 2012